Equine-Assisted Men~~tal~~ ~~Health~~
for Healing Tra~~u~~

Clinicians have long recognized that trauma therapy provides a pathway to recovery, and *Equine-Assisted Mental Health for Healing Trauma* provides that pathway for those who work with horses and clients together. This book demonstrates a range of equine-assisted mental health approaches and step-by-step strategies for facilitating recovery from trauma for children, adults, and families. Chapters address topics such as chronic childhood trauma, accident-related trauma, complex trauma and dissociation, posttraumatic growth in combat veterans, somatic experiencing and attachment, eye movement desensitization and reprocessing (EMDR), reactive attachment disorder (RAD), relational trauma, and sexual trauma. Experts also provide case studies accompanied by transcript analyses to demonstrate the process of trauma healing. Clinicians will come away from the book with a wealth of theoretical and practical skills and an in-depth, trauma-informed understanding that they can use directly in their work with clients.

Kay Sudekum Trotter, PhD, LPC-S, RPT-S, NCC, CEIP-MH, is a licensed professional counselor supervisor, author, speaker, and consultant, as well as the founder of Kaleidoscope Behavioral Health in Flower Mound, Texas, where she has developed and taught animal-assisted therapy workshops. Dr. Trotter's groundbreaking research led to one of the first published studies on the effectiveness of equine-assisted mental health. She is the author of *Harnessing the Power of Equine Assisted Counseling: Adding Animal Assisted Therapy to Your Practice*.

Jennifer N. Baggerly, PhD, LPC-S, RPT-S, is a professor of counseling at University of North Texas at Dallas, a licensed professional counselor supervisor, and a registered play therapist supervisor who also provides counseling at Kaleidoscope Behavioral Health. She is a former chair of the board for the Association for Play Therapy. Dr. Baggerly has taught and provided counseling for children for over 20 years. Her other books include *Counseling Families: Play-Based Treatment*, *Group Play Therapy: A Dynamic Approach*, and *Child-Centered Play Therapy Research: The Evidence Base for Effective Practice*.

Equine-Assisted Mental Health for Healing Trauma

Edited by
Kay Sudekum Trotter and
Jennifer N. Baggerly

Routledge
Taylor & Francis Group

NEW YORK AND LONDON

First published 2019
by Routledge
711 Third Avenue, New York, NY 10017

and by Routledge
2 Park Square, Milton Park, Abingdon, Oxon, OX14 4RN

Routledge is an imprint of the Taylor & Francis Group, an informa business

Library of Congress Cataloging-in-Publication Data
A catalog record for this title has been requested

ISBN: 978-1-138-61269-3 (hbk)
ISBN: 978-1-138-61274-7 (pbk)
ISBN: 978-0-429-45610-7 (ebk)

Typeset in Perpetua
by Out of House Publishing

Contents

About the Editors   vii

About the Contributors   ix

Preface   xii

SECTION ONE
Trauma Originating in Childhood   1

1 Integrating Somatic Experiencing® and Attachment into
  Equine-Assisted Trauma Recovery   3
  SARAH SCHLOTE

2 Treating Structural Dissociation through Equine-Assisted
  Trauma Therapy: Working with the Parts System   19
  SARAH SCHLOTE AND ILKA PARENT

3 Increasing Tolerance for Calm in Clients with Complex
  Trauma and Dissociation   44
  SARAH JENKINS

4 Natural Lifemanship's Trauma-Focused EAP for Reactive
  Attachment Disorder   54
  BETTINA SHULTZ-JOBE, KATE NAYLOR, AND TIM JOBE

5 Working with Relational Trauma: Limbic Restructuring through
  Equine-Facilitated Psychotherapy   69
  PHILIPPA WILLIAMS

6 Equine-Assisted Group Therapy for Adolescent Sexual Trauma
  Survivors: Development, Implementation, and Outcomes   84
  KIRBY WYCOFF AND VIRGINIA MURPHY

  7 Experiential Equine-Assisted Focal Psychodynamic
     Psychotherapy: Addressing Personality and Attachment in
     Clients with Chronic Childhood Trauma   107
     GÉZA KOVÁCS

SECTION TWO
Trauma Occurring during Adulthood   123

  8 Equine-Assisted Therapy for Trauma – Accidents   125
     NINA EKHOLM FRY

  9 Families and Trauma   140
     REBECCA F. BAILEY AND ELIZABETH BAILEY

 10 Natural Lifemanship's Trauma-Focused
     Equine-Assisted Psychotherapy (EAP): Equine-Connected
     Eye-Movement Desensitization and Reprocessing (EC-EMDR)   154
     BETTINA SHULTZ-JOBE, KATHLEEN CHOE, AND TIM JOBE

 11 Warrior PATHH: Integrated Equine-Assisted Psychotherapy for
     Posttraumatic Growth in Combat Veterans   171
     ROB PLISKIN

 12 Treating Combat-Related Posttraumatic Stress Disorder
     through Psychodynamic Equine-Assisted Traumatherapy   186
     ILKA PARENT

     Appendix 1: General Trauma-Informed Therapy Trainings   195
     Appendix 2: Trauma-Informed Equine-Assisted Mental Health Trainings   203
     Index   207

About the Editors

Figure 0.1 Dr. Kay Trotter

Dr. Kay Sudekum Trotter

Dr. Kay Trotter is the founder of Kaleidoscope Behavioral Health, a group practice providing services to the whole family: children, teens, and adults. She has taught and spoken professionally on child development, such as treating anxiety in children, play therapy, parenting, and equine-assisted mental health. Dr. Trotter has worked with children and their families over the last 20 years. She is a Licensed Professional Counselor Supervisor, Registered Play Therapist Supervisor, National Certified Counselor, and Certified Equine Interaction

Professional—Mental Health. Dr. Trotter currently serves on the Medical City Lewisville Board of Trustees and is the Past-President of the North Texas Chapter of Play Therapy. Dr. Trotter earned her master's degree and PhD from the University of North Texas, with an emphasis on Play Therapy and Animal Assisted Therapy—Equine. Her PhD dissertation became groundbreaking research, and is one of the first published studies on the effectiveness of equine-assisted mental health. Contact Dr. Trotter: Kay@KayTrotter.com

Figure 0.2 Dr. Jennifer Baggerly

Dr. Jennifer N. Baggerly

Dr. Jennifer N. Baggerly is a Professor of Counseling at the University of North Texas at Dallas. Dr. Baggerly is a Licensed Professional Counselor Supervisor and a Registered Play Therapist Supervisor who also provides counseling at Kaleidoscope Behavioral Health. She served as Chair of the Board of Directors for the Association for Play Therapy from 2013 to 2014 and was a member of the board from 2009 to 2015. Dr. Baggerly has taught and counseled children for over 20 years. Her published books include *Counseling Families: Play-Based Treatment*, *Group Play Therapy: A Dynamic Approach*, and *Child-Centered Play Therapy Research: The Evidence Base for Effective Practice*. Dr. Baggerly's multiple research projects and over 60 publications have led to her being recognized as a prominent expert in children's counseling. Contact Dr. Baggerly: jennifer.baggerly@untdallas.edu.

About the Contributors

Elizabeth Bailey is a registered nurse, board certified in psychiatric-mental health care. She worked at the Resnick Neuropsychiatric Hospital at UCLA for 11 years. She recently completed a master's program in clinical psychology and is in the process of becoming licensed as an MFT in California. She occasionally works with Transitioning Families in the capacity of psychiatric RN, and is currently working on a second book with her sister, Dr. Rebecca Bailey. Contact Elizabeth: Ebaileyla@yahoo.com.

Dr. Rebecca F. Bailey, PhD, developed Transitioning Families, a family-based program for therapeutic reunification and reintegration. She is a nationally recognized expert in non-familial and familial abduction. Dr. Bailey is a consultant to the National Center for Missing and Exploited Children and is an active member of the Association of Family and Conciliation Courts as well as the International Association of the Chiefs of Police. Contact Dr. Bailey: Drbailey@transitioningfamilies.com.

Kathleen Choe, MA, LPC-S, NLC-C, has a Master of Art's degree in Marriage, Family and Child Counseling from Azusa Pacific University. She is a Licensed Professional Counselor and Supervisor as well as a Natural Lifemanship Certified Clinician and Trainer with over 20 years of experience in the counseling field. Her focus is treating eating disorders and trauma utilizing EMDR and equine-assisted psychotherapy. Contact Kathleen: Counseling@kathleenchoe.net.

Nina Ekholm Fry, MSSc., CCTP, is the Director of Equine Programs at the Institute for Human–Animal Connection and Adjunct Professor at University of Denver, where she leads the Equine-Assisted Mental Health Practitioner Certificate program. Nina is a certified clinical trauma professional and consults on psychotherapy services with horses nationally. She has a particular interest in equine welfare issues, both in equine-assisted services and for human–horse interactions in general. Contact Nina: Nina.ekholm-fry@du.edu.

Sarah Jenkins, MC, LPC, CPsychol, is an EMDR International Association (EMDRIA) EMDR Training Provider & Consultant, Equine-Assisted

Therapist, and lifelong horsewoman. Sarah created EquiLateral, the Equine-Assisted EMDR Protocol, and the first EMDRIA approved training in Equine-Assisted EMDR. A trauma and dissociation specialist and highly sought after international speaker, Sarah provides consultation and education on EMDR, structural dissociation theory, along with the ethics and best practices of EAP with complex trauma and dissociation. Contact Sarah: Sarah@dragonflyinternationaltherapy.com.

Tim Jobe, BS, has spent the last 50 years learning from the horse how to build a connected relationship that seamlessly transfers to human relationships. For the last 30 years he has partnered horses and people while developing a model of therapy that is healing for both. He and his wife, Bettina Shultz-Jobe, developed the Natural Lifemanship model of TF-EAP in which they continue to train and certify individuals across the globe. Contact Tim: Tim@naturallifemanship.com.

Dr. Géza Kovács is a clinical psychologist at SPELpsychologen in the Netherlands. He has been a licensed therapist (BIG) for 18 years and is a board member of the animal-assisted psychotherapy department. As well as his clinical work he has recently attended a PhD project at the Open University Netherlands in which the effects of equine-assisted psychotherapy are investigated. Contact Dr. Kovács: G.kovacs@spelpsychologen.nl.

Virginia Murphy, PsyD, is a licensed psychologist with clinical interests in the treatment of trauma among children, trauma informed care, case formulation, and cognitive-behavioral therapies for mental health disorders affecting children and adolescents. Dr. Murphy has worked at various levels of mental health care, including outpatient care, day hospitals, and inpatient units. Currently, she provides mental health care in a residential facility for at-risk youth. Contact Dr. Murphy: Murphyvb1970@yahoo.com.

Kate Naylor, MA, LMFT, NLC-C, EP, holds a Master of Arts degree in Counseling from St. Edward's University. She is a Licensed Marriage and Family Therapist as well as a Natural Lifemanship Certified Clinician, Equine Professional, and Trainer. Kate offers traditional and equine-assisted psychotherapy for parents and families in the Austin, Texas area, as well as co-leading trainings in the Natural Lifemanship model throughout the country. For more information, please visit kategosenaylor.com. Contact Kate at: Kate@naturallifemanship.com.

Ilka Parent, MS, Dipl-Psych, is a Clinical Psychotherapist, Traumatherapist, and founder and owner of Minds-n-Motion. Ilka has been a world leader in getting psychodynamic equine-assisted traumatherapy implemented as a treatment modality for members of the armed forces. She specializes in working with combat-related trauma and complex PTSD. Ilka is an avid advocate for trauma-informed care, promoting further research and advocating for horses' wellbeing in equine interaction programs. Contact Ilka Parent: Ilka.parent@mindsnmotion.net.

Rob Pliskin, MSSA, LSW, CDCA, is an International NHS Clinician, EAGALA (Duel Certified) Professional. In 1998 Rob began his exploration of equines and healing while gentling wild horses and burros in the American West. Rob co-founded the EAP program at Big Heart Ranch in Malibu, CA for adolescents in 2005. Since 2010 Rob has been an adjunct instructor at Lake Erie College, teaching equine-assisted therapy. Rob holds Advanced Certification as an EAGALA Mental Health Professional and Equine Specialist. Contact Rob: Robpliskin@icloud.com.

Sarah Schlote, MA, RP, CCC, SEP, is the creator of EQUUSOMA™ and the EquuSpirit: Healing with Horses program, and founder of The Refuge: Centre for Healing and Recovery. A Somatic Experiencing Practitioner and EMDR therapist with training in somatic touch work, attachment ruptures and repair, structural dissociation, polyvagal theory, Body Memory Recall, and other approaches, she is devoted to educating professionals about trauma-informed practice and integrative trauma treatment. For more information see www.equusoma.com and www.healingrefuge.com. Contact Sarah: Sarah@healingrefuge.com.

Bettina Shultz-Jobe, MA, LPC, holds a Master of Arts degree in Counseling and is a Licensed Professional Counselor. She is trained in a variety of experiential, body-based, equine, and trauma therapies, and has served a variety of clients for over 15 years. She and her husband, Tim Jobe, developed the Natural Lifemanship model of TF-EAP in which they continue to train and certify individuals across the globe. Contact Bettina: Bettina@naturallifemanship.com.

Philippa Williams is a registered Equine Facilitated Psychotherapist (EFP) and Supervisor (LEAP Senior). She is an experienced psychologist, whose research interests lie in body–mind processes and attending to the body when working with trauma. Alongside her EFP work, Philippa has extensive experience and training at doctoral level, providing psychological and psychotherapeutic interventions and supervision for a broad range of presenting issues. Her experience, love and passion for horses also enables her to share tools and techniques that help to attend to the care and needs of the therapy horse. Contact Philippa: info@equineenlightenment.co.uk.

Dr. Kirby Wycoff, Psy.D., NCSP, is an Assistant Professor of School Psychology at Worcester State University in Central Massachusetts and a Nationally Certified School Psychologist. She is a former member of the Governing Board of the American Psychological Associations Section on Human-Animal Interactions. Dr. Wycoff teaches and supervises graduate students and her clinical work and research focuses on at-risk children, human–animal interactions, and trauma-impacted youth and families. Contact Dr. Wycoff: Kwycoff@worester.edu.

Preface

What do equines and trauma survivors have in common? They both had the experience of being prey. Equines are prey of predators such as wild animals (wolves, coyotes, mountain lions, bears, etc.) and humans. Trauma survivors are prey of predators such as abusive parents, sexual perpetrators, criminals, enemy soldiers, disasters, and accidents. What can trauma survivors learn from equines? Equines model majestic power, stealth strength, and watchful waiting despite possible threat. What can mental health providers learn from equines? Equines teach mental health providers how to be a patient witness, move with a gradual approach, and respect an empowered will or choice in the context of a safe relationship. This groundbreaking book expounds on this dynamic healing experience between equines, trauma survivors, and mental health providers by harnessing equine-assisted mental health with trauma-informed treatment.

Trauma-informed treatment is becoming a standard of practice in mental health. The Substance Abuse and Mental Health Services Administration (SAMHSA, 2014) describes trauma-informed care as realizing the widespread impact of trauma, recognizing the signs and symptoms of trauma in individuals, integrating knowledge about trauma into policies and practices, and resisting re-traumatization. Rather than a prescribed set of procedures, SAMHSA (2014) encourages mental health professionals to follow six trauma-informed principles of "(1) safety, (2) trustworthiness and transparency, (3) peer support, (4) collaboration and mutuality, (5) empowerment, voice, and choice, and (6) cultural, historical, and gender issues" (p. 10).

The authors in this book exemplify these trauma-informed principles. Their commitment to safety, collaboration, and empowerment are illustrated in case examples of clients who have survived trauma and are thriving after participating in trauma-informed equine-assisted mental health. The authors' depth of understanding of trauma is matched by their compelling stories of how equines (horses and donkeys) facilitate safe relationships, restoration, and reconnection for their clients.

A variety of types of trauma are addressed in this book. The first section focuses on trauma originating in childhood such as complex trauma, dissociation, attachment issues and disorders, relational childhood trauma, and adolescent sexual trauma. The second section focuses on trauma originating in adulthood such as accidents, families, and veterans. These topics are conceptualized from a variety of theoretical approaches including interpersonal neurobiology, attachment, psychoanalytic, family systems, trauma focused cognitive behavior therapy, and eye movement desensitization and reprocessing (EMDR). This book offers a wealth of resources dedicated to the practice of trauma-informed care. We have included the authors' favorite trauma-informed trainings options for the reader to explore. Both recommended general *Trauma-Informed* trainings and specific *Trauma-Informed Equine-Assisted Mental Health* trainings resources are included.

Ethical considerations in equine-assisted mental health are covered in the individual chapters in this book. For an in-depth exploration of ethical issues please see Trotter & Baggerly, 2018. For clients with trauma histories, mental health professionals must also be aware that touch and sudden movement may be a trigger. Securing informed consent, thoroughly explaining procedures, teaching safety and stabilization skills to use when overwhelmed, and asking for ongoing client feedback are an important part of ethical practice.

We are confident this book will enrich your practice of equine-assisted mental health with trauma survivors. You will be part of a new breed of trauma-informed equine-assisted mental health professionals who witness the transformative power that equines offer in healing trauma.

Warm regards,

Kay Trotter and Jennifer Baggerly

References

Substance Abuse and Mental Health Services Administration. (2014). SAMHSA's Concept of Trauma and Guidance for a Trauma-Informed Approach. HHS Publication No. (SMA) 14-4884. Rockville, MD: Substance Abuse and Mental Health Services Administration.

Trotter, K. S. & Baggerly, J. N. (2018). Ethical considerations in equine-assisted interventions: meeting the needs of both human and horse. In K. S. Trotter & J. N. Baggerly (Eds.), Equine-assisted mental health interventions: harnessing solutions to common problems. Abingdon: Routledge.

Trauma Originating in Childhood

1 Integrating Somatic Experiencing® and Attachment into Equine-Assisted Trauma Recovery

Sarah Schlote

Introduction

Chronic Stress and Trauma

Often masquerading as a host of other mental and physical health challenges, the widespread impact of chronic stress and trauma as well as their role in adult disease are finally being recognized by the mainstream. In its groundbreaking research study with Kaiser Permanente, the Center for Disease Control found that two-thirds of adults have suffered from at least one type of adverse childhood experience (ACE), and that there was an 87% chance of having experienced two or more kinds of ACE (Karr-Morse & Wiley, 2012). Regardless of the type of adverse experience or trauma, the impacts can be significant and life altering. Potential impact includes an increased likelihood of addictions, eating disorders, suicidality, anxiety, depression, chronic shame, and dissociation, along with sexual and relationship issues. Trauma is also correlated with increased risk for complex health conditions such as autoimmune disorders, obesity, pain syndromes, chronic fatigue, gastrointestinal issues, pelvic issues, respiratory issues, allergies, heart disease, and cancer, among other challenges. Western medicine still typically treats mental and physical health as separate entities, but a growing body of trauma experts is proposing that when trauma is addressed and healed, mental and physical health both improve (Levine, 2010; Scaer, 2001/2014).

Impact on Attachment

From an early developmental standpoint, we are reliant on our primary caregivers not only for physical survival, but also to soothe distress to ensure experiences do not exceed our window of tolerance. Through consistency, attunement, responsiveness, touch, and play, our nervous systems learn to settle, become accustomed to experiences that broaden our tolerance, and internalize a sense of safety and security that are foundational to future growth. Through our caregivers' regulation and presence, our brains and bodies can focus on the act of living because our needs are met. As we settle and thrive, our caregivers settle further as well, which supports bonding through a process known as co-regulation. However, when our caregivers are unable to provide this source of co-regulation, attachment ruptures lead to pervasive patterns of hyperarousal and hypoarousal as our organism tries its best to regulate despite lacking the neural platforms and capacity to do so (Kain & Terrell, 2016; 2018). A similar situation occurs with regards to shock trauma, which refers to incidents that happen when it was not possible to mount a successful defensive response, resulting in a tremendous amount of survival energy mobilized as procedural (or body) memory, stuck in the queue with nowhere to go (Levine, 1997, 2010; Payne & Crane-Godreau, 2015).

Unresolved traumatic stress physiology can wreak havoc on one's mind, body, emotions, and relationships. When it is not possible to orient, fight, or flee an impending threat, or find someone to protect us or soothe our distress, the only options involve utilizing the high-tone dorsal vagal response, implicated in the freeze state and dissociation (tonic immobility or collapsed immobility), or ventral vagal social engagement strategies (Porges, 2007; Walker, n.d) such as fawning, complying, submission, or caretaking. A range of destructive management strategies (e.g., addictions, eating disorders, self-blame) may be drawn upon to approximate regulation, ward off potential future threats, prevent rejection and further pain, and cope with survival and attachment dilemmas (Kain & Terrell, 2016, 2018).

Neuroception, our unconscious sorting system that allows us to detect safety or threat, becomes over- or under-responsive, leaving survivors feeling perpetually in danger or unaware they are at risk (Porges, 2007). Not surprisingly, all this stacked survival energy left in the body results in persistent insecure attachment patterns and a vast array of somatic symptoms. Trauma survivors often spend their lives using their energy to manage the chaos within or contending with numbness or disconnection. The sheer fatigue of having had to do so for so long results in little energy left for living. Safety, comfort, pleasure, ease, and goodness are unfamiliar or uncomfortable luxuries that the body and the personality have difficulty taking in or even recognizing (Levine, 1997, 2010; Kain & Terrell, 2016). The majority of the impacts resulting from trauma and attachment injuries apply not only to humans, but also other mammals, including equines. Species-related differences notwithstanding, overall the impact of adverse experiences shows startlingly familiar and consistent patterns across mammals from a neurobiological, behavioral, and relational standpoint. This makes a trauma lens to working with both humans and animals like horses, donkeys, mules, and hinnies a necessity (see Schlote, in press, for a longer literature review and an outline of how to apply trauma and attachment principles to horsemanship as well as equine-assisted practice).

Equine-assisted therapy and learning approaches have been used with trauma survivors since their inception. However, this has not always been undertaken in a trauma-informed way with full appreciation for the complexities and nuances involved, resulting in inadvertent traumatic re-enactments or sending participants and equines beyond their thresholds in spite of the best of intentions. "Trusting the process" in this work often implies that the therapist must take a backseat to what is unfolding, which can result in following a client into dysregulation, dissociation, and overriding if a foundation of stabilization and containment has not been established first, as promoted by best practices and staged models of trauma treatment (Herman, 1997). Indeed, trauma therapy of any kind, equine-related or otherwise, requires the skillful and nuanced ability to know when to follow and when to lead, especially if a client lacks the inner capacity to self-regulate and recognize the edges of their own window of tolerance. This is relevant to the animals as well, who also have the capacity to get activated into fight or flight, overwhelmed, and override through appeasement, submission, freeze, or dissociation in their interactions with humans. The literature of trauma-informed care, with its emphasis on fostering *safety, consent, choice, voice, empowerment, trust, collaboration, and compassion*, provides an ethical framework for conducting any equine-based interventions in such a way that the wellbeing of all human and equine participants is honored—whether or not trauma treatment is the focus. These values, along with an understanding of attachment rupture and repair, trauma psychophysiology, polyvagal theory, and principles and techniques drawn from Somatic Experiencing®, form the basis of the EQUUSOMA™ (Schlote, 2017) approach.

EQUUSOMA™ Biological Explanation

> In dreams, mythical stories, and lore, one universal symbol for the human body
> and its instinctual nature is the horse.
>
> (Peter A. Levine 1997, p. 66)

Dr. Levine's research into mammalian stress physiology and the activation cycle of defense responses extends our understanding of the window of tolerance model proposed by Siegel (1999) and helps explain why wild animals are routinely exposed to threat but rarely experience trauma. When faced with novelty in the environment, our first response is to arrest/startle and orient to the source of the stimulation. Herd mammals turn to group members to confirm or disconfirm whether or not there is danger, and also rely on one another for survival efforts and safety. If a threat is identified, both horses and humans will seek safety through connection or engage in specific defensive actions (fight/flight). When these are not possible, mammals can also resort to fawning (relate, appease, submit, tend, and befriend behaviors) or freezing (immobility). The main difference between domesticated species and our wild cousins is that they are generally not exposed to the same long-term stressors as humans and domesticated animals are. They are also typically free to engage in natural behaviors and protective actions, and move through the immobility response by shaking and discharging whatever thwarted survival energy is left in the system to return to a state of balance (Levine, 1997, 2010, 2015; Kozlowska et al., 2015; Payne & Crane-Godreau, 2015; Scaer, 2001/2014).

This is not always the case for humans and other domesticated or captive species. First of all, punishment, confinement, shame, or social norms prevent the full enactment of defensive responses and other natural behaviors. Secondly, attachment ruptures (like abuse, abandonment, neglect, early weaning, isolation from others, and chronic misattunements between humans or horse and human) result in a loss of co-regulation and ability to accurately gauge safety or threat, meaning that the nervous system often remains in hyperarousal or shutdown even when this is no longer necessary. Finally, humans in particular have a highly developed neocortex, which in Western cultures tends to judge, fear, and suppress instinctual behaviors such as the tremors associated with the discharge of survival energy when coming out of a state of immobility or freeze.

Porges' (2007) polyvagal theory also adds an important element to consider when working with survivors of trauma. Originally, the autonomic nervous system (ANS) was viewed as having two branches, where sympathetic and parasympathetic states were limited to reciprocal action (i.e., that when one is stressed, one cannot also be in a state of relaxation, and vice versa). In this model, the stress response is often incorrectly portrayed as being a negative experience, associated with fear, pain, confusion, or distress, and that down-regulating via the relaxation response is preferable. However, stress can be experienced positively or negatively, depending on what is happening, and the sympathetic response is also involved with excitement, vigorous play, sexual activity, exercise, and other experiences that might be deemed pleasurable. Furthermore, the parasympathetic state is not always adaptive, and individuals stuck in chronic hypoarousal need support to up-regulate back into a window of tolerance of aliveness.

Porges (2007) and others have proposed that the ANS actually consists of three branches that can vary independently or in the same direction, at different intensities. According to the polyvagal theory, the sympathetic nervous system is still the body's equivalent of a gas pedal, but the parasympathetic nervous system consists of two different types of brakes to support settling: the "freeze" or dorsal vagal complex (DVC, conservation, and shutdown), and the ventral vagal complex (VVC, social engagement and attachment relationships). At any given point, each of these states is like a dial, with varying levels of intensity or tone co-occurring. For instance, play usually involves a certain amount of sympathetic nervous system (SNS) arousal plus VVC social engagement, which moderates the experience. When play starts to become overwhelming or distressing (such as when tickling ceases to be fun), the amount of SNS arousal increases into anger or panic (fight or flight mobilization), VVC decreases (social engagement is withdrawn when the person is viewed as threatening or the experience is no longer enjoyable), and there would be a certain amount of DVC that occurs as the individual shuts down or experiences helplessness in the face of activation without relief.

Similarly, immobility or stillness can also be experienced as pleasurable or threatening, depending on what is going on. For kittens being carried by the scruff of their necks by their mothers, the limp immobility that is experienced is not coupled with fear, and they come out of immobility easily once placed on the ground again (a phenomenon known as self-paced termination; Levine, 2010). This is also true of other situations, like the stillness experienced when resting and digesting, following orgasm, when nursing an infant, or even during certain spiritual practices like meditation.

However, under certain circumstances, immobility or stillness as in the previous examples is over-coupled with fear, terror, or helplessness. Under conditions of repeated fear and restraint, it takes humans and other mammals much longer to come out of the "freeze" response. As stated by Levine (2010), "the potentiation of immobility by fear can lead to a self-perpetuating feedback loop causing an essentially permanent quasi-paralysis in the traumatized individual. This condition, I believe, underpins several of trauma's most debilitating symptoms, especially numbing, shutdown, dissociation, feelings of entrapment, and helplessness" (p. 54). Should an individual enter into a state of dorsal vagal shutdown while terrified and restrained in some way, he or she will likely emerge from the freeze state in an equally frenzied, disorganized, or violent way, as he or she taps into the high state of bound SNS arousal (fight or flight energy) that was locked in the queue when the person entered freeze in the first place; "as they go in, so they come out" (Levine, 2010, p. 62). This is as true for humans as it is for other mammals, including horses, who can also come out of freeze or dissociation the way they went in. This phenomenon is biologically appropriate and necessary; indeed, "as a captured and terrified animal comes out of immobility, its survival may depend on its violent aggression toward the still-present predator [. . .] or to flee in frantic desperation" (p. 64).

As a result, moving in and out of immobility or freeze is a delicate process that requires a graduated approach so that primal, body sensations associated with rage or terror are experienced slowly to prevent becoming overwhelmed as the organism comes back into aliveness. This is especially true if chronic states of immobility and unresolved charge in the body have led to complex health syndromes that get aggravated when experiencing too much survival energy at once (such as fibromyalgia flares, migraines, and so on). Working in an incremental way also allows space to work with any associated shame and self-loathing connected to the freeze response and underlying thwarted impulses towards rage or escaping. For example, a client who long ago shut down their fight response and lives in a state of functional freeze may have difficulty with activities that invite them to explore boundaries and assertiveness with horses because these require them to move out of hypoarousal and tap into self-protective movements and intensity that may be over-coupled with fear or shame. Faced with the sudden flooding of hyperarousal, the client might either try to override the unleashed activation for the sake of doing the activity, or go back into a rigid or collapsed state of shutdown or defeat ("I can't"). Similarly, a horse that has been functionally frozen for a long time may begin to express "acting out" behaviors when thawing out of a freeze or dissociated state as it begins to recognize that it has choice and a voice. If this is not understood as normal and worked with constructively, the risk—as with humans—is that the survival energy will again be shut down out of fear or submission, resulting in a ticking time bomb of unresolved bound charge lurking beneath the surface.

EQUUSOMA™ Description

Equine-assisted trauma recovery can provide some of the conditions required to restore a sense of regulation, safety, and connection in relationship. It works carefully through survival responses in the nervous system to facilitate "feeling felt" through the presence of equines as well as embodied, attuned, and regulated human facilitators. At the base of the EQUUSOMA™ approach is Levine's nuanced nine-stage Somatic Experiencing® model (Levine, 2010), which involves the following components and roadmap for equine-based work in alignment with the window of tolerance:

1. Establish an environment of relative safety.
2. Support initial exploration and acceptance of sensation.
3. Establish "pendulation" and containment: the innate power of rhythm.
4. Use titration to create increasing stability, resilience, and organization.
5. Provide a corrective experience by supplanting the passive responses of collapse and helplessness with active, empowered, defensive responses.
6. Separate or "uncouple" the conditioned association of fear and helplessness from the biological immobility response.
7. Resolve hyperaroused states by gently guiding the "discharge" and redistribution of the vast survival energy mobilized for life-preserving action while freeing that energy to support higher-level brain functioning.
8. Engage self-regulation to restore "dynamic equilibrium" and relaxed alertness.
9. Orient to the here and now, contact the environment and reestablish the capacity for social engagement. (pp. 74–75)

Pendulation refers to the body's natural oscillation between stress arousal or trauma activation and its subsequent deactivation—the ebb and flow, rise and fall, or constriction and expansion of the organism. Somatic Experiencing® helps build the capacity for progressively larger pendulations or thresholds of activation, self-protective responses, relational intimacy, or even positive affect (including activities involving equines) without having to override, get flooded, freeze, or dissociate to cope. While these responses can and will occur, the goal would be for them to progressively decrease over time as inner capacity and resilience are developed, resulting in a different experience of oneself and relationship. This requires the joint techniques of mindfully *micro-tracking* subtle bodily sensations and movement impulses and *titrating* at lower thresholds of intensity before proceeding to higher ones. These skills can be applied to any equine-facilitated activity, from observing at a distance all the way through to more involved equine interactions. As clients grow their window of tolerance for moving through activation–deactivation cycles (that is, as they build the capacity to tolerate incrementally larger negative and positive experiences of arousal and attachment connection, and engage in actions that require greater agency and assertiveness), they develop a sense of embodiment, competency, and triumph.

Thresholds of Intensity Model

This work also relies on the therapeutic presence of human and equine co-facilitators in service of offering *co-regulation*: an opportunity to "ping" off other regulated beings (Kain, 2015), check in with the "herd" to get a more accurate gauge of safety or threat, determine whether mobilizing for action or settling is deemed warranted, and either take action or settle into activities that are enjoyable or nourishing. For those who experienced trauma, safety, settling, and pleasure may be unfamiliar experiences. If caregivers were the source of harm, were unresponsive or inconsistent, or struggled themselves with anxiety or anger, the message a child's nervous system receives from the other bodies surrounding him or her is that the world is a dangerous place, there is always something to be on guard about, and "I have to go it alone." This state of hypervigilance can result in a negativity bias where everything is deemed a threat, even if it is not, and a sense of wariness or anxiety when feeling calm or experiencing pleasurable moments. The opposite can also be true, where a person's noticing systems become hypoaroused and awareness of threats is compromised, resulting in greater risk of harm due to inattention. In either case, it becomes difficult to trust one's own perception and ability to make sense of the world. The quality of the attunement, regulation, and presence of the organisms, both human and equine, that support the process allows

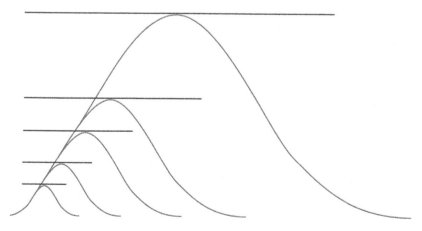

Figure 1.1 Thresholds of Intensity Model

for a remapping of one's neuroception. This also allows for greater flexibility and range of responses in the world (other than always "on" or always "off"), including shared experiences of settling, calm, pleasure, play, gratitude, confidence, and joy.

These shared corrective emotional and bodily experiences mediated by social engagement and the ventral vagal system in turn support organization, regulation, and coherence in the nervous system of clients (Baldwin, 2015; Geller & Porges, 2014; Kain & Terrell, 2016, 2018; Stanley, 2016). Social engagement is further enhanced by attending to the core components of attachment in order to repair relational ruptures by restoring a sense of *safe haven* and *secure base* with the animal(s) and human facilitator(s). In addition, this experience helps clients work through activation associated with *proximity and separation*, the natural arrivals and departures in relationships (Ainsworth & Bowlby, 1991; Kain & Terrell, 2016, 2018).

As a result, the materials needed will depend on the activity and do not require any specific tools or items beyond therapists' skillful awareness of the aforementioned principles, their attunement, and their ability to attend to psychophysiology of the client, animal, and themselves. If working in a co-facilitation team, the equine professional's regulation and presence are equally important to both the client and the animals, even if his or her focus is primarily the animal's experience, responses, needs, and wellbeing. Finally, the dynamic between the equine professional and therapist also needs to be monitored, in order to prevent or address any inadvertent family of origin transference and re-enactments, or co-dysregulation, and to maintain relational safety for all involved.

Case Example 1

Amanda (*pseudonym*) is a 43-year-old female of mixed ethnicity with a college diploma and significant early developmental trauma as well as shock trauma. She struggled with dysregulation, dissociation, anxiety, passivity, lack of somatic awareness and boundaries, a pervasive belief that she did not deserve to exist, and a pattern of disorganized attachment. Amanda also experienced pain in her neck and shoulders, and had irritable bowel syndrome. She had done talk-based therapies for many years, with mixed results. She attended therapy sessions of Somatic Experiencing® and attachment-focused therapy for approximately eight months prior to adding in EQUUSOMA™ sessions at a local farm. The following transcript reflects movement through Levine's nine stages to demonstrate the process. However, for many clients working through all the steps in one session would not necessarily be a realistic expectation. Instead, therapists can work with clients over time as their capacity for higher thresholds of positive and negative arousal increased. This session took place with a cross-trained therapist with experience in horsemanship. Yet, this process can easily be adapted to include an equine professional.

Transcript Analysis of Case Example

The following transcript analysis is about a pseudonym composite client:

Table 1.1 Case Example Transcript

Transcript	Analysis
(Step 1: The therapist has already helped the client orient to present time and the farm environment through sensory awareness exercises, and provided psychoeducation about the process to support settling and begin building safety through informed consent, choice, transparency, and pacing. The transcript picks up following these initial moments, and includes two pendulations of activation–deactivation, following the nine-step process twice.)	
Therapist: As you anticipate the possibility of approaching Brando (horse), what do you notice? *(the horse is grazing a distance away)*	**Step 2:** The process of tracking sensations and titrating the experience begins at the lowest point in the sequence of exploring proximity, before even approaching the horse.
Client: That I'm excited to meet him. *(however, therapist notices the client's eyes are darting around, her posture is braced, and that she is shifting her weight from foot to foot)*	The body story conveys a different tale than the verbal story, as the client disregards and overrides her internal experience of discomfort. It would be easy at this point to disregard the discrepancy and rush into relationship to get the activity done, at the risk of creating a re-enactment of misattunement for both the client and the horse.
Therapist: I'm curious about what your body is saying right now. What's happening on the inside?	**Steps 2 and 4:** The therapist notices the over-coupled excitement and hypervigilance and pauses the process to explore it.
Client: There's a tension in my chest and stomach and I can't really focus.	**Step 2:** The client begins to bring awareness to the underlying anticipation activation.
Therapist: Let's slow things down for a moment and pause here. How might you describe the tension? Does it have a size, shape, color, texture, or sense of dimension or movement?	**Steps 2–4:** The therapist guides the client in developing interoception, the ability to mindfully notice what is happening inside with curiosity. Slowing the process down titrates things further and helps with building safety and security together.
Client: It's like a tight knot right in the middle, the size of a grapefruit, with pangs that radiate out from the center …	**Step 3:** The client describes their activation with interest and notices rhythm, movement and dimensionality in what is taking place inside.

(continued)

Table 1.1 Case Example Transcript (Cont.)

Transcript	Analysis
Therapist: What happens as you track the edges of that sensation where it's less intense?	**Step 4:** Focusing on the periphery of the sensation helps titrate it further so the client can explore it with less apprehension.
Client: It stays the same ... I feel like I need to back away.	**Step 5:** The client recognizes an underlying self-protective impulse to flee, which was hinted at with the foot movements and body posture but masked by her pattern of overriding. The client begins to connect with a sense of underlying rhythm in the nervous system and activation around closeness/proximity.
Therapist: I wonder what might happen if you were to allow your body to move the way it wants to right now? *(client moves back a few feet and at a different angle).* Does that feel like the right spot? How do you know?	**Step 5:** The therapist encourages the client to mobilize and complete a self-protective movement, and to notice what's different as a result of engaging in the action. The therapist is supportive and offers permission to the client to have agency as opposed to feel helpless.
Client: I don't feel as nervous now, but there's still some tightness in my chest.	**Step 7:** Engaging the impulse to flee in a small way allowed some of the survival energy to dissipate.
Therapist: What happens next as you pay attention? If you like, track the edges of the sensation again and follow what changes.	**Steps 4, 7–8:** The therapist titrates the experience to allow the activation time to move through.
Client: *(after a few moments)* It's not so tight now. It's starting to fade a little *(exhales).*	**Steps 3, 7–8:** The client stayed with a pendulation of activation until it deactivated, which is different from overriding, complying, panicking, or becoming overwhelmed and shutting down. The therapist's grounded attunement offered the support and confidence to allow this to unfold.
Therapist: That's it, notice what's shifting. *(a few moments pass)* How are things now?	**Step 8:** The therapist encourages the client to stay with the deactivation of the remainder of the survival energy in the body until equilibrium is restored.
Client: *(able to look the therapist in the eyes)* I'm feeling calmer. I hadn't realized how much I go along with things even though I'm uncomfortable.	**Step 9:** As the client returns to baseline and re-enters their window of tolerance, she is able to make meaning from the experience and has more capacity for social engagement.

Table 1.1 Case Example Transcript (Cont.)

Transcript	Analysis
Therapist: What happens now when you think of approaching Brando?	**Steps 2–3:** Now that the client has moved through the initial pendulation (steps 1–9), the therapist revisits the original invitation to see if there is any remaining charge.
Client: *(checks in internally)* There's barely any tension there now. I'm interested in getting a bit closer.	The idea of approaching is less daunting now that the client has more choice and feels less helpless in the face of her inner activation. She has a sense that what goes up must come down, and that she can move through the activation until it resolves, which is different from getting stuck in it or having to go along with things she is not comfortable with.
(Before they have a chance to observe Brando's body language to see if the desire for contact is mutual, he moves slowly toward them instead from a distance away.)	
Therapist: What's happening now? **Client:** What if he comes too close? *(client appears frozen in place but still engaging with the therapist)*	**Step 6:** Without the element of choice, the client begins to experience the familiar state of freeze (immobility with fear) in the face of closeness/proximity, which underlies their chronic passivity.
Therapist: I will ultimately make sure that doesn't happen. See what happens as you track what's happening inside, and notice if there's any movement your body might like to make, if it could.	**Steps 2–6:** The therapist's statement provides a corrective experience affirming that she will protect the client, offering a repair for past attachment ruptures where caregivers did not do so (secure base). This allows the client time to sort out what to do next without pressure, time often being what was lacking in past traumatic events. Mobilizing active defenses is challenging for the client. The client was unable to self-protect effectively in the past, resulting in immobility, submissiveness, and helplessness, so agency is over-coupled with shame and fear. Allowing time to explore what movements the body might like to make now provides a different option and outcome than what may have occurred in the past, with the eventual goal of the client being progressively able to assert herself more confidently.
Client: *(makes an awkward attempt to flap her arms, but does so rigidly like a penguin and cannot raise them much above her waist. However, this gets Brando's attention and he pauses nonetheless)*	**Steps 5–7:** Tapping into procedural memory associated with the fight response (needed for asserting boundaries) is often challenging for trauma survivors. Exploring smaller titrations of a

(continued)

Table 1.1 Case Example Transcript (Cont.)

Transcript	Analysis
Therapist: I noticed that Brando stopped in response to your movement, even though that was unfamiliar for you. What's happening inside?	movement and tracking through the associated sensations until deactivation occurs is important to building capacity for larger manifestations of such self-protective
Client: My arms are tingling and my chest is pounding and my eyes are locked on him. **Therapist:** *(reassuringly)* That's right see what happens as you allow the sensations to pass through you and release.	actions. This is especially true if clients were punished or harmed for trying to protect themselves or even for voicing their needs or feelings. Had the client not been able to engage in any movements in that moment (had the immobility response been more intense, and had the client not done months of Somatic Experiencing® prior to coming to the farm), the therapist would have asked the horse to pause, allowing time for the client to track the sensations associated with the freeze first, to allow the unwinding of the fear to take place before engaging in any movements. Gradual titration in and out of immobility is important to not overwhelm the client by connecting with underlying fight or flight energy too quickly. However, because this client had built up some prior experience with moving in and out of immobility, it was possible to engage in an attempt at a movement in this example. With other clients, slowing down the process further would be a necessary first step, especially if shame was further reinforcing the freeze response.
Client: *(tracks sensations for a few moments)* The tingling is easing off a little, my chest isn't pounding as hard, and my eyes aren't straining as much now *(exhales)*. I feel more aliveness. **Therapist:** What are your eyes noticing now? **Client:** They seem softer. Brando doesn't seem as scary to me now. The pasture also seems a lot larger than it did a few moments ago.	**Steps 8–9:** The client is experiencing the benefit of having stayed present through a second titrated pendulation of activation–deactivation following the immobility (dorsal vagal) response: thawing out of freeze, she mobilized energy, was successful in her attempt to self-protect (Brando stopped), which allowed her to settle and return to a state of exploratory orienting to her surroundings. As her gaze softens and she is able to socially engage (ventral vagal response), her neuroception recalibrates from immediately sorting for threat to recognizing cues of safety.
(Brando is a few feet away, still calm, and licks and chews in response to the client's experience, a sign that he has shifted from sympathetic arousal into a more parasympathetic state as well.)	

Further equine-based activities with the client also followed a similar process, involving tracking activation, titrating at lower thresholds first before progressing to higher ones, and uncoupling fear, shame, and judgment from instinctual responses and impulses. The goal of the process is to experience a *renegotiation*, as opposed to a re-enactment or unhelpful reliving of situations reminiscent of past traumatic experiences. As defined by Levine (2015),

> Renegotiation occurs primarily by accessing procedural memories associated with the two dysregulated states of the autonomic nervous system (hyperarousal/overwhelm or hypoarousal/shutdown and helplessness) and then restoring and completing the associated active responses. As this process progresses, the client moves from hypo- or hyper-arousal, toward equilibrium, relaxed alertness, and a here-and-now orientation.
>
> (pp. 43–44)

Aside from working through the organism's charge and biological completion of self-protective actions, an additional form of renegotiation occurs at the level of the attachment dynamic with the therapist and the horse. First, the therapist demonstrates somatic attunement to the client and horse's experience, offers therapeutic presence through his or her own self-regulation, and more actively mediates the process in the early stages to foster safety, choice, and empowerment. Then, the repair of past attachment ruptures can begin to take place as the client has a different experience of a human as trustworthy (secure base) and the environment as predictable (safe haven). The budding relationship of mutuality and respect with the horse also provides an opportunity to explore self-protective impulses and the components of attachment, as well as experience responsive attunement, which might be less daunting to do than with humans.

Over time, as the client's capacity, regulation, and resilience grew, she required less intervention from the therapist—that is, less directing and more following what was unfolding organically. She was able to engage in progressively larger and more flexible mobilizations of self-protective responses, tolerate change and spontaneity, and experience more fluidity and enjoyment in her relationship with the horse. Increasing experiences of healthy social engagement further supported coherence in her nervous system. Gradually moving beyond immobility into utilizing the survival response energy that was locked in her body, Amanda eventually noted a reduction in physical symptoms as constricted areas in her body released. She also experienced a greater sense of embodiment and reclaimed a felt sense of rightfully inhabiting space in this world, culminating in the ending of abusive and toxic relationships she was tolerating in her life.

Case Example 2

Valerie (pseudonym) is a 52-year-old survivor of childhood sexual abuse, struggling with posttraumatic stress disorder (PTSD) as a result of her work as a police officer. Her occupational-based trauma results not only from the impact of the work itself but also betrayal by her work partner and targeted micro-aggressions, bullying, and assaults against her person because she does not conform to traditional gender roles. She presented with hypervigilance, guardedness, and distrust; a survival pattern of intellectualizing; being energetically "large and in charge"; and masking emotion in spite of being a very sensitive individual (in part due to her professional training and in part due to trauma). She struggled with periods of strong somatic activation and dysregulation, depression, and intermittent suicidal ideation. In one of our early sessions, Val arrived at the farm only to come upon a dog trapped under one of the boarders' vehicles. In that moment, we all entered into crisis mode and Val took charge of the scene in keeping with her former role as a first responder, mobilizing a full-out protective response. When the dog was safe, she was able to finally be a client and work through the charge associated with suddenly finding herself in a similar helping role to that which had contributed to her PTSD. Recognizing the importance of shifting from re-enactment to renegotiation, we went out to the horses to support deactivation of her nervous system with the support of an attuned human and the herd, something that may not have had the chance to happen before given the invalidating environment she was accustomed to. As we began to track through her discharge of sensations, horse after horse dropped to the ground and rolled shortly after we arrived in the pasture, as though they too were "letting down" along with us.

Val experienced numerous powerful moments with the herd like this over time, often remarking about the similarities between certain horses and former coworkers who tended to posture or push boundaries to establish dominance within her human herd. She had been to the farm for about five EQUUSOMA™ sessions before the following experience took place showing the principles of Somatic Experiencing® and attachment theory in action. The appointment began unusually, with a number of horses urinating in succession as we entered the large pasture and paused to ground and orient to our surroundings, as though priming us for the theme of the session about to unfold. After taking the time to settle and tune into being present, we carefully approached a row of three geldings, moving forward only when she felt a sense of draw or attraction within herself or when the horses' body language showed a sense of curiosity or receptivity, and pausing when she noticed signs of aversion or activation in herself or the animals. Once greetings had been shared with the geldings, another group of three geldings came and positioned themselves in a row on our other side, with another gelding holding up the rear of this equine version of the "thin blue line." Given that these horses lived in a large mixed herd, it was unusual that no mares took part in the equine "shield"—symbolic of the gender imbalance in the police force, perhaps, while also providing an opportunity for her to experience the support of gentle masculine energy.

Val was drawn to one horse in particular mid-lineup named Harley who seemed just as interested in her. The majority of the session consisted of Val and Harley negotiating the boundaries of their relationship by small, titrated increments, beginning with standing in close proximity without touching. She then explored if he would be open to receiving physical contact from her by approaching her hand then pausing when she would see him brace, and resuming her approach only when he relaxed (thresholds of intensity). Val had learned about titration and tracking pendulations of activation and deactivation at gradually higher levels, and it was mesmerizing to observe her attunement to his body language as she worked through whatever discomfort he had around proximity and entering into connection (as noted above, insecure attachment typically involves somatic and emotional activation associated with "arrivals" or "departures" in relationship). He eventually dropped his head, nuzzled his face into her chest, and cocked a leg along with the rest of the horses in the line, and Val was able to stroke his face and neck. When I checked in with her about what she was noticing inside herself, she sounded choked up and answered that she wasn't sure if showing her emotions would be too much of an imposition on him. She eventually reached an optimal threshold, allowed herself to cry and lean into Harley, who stayed with her as she herself experienced her own release, facilitated by the safety and security of his presence (safe haven and secure base). They enjoyed more moments of calm connection surrounded by the other horses in the lineup as her emotions ebbed, flowed, and settled.

Shortly after letting her know that we would be starting to wrap up in the next few moments, the grouping of horses began to dismantle and move away. Just then, a different horse quickly approached the original trio from behind and shoved himself into Harley to move him out of the way. Interestingly, Harley shifted his weight, sidestepping us and backing away out of our space instead of following the chain reaction of forward movement and colliding into us. Val was struck by this respect for her boundaries, which seemed only natural given how much she attended to the subtle expression of his boundaries earlier in the session. As we walked towards the gate, more horses began to urinate a short distance away, still more releasing. It is interesting to note that Harley is considered by many to be pushy, disrespectful, and unpredictable, which did not at all match our experience of him that day. Likewise, I wonder if Harley's experience of humans as being attuned and responsive to his non-verbal cues was also different from his typical experience of people. The renegotiation in the session was therefore twofold: 1) both Val and Harley had the opportunity to experience the titrated buildup, deactivation, and completion of charge to build capacity for connection and secure attachment (as opposed to experiencing the re-enactment of having to override, act out, or shut down to be in misattuned relationship); and 2) Val also experienced the backup of a team of calm and accepting male "coworkers" and an equine "partner" who supported a fuller expression of her selfhood and quite literally had her back when push came to shove.

References

Ainsworth, M.S. & Bowlby, J. (1991). An ethological approach to personality development. *American Psychologist*, 46(4), 333–341.

Baldwin, A.L. (2015, November 14). *Heart-to-Heart Communication with Horses*. HeartMath Institute webinar. Available online: www.heartmath.org/resources/downloads/heart-heart-communication-horses/.

Geller, S. & Porges, S. (2014). Therapeutic presence: Neurophysiolgical mechanisms mediating feeling safe in therapeutic relationships. *Journal of Psychotherapy Integration*, 24(3), 178–192.

Herman, J. (1997). *Trauma and Recovery*. New York: Basic Books.

Kain, K.L. (2015). *Touching Trauma: Touch Skills Training for Trauma Therapists*. Victoria, BC: Author.

Kain, K.L. & Terrell, S.J. (2018). *Nurturing Resilience: Helping Clients Move Forward from Developmental Trauma — An Integrative Somatic Approach*. Berkeley, CA: North Atlantic Books.

Kain, K.L. & Terrell, S.J. (2016). *Somatic Resilience and Regulation: Early Trauma* [training]. Victoria, BC: Author.

Karr-Morse, R. & Wiley, M.S. (2012). *Scared Sick: The Role of Childhood Trauma in Adult Disease*. New York: Basic Books.

Kozlowska, K., Walker, P., McLean, L., & Carrive, P. (2015). Fear and the defense cascade: Clinical implications and management. *Harvard Review of Psychiatry*, 23(4), 263–287.

Levine, P.A. (1997). *Waking the Tiger: Healing Trauma*. Berkeley, CA: North Atlantic Books.

Levine, P.A. (2010). *In an Unspoken Voice: How the Body Releases Trauma and Restores Goodness*. Berkeley, CA: North Atlantic Books.

Levine, P.A. (2015). *Trauma and Memory*. Berkeley, CA: North Atlantic Books.

Payne, P. & Crane-Godreau, M.A. (2015, April 1). The preparatory set: A novel approach to understanding stress, trauma, and the body mind therapies. *Frontiers in Human Neuroscience*, published online at: http://journal.frontiersin.org/article/10.3389/fnhum.2015.00178/full.

Porges, S.W. (2007). The polyvagal perspective. *Biological Psychology*, 74(2), 116–143.

Scaer, R. (2001/2014). *The Body Bears the Burden: Trauma, Dissociation and Disease*. New York: Routledge.

Schlote, S. (2017). *EQUUSOMA Equine-Facilitated Trauma Therapy*. Retrieved from https://equusoma.com/about/approach/.

Siegel, D.J. (1999). *The Developing Mind: How Relationships and the Brain Interact to Shape Who We Are*. New York: The Guilford Press.

Stanley, S. (2016). *Relational and Body-Centered Practices for Healing Trauma: Lifting the Burdens of the Past*. New York: Routledge.

Walker, P. (n.d.). *The 4 Fs: A Trauma Typology in Complex PTSD*. Retrieved from: http://pete-walker.com/fourFs_TraumaTypologyComplexPTSD.htm.

2 Treating Structural Dissociation through Equine-Assisted Trauma Therapy

Working with the Parts System

Sarah Schlote and Ilka Parent

Introduction

According to the Sidran Institute (2010), as many as 99% of individuals who develop dissociative disorders have a history of adverse childhood experiences at sensitive periods in early development that were either overwhelming, repetitive, or life threatening in some way. This trauma can include severe emotional, physical, or sexual abuse by caregivers, as well as medical and surgical procedures such as war; childhood sex trafficking; brainwashing, indoctrination, torture, ritual abuse, or programming in sects, cults, or terror organizations; political imprisonment; coercive persuasion, and other forms of mind control (American Psychological Association, 2013). Although many individuals experience occasional moments of disconnection or dissociation that do not interfere with life in a significant way, the *Diagnostic and Statistical Manual of Mental Disorders (DSM V)* characterizes dissociative disorders as "a disruption of and/or discontinuity in the normal integration of consciousness, memory, identity, emotion, perception, body representation, motor control, and behavior" where "symptoms can potentially disrupt every area of psychological functioning" (APA, 2013). These include dissociative identity disorder (DID), dissociative amnesia, depersonalization/derealization disorder, other specified dissociative disorder (OSDD), and unspecified dissociative disorder. Although a detailed analysis of each of these categories is beyond the scope of this chapter, the description of the most common symptoms comprising complex traumatic dissociation is as follows (APA, 2013; Steinberg & Schnall, 2001):

- Unbidden intrusions into awareness and behavior, with accompanying losses of continuity in subjective experience, such as:
  - Identity disturbance, confusion, alteration, or fragmentation
  - Dissociative trance (acute narrowing or complete loss of awareness of immediate surroundings that manifest as profound unresponsiveness or insensitivity to environmental stimuli)
  - Depersonalization and derealization (sense of unreality or detachment from one's mind, self, body, surroundings, or present time)
  - Perceptual disturbances (time slowing, objects, or people seeming larger or farther away)

- Inability to access information or to control mental functions that normally are readily amenable to access or control (such as gaps in recall or amnesia of events, aspects of events, periods of time, or of identity)

Of particular interest are the impacts to identity that can occur, whereby a person may have had to split off or disown certain aspects of their own experience (emotions, sensations, pain, action impulses, self-protective responses, needs, sensory perceptions, and memories) in order to survive challenging life circumstances.

Many theories exist to describe this process of compartmentalization. Peter Fonagy (Fonagy et al., 2008), a Hungarian-born psychoanalyst, put forth a detailed theory on mentalization and one's resulting ability to regulate affect based on one's primary relationship experiences. Mentalization is defined as the ability to make and use mental representations of one's own and other people's emotional states, which is dependent on receiving sufficient parenting by primary caregivers. He defines insufficient parenting as the caretakers' inability or unwillingness to identify and/or detect emotional processes in themselves and others; to understand, reflect back, and articulate emotions, giving the child the opportunity to successfully identify himself or herself; and to detect and to articulate his or her own emotional states. An individual's attachment style and ability to mentalize affect his or her ability to form a self-concept, which later affects their ability to sustain relationships.

Fonagy's view is similar to the perspective put forth by John Bowlby related to attachment theory, which states that human development is dependent upon the ability to form a safe and secure attachment to a primary caregiver. In early development, humans (and, indeed, mammals in general) rely on consistent attunement and responsiveness by caregivers in order to be fed, kept warm, dry, clean, and soothe distress. Bowlby (1982) suggested that the attachment relationship is both the source of emotional regulation, as a result of co-regulation in the presence of an attuned caregiver, and is also how children develop internal working models of relationships. The more consistently caregivers can respond to the needs of the child, the more a child is able to tolerate uncomfortable emotional arousal by either seeking out the support of others or through their own attempts at self-regulating. The reverse is also true. Inconsistent, neglectful, or abusive parenting results in emotion dysregulation and the internalized belief that one's needs, emotions, or impulses are unacceptable, shameful, or wrong. As stated by Levine and Kline (2007),

> because infants and children are less able to defend themselves, they are more vulnerable than adults to retaining an excess of highly charged arousal energy. Without specific and directed help from caring adults, the unresolved energy eventually finds expression in a wide array of behaviors and symptoms. Children have a very limited behavioral repertoire to deal with life's stresses and difficulties.
>
> (p. 41)

That is, when emotions, needs, or impulses are unmet or invalidated, a child's options are to act out or "act in," which can range from numbing, shaming, complying, pleasing, caretaking, or otherwise sublimating what was deemed to be unacceptable by others. In infants, the options are even more limited; when the attachment cry is not successful, the only option is to freeze or shut down. These types of experiences set the foundational conditions for dissociation and fragmentation as ways to manage that which was overwhelming or disapproved of (Kain & Terrell, 2016).

Van der Kolk (1997) describes compartmentalization as an adaptation where the isolated fragments are stored separately in order to be able to manage what was at one point personally overwhelming to oneself or unacceptable to others, and avoid further pain, harm, or rejection. For many, "having to go away" or shut down certain aspects of oneself became the only way to preserve relationship, resulting in difficulty being aware of oneself while also being aware of others. The two simply could not exist simultaneously at an earlier point in development. Similarly, dissociation may also have been the only way to survive being in one's body, the home of so many painful experiences, short of leaving one's body altogether by ending one's life. Dissociation and fragmentation are also potent ways to cope with overwhelming circumstances through non-realization, in order to be able to continue to attend to daily living activities. As a result, a person may only have access to certain aspects of their experience at any given point, resulting in a discontinuity in their sense of self and the world (van der Hart et al., 2006).

Understandably, complex trauma-related dissociation can involve "distinct identity or personality states, each with its own relatively enduring pattern of perceiving, relating to, and thinking about the environment and self" (APA, 2013), to varying degrees along a continuum. Clinicians and clients have a variety of different words for describing these states, including "parts" (or "personality parts," "parts of the self," "emotional parts"), "self states," "alters" (or "alter personalities," "alter identities"), "aspects of self," "ways of being," "selves," "little parts," "inner child(ren)," and so on, depending on their theoretical orientation with regards to ego state work. Sometimes, parts are named by clients for the role or function that they hold within the inner system (such as carrying a particular emotion, unmet need, or defensive response), such as "inner critic," "the rage beast," "the terrified child," "shame monster," "the saboteur," "the lawyer," "the protector," "the bully," "wonder woman," etc. Some clients resonate strongly with the idea of parts and are receptive to engaging with these different aspects of themselves. Yet other clients have a strong avoidance or phobia of the different parts of the personality as a result of over-coupled fear, shame, and confusion about the often-conflicting inner emotions, needs, and experiences that were long ago deemed unacceptable or overwhelming.

Ego state work comprises a broad category of different approaches that share certain foundational views around how the personality can be structured in response to life experiences and worked with to support greater awareness and functionality in day-to-day life. Most ego state models recognize that the states, alters, or parts were an adaptation required to protect the whole inner system of the person at some point in the past, which can result in inner conflict, chaos, stagnation, or dysfunctional behavior when they continue to take over in the present. While there are similarities between these approaches, the structural dissociation model originally proposed by Pierre Janet in the late 1800s and expanded upon by van der Hart et al. (2006) is noteworthy in that it involves a detailed theory of dissociation related to trauma (Martin, 2017). This structural dissociation model serves as a foundation for this chapter. While a thorough review of this model is beyond the scope of this chapter, it bears mentioning that structural dissociation distinguishes between apparently normal parts (ANP), which are the aspects of self that serve as the functional adult self that interfaces with everyday life, and the emotional parts (EPs), which consist of the various split-off emotions, behaviors, bodily sensations and impulses, survival responses, and traumatic memories. In more simple cases of structural dissociation, there is commonly one ANP with one or more EPs, whereas in more complex cases there can be more than one ANP with multiple EPs. The ANP tries to maintain appearance of normality ban through avoiding, detachment, or numbing, but can nonetheless experience intrusions from the EPs, which are considered to be incorrectly time oriented (or stuck in "trauma time") and view present-day experiences through the lens of maladaptive thoughts, beliefs, emotions, and activation (Martin, 2017; van der Hart et al., 2006). Parts vary in type and function, and can include (but are not limited to):

> (1) host parts; (2) child parts; (3) protector and helper parts; (4) internal self-helpers; (5) persecutor parts, based on introjects of perpetrators; (6) suicidal parts; (7) parts of the opposite sex; (8) promiscuous parts; (9) administrators and obsessive-compulsive parts; (10) substance abuse parts; (11) autistic and handicapped parts; (12) parts with special talents or skills; (13) anesthetic or analgesic parts; (14) imitators and imposters; (15) demons and spirits; (16) animals and objects such as trees; and (17) parts belonging to a different race.
>
> (van der Hart et al., 2006, pp. 79–80)

Some of these expressions and categories are also often used with and by individuals who do not meet the criteria for a formal diagnosis, but nonetheless experience different conflicting response patterns and emotional states in various moments of their lives, and who find an ego state framework helpful for relating to their inner dynamics. Indeed, we all have ego states and, as stated by Steele, "all dissociative states are ego states; not all ego states are dissociative parts" (in Shapiro, 2016). As a result, this chapter will have applicability for a wider range of clients than those who fit the criteria of a more formal dissociative disorder.

Parts work as a treatment approach to working with complex dissociation has a number of goals, which include fostering awareness of and co-consciousness between parts of the personality; integration, cooperation or diplomacy amongst aspects of the self; as well as regulation, empathy, self-compassion, embodiment, and agency. It is important to note that the goal in bringing awareness to the parts system is not to further fragment the personality or collude with the ANP's belief of separateness (i.e., that the EPs are not part of the oneself or one mind). Instead, parts work seeks to make sense of the inner unconscious dynamics that are already occurring, with the belief that people are whole as individuals and have the ability to develop a more cohesive and functional sense of identity. To achieve this end, the ANP needs to gain the trust of the other disowned parts of the personality. This is done slowly to not exceed the client's window of tolerance, by empathizing with the emotional parts' distress with compassion, validating that their self-protective efforts were necessary in the past under the original conditions when the fragmenting occurred, and updating the parts with adaptive information by orienting them to evidence of the present time and adult state (helping them shift out of "trauma time"); in essence, being the adult they needed when they were younger. However, resistance and avoidance are common defensive responses to the idea of letting down one's guard and not engaging in defensive strategies as a default, and trusting the "new management" at the helm.

Once the parts system has been treated "enough," then trauma processing using different approaches such as EMDR or Somatic Experiencing® becomes possible. Attempting trauma processing before addressing the structural dissociation can result in treatment delays, derailing or looping when the EPs attempt to thwart the process to maintain inner stability (Martin, 2017). This is consistent with other staged models of trauma treatment, whereby safety and stabilization needs to occur first before addressing traumatic material, which then sets the conditions for the resolution of the personality fragmentation and supports integration to occur (Herman, 1997; International Society for the Study of Trauma and Dissociation , 2011; Paulsen and Lanius, 2014). This complex and nuanced process, which is outlined in great detail in other sources (van der Hart et al., 2006; Boon et al., 2011; Martin, 2017; Lanius et al., 2014), takes time, patience, and further training and supervision is required.

Parts Work and Equine-Assisted Trauma Therapy

Combining parts work for structural dissociation with equine-assisted interventions is a natural pairing on a number of levels. As noted, many symptoms of complex post-traumatic stress disorder originate from traumatic events that occurred in a relational context. As such, treatment needs to focus on addressing the trauma content in a relational context—typically a therapist and the client. That in itself often poses a challenge, as trusting another human being can be difficult, which is where the value of building relationships with horses comes in. The fundamental biological structures and functions that serve to regulate social relationships in equines are identical to those in humans and, indeed, all mammals. Generally, studies on human–animal interactions have noted a so-called "social catalyst effect" in that having an animal present in a therapeutic setting facilitates building a therapeutic alliance with clients (Julius et al., 2014). Studies also show that connecting with animals is associated with reduced sympathetic arousal in the hypothalamus–pituitary–adrenal axis as well as increased oxytocin levels (Handlin et al., 2011; Odendaal & Meintjes, 2003; Pendry et al., 2014). Oxytocin, released through bonding and attachment, influences and helps regulate social behavior, fear, stress, and pain, and fosters tranquility, well-being, memory, and learning. Oxytocin also induces states of rest and digest as well and a state of calm that supports connection. In the presence of supportive humans and horses, cortisol levels do not rise as much and situations are less likely to be perceived as threatening—presumably due in part to an increase in oxytocin levels in the brain. One can easily conclude that "true" relationships between humans and equines are possible and that oxytocin is released in those interactions.

Because of past attachment ruptures, trusting a human therapist can be a daunting task. However, certain younger parts may feel more trusting of the human facilitators when they observe them treating the animals with respect, consideration for their needs, and attunement to their responses in the moment. Witnessing the humans' responsiveness toward other vulnerable creatures provides a corrective emotional experience, setting the tone for the repair of past attachment ruptures. This in turn can support distrusting parts of the personality to be open to the possibility that the human facilitators might be a source of safety and security. This kind of remapping or renegotiation of relationship expectations may be especially true of clients who witnessed animal abuse, or who themselves felt preyed upon by human predators, and who would be sensitive to noticing submission, coercion, distress, or shutdown in others. In addition, certain parts of the personality might not feel safe to emerge in the presence of a human therapist alone, but may be more likely to come forth in relationship with a horse, donkey, or mule. In addition, just as a therapist seeks to build a relationship with all the parts of the client, so too can the different parts of the client each build a relationship with the horse(s). Observing the relationship dynamics between an animal and different parts of a client's personality offers opportunities to work through specific attachment, behavioral, emotional, sensory, and cognitive difficulties related to each particular part.

Additionally, observing herd dynamics can provide an opportunity to normalize the different roles of the parts within a client's inner system. This kind of exploration and discussion can help alleviate shame associated with fragmentation, painful emotions, needs, and self-protective actions or reactions, by acknowledging how those were adaptive and necessary for the survival of one's entire inner "herd." It can also be enlightening for clients to learn that herd dynamics and behaviors do not always reflect the natural behaviors of horses in the wild, but in fact reflect captivity conditions including exposure to stressors that horses have had to adapt to in various ways, similar to clients. This supports the goal of helping the ANP to soften and extend compassion toward oneself and one's EPs for what was necessary to cope and survive. Observing herds in this way can also support the process of identifying specific parts as well, similar to the inner meeting space or Fraser's dissociative table technique (Boon et al., 2011; Fraser, 1991; Martin, 2012). An example will be provided below.

Individuals facing traumatic dissociation have difficulty maintaining dual awareness. That is, they have difficulty holding awareness of self and other simultaneously, connecting with past traumatic material while remaining anchored in the present (instead of getting lost in trauma time), sensing their bodies while engaging in certain activities, thinking analytically, or feeling certain emotions, and so on. Building a relationship with a horse offers many opportunities to develop dual awareness through the directed guidance of the facilitators, inviting the client to expand their awareness to include the missing elements in a gradual, titrated way throughout the course of different equine-based activities. This might require sequential focus at first, shifting back and forth between two different points of focus, until the client is able to hold awareness more or less simultaneously. This supports greater capacity for embodiment as well as present time orientation.

Internalizing and reinforcing inner resources (such as strength, courage, softness, calm, assertiveness, playfulness, and so on) and increasing the capacity to tolerate positive affect are an important part of parts work and trauma work in general (Shapiro, 2016). In the process of building relationship with an equine, the animal may come to represent a powerful archetype for the client of such a resource quality, trait, emotion, sensation, or action that they want to access within themselves. Similarly, a positive experience in the context of equine-focused activities involving the client's own skills and capacity can also serve as a potent memory resource to be able to recall and sense after the fact. Internalizing these resources can also help shift the structure of the client's inner landscape, strengthening his or her sense of a capable adult self, or providing a counter-response to persecutor parts that torment and continue to reenact past abuse toward the self.

Engaging in activities with horses allows clients with structural dissociation to restore a sense of awareness of self and insight into their present. Through the interaction with the horses, clients are invited to examine projections related to the therapeutic alliance with the human therapist and instead place their projections onto the horses for exploration and resolution. Symbols can be used in the sessions whereby clients are asked to create or build a situation representing their internal images or system using objects found around the farm or in the arena. Clients with structural dissociation often struggle with abstract concepts and at times may not be able to put some of their experience into words, which is especially true for those whose trauma or attachment ruptures occurred before language was developed. By using symbols and labeling the horses and various items, a stage representative of their inner world is created in the theater of the farm, similar to drama therapy processes of psychodrama, therapeutic enactment, and family constellations. As the horses move freely around "on stage," self- and object representations based on individual mentalization concepts may be experienced directly by the client in the here and now, along with the experience of regulation in relationship with the horses. The horses' reactions are reflected back to clients, which allows them to gain insights into another being's responses to their nonverbal cues. Experiencing interactions with horses on a stage that represents the clients' real life facilitates an insight into everyday behaviors that they may not be able to verbalize or bring to consciousness. In some cases, the projections being mirrored are not simply metaphors placed on the horses, but are representative of the actual relationship dynamics with the horses themselves, which further allows for corrective emotional and relational experiences to take place with the animals and therapist.

Description of Technique

Working with complex dissociation requires a toolkit of various techniques that are beyond the scope of what can be described in this chapter. However, one of the first principles that can be summarized here is working with a staged model of trauma treatment, focusing first on safety and stabilization before moving toward deeper processing or more intense activities (Herman, 1997; International Society for the Study of Trauma and Dissociation 2011). This principle applies even if one is not providing trauma therapy, and the focus instead is on offering experiential learning activities for trauma-affected clients. A recent example shared by Ilka Parent (2016) describes what can happen in equine-based programs without an understanding of dissociation and how to proceed in a trauma informed way:

> A few months ago I was approached by a person from out of country who had attended equine-assisted psychotherapy with a person certified in Equine Assisted Therapy and Learning. This person was desperate: during the course of his personal growth seminar, he had become aware of past events. During the seminar, he was encouraged to explore his issues deeper by focusing on the metaphors he had used during the equine activity. He reported that he had "lost time" during the activity and "has not felt right" since then. The experience made him aware of things he had long forgotten. He said that the people who conducted this workshop did not help, but rather told him to "trust the process" and "trust the horses" and eventually were oblivious to the abyss he had fallen into.
>
> (n.p.)

Working with complex dissociation in the context of equine-focused programs requires the ability to recognize any signs of dissociation in the first place, build emotion regulation and time orientation skills, foster dual awareness, and not work at higher thresholds than a person is ready for and capable of handling. This process also involves being able to engage in a dialogue about the ways dissociation can manifest, its self-protective purpose, identifying aspects of one's personality along with the roles they played in allowing a person to survive their circumstances, and redefining roles within the system. Through this process, support is given in the hope that an empathetic inner adult witness will emerge and relate compassion to the parts. The overall goal consists of greater integration of the personality, with a reduction or elimination of parts fragmentation and switching; an increase in co-consciousness and internal collaboration; and a more functional experience of one's ego states.

Techniques and Case Examples

The following case examples that illustrate three techniques have been adjusted to protect the privacy of the clients and other persons involved in the sessions, if relevant. In some cases, the transcripts reflect a composite client combining excerpts and details from a few different people and sessions to preserve anonymity.

Case Example 1: Meet the Inner Herd: Identifying Parts and Purposes

Emma (pseudonym) is a 26-year-old female who experienced abuse and neglect from her foster parents and extended family members, and being harassed and stalked by the partner of a former friend. She experienced difficulty with recognizing and regulating emotions, trusting others' intentions, and shifting from an external to an internal locus of control. She also would quickly switch between ego states when triggered, avoided, or denied certain feelings, and was resistant to various attempts at treatment. She had some prior experience with horses as a teenager and was comfortable spending time in their presence. The following excerpt is drawn from one of her early sessions at the farm, while observing and mingling with a herd at liberty, and integrates the inner meeting space technique (an adaptation of Fraser's dissociative table method; Fraser, 1991) as an introduction to helping her understand her inner parts system. Martin (2012) outlines the eight recommended steps when working with this particular technique, which will be outlined in the analysis below.

Transcript Analysis of Case Example

The following transcript analysis is about a pseudonym client:

Table 2.1 Case Example Transcript

Transcript	Analysis
Therapist: As we spend time with the horses in their environment, I'm curious about what you notice about their interactions.	**Step 1: Psychoeducation and introduction.** Therapist invites the client to observe the herd dynamics. The client begins to reflect back about what she observes.
Client: They all have different personalities and ways of relating or acting. That one over there seems really aloof and is always looking away, almost as if it was on guard, you know?	
Therapist: What do you notice happens for the other horses in response to that horse's behavior?	

(continued)

Table 2.1 Case Example Transcript (Cont.)

Transcript	Analysis
Client: They seem to be mostly calm and relaxed. A few are looking around as well, but mostly they are grazing and just focusing on eating. *(A horse approaches her and nuzzles her hand.)* This one is really curious.	
Therapist: In horse herds, different horses take on different roles at different times. This is similar to how we can feel and act differently in different situations. Some horses take on a sentinel role, on the lookout while others graze or take turns lying down and having a nap. Or being social. It's easier to do those things when not feeling threatened or on guard.	**Step 1: Psychoeducation and introduction.** The therapist provides some education about roles in horse herds, and introduces a trauma lens to normalize certain responses and behaviors as adaptive given external conditions or stressors. This models empathy for the ways one had to cope to survive to begin to address shame, especially if the client has a phobic response to identifying certain disowned parts of their personality (needs, emotions, sensations, action impulses, etc.).
Client: Kind of like they're protecting the others.	
Therapist: Yes, that's right. Sometimes some horses will defend other horses too when there are conflicts, or when a foal needs protection by its mother. *(Two horses enter into an intense skirmish a short distance away over a particular pile of hay.)*	
Client: That horse looked like it was bullying the other horse. Why was it that mean?	
Therapist: Horses in captivity experience a lot of stressors that horses in the wild don't face. In the wild, the herd's survival is dependent on group cohesion, resorting to survival responses like fight or flight only when necessary. In captive horse herds like this one, the horses have often faced different stressors and challenging experiences, like being weaned too young, social deprivation, and not learning the nuances of herd communication, being separated from friends when moving to different barns or being kept with other horses they don't get along with, adverse training methods, competitive situations involving food or resources, or being kept in a small paddock or confined in stalls. Conflict behaviors are more common between	

Table 2.1 Case Example Transcript (Cont.)

Transcript	Analysis
herd members sometimes as a result. Sometimes horses are naturally a bit more dominant, but other times aggression is a learned behavior. An adaptation.	
Client: *(Seems thoughtful for a few moments.)* I bully myself a lot. *(She then notices a horse decide to lie down nearby in a pile of hay and begins to giggle in a more childlike tone.)* He's having breakfast in bed!	The therapist notices the ego state switching and uses this to prepare to move in the direction of exploring the idea of parts.
Therapist: *(Laughs as well.)* Horses only lie down or eat when they are feeling safe and not threatened. **Client:** That horse feels safe enough with me here to do that? I'm really touched. **Therapist:** When there's trust and a sense of safety, it's easier to let one's guard down. When that trust is not there, or if there's a perception of danger, the focus is more on self-protection than bonding, feeding or playing. **Client:** That sounds a lot like me.	**Step 1: Psychoeducation and introduction.** The therapist shares about what is possible when different members of the herd feel safe. This idea plants a seed for later on, when exploring how the client's emotional parts might begin to trust the client's adult ego state and eventually let down their guard in order to experience calm or pleasurable states or safe interactions.
Therapist: *(Nodding.)* I was wondering if you'd be interested in trying an exercise to explore this further. **Client:** *(Nods in agreement.)* Sure. What do you mean? **Therapist:** Sometimes we have conflicting feelings or reactions to things. Our personality can be made up of different aspects or parts, representing different beliefs, emotions, needs, behaviors, or reactions to our circumstances. Sometimes it feels like our emotions or reactions aren't our own, or we feel torn between two ways of feeling about or reacting to a particular situation. We all have parts like this to varying degrees. It can be useful to have a way to talk about these parts of yourself, to help address what is bothering you. **Client:** Ok, that makes sense. You just described me in a nutshell.	**Step 1: Psychoeducation and introduction.** Therapist begins to describe the rationale for identifying parts to normalize and set the stage for the upcoming activity.

(continued)

Table 2.1 Case Example Transcript (Cont.)

Transcript	Analysis
Therapist: Before we begin, let's move a bit further away so we can watch the horses at a distance. *(The therapist and client move away, and sit down. The therapist then leads the client in a grounding practice for settling and calm, inviting the client to feel the support of the ground, and take in soothing sensory details in the environment.)*	**Step 3: Get your client into a calm state.** It is important to make sure that the client has emotion regulation skills to draw on. According to Martin (2012), "an internal calm state decreases the adult part's resistance to the emotional parts (EPs) and increases the EPs' willingness to participate and become present. If the client is activated into dysfunctionally stored material, this technique will be harder to implement as fewer parts may be willing to come to the table. You will have to work to deactivate the distress before you can return to identifying the parts" (p. 180).
Therapist: Do you remember the calm place exercise? *(Client nods.)* Let's create a different visualization of a place where we might invite the different parts of your personality to come forward. This might look like a meeting room with tables, or look like a different place altogether where you might imagine being able to do a roll call, as it were, of the different aspects of yourself, so we can get a sense of your inner "system"—sort of like getting to know the different personalities and roles within a herd.	**Step 2: Establish that the client can visualize.** This was already done prior to this activity. If the client has difficulty visualizing, then simply observing the herd dynamics and inviting the client to list the different parts will suffice. If the client's calm place visualization is being at the farm, then a different internal meeting place will need to be established so that the farm can remain a separate resource for the client. However, in some cases it might be that the client has a separate calm place and their chosen visual for a meeting place would be a horse paddock, indoor arena, or round pen. Alternately, a client might select a calm place in one part of the farm, and a different contained area at the farm for the meeting place. There are many possible iterations.
Client: I think I'd like my inner meeting place to be the riding ring. *(Client and therapist explore the details of the image to bring in as much sensory detail as possible, so that the client can recall this image easily later.)*	**Step 4: Develop the meeting place imagery.** **Step 5: Vivify the imagery.** **Step 6: Instruct the adult part of self to enter the imagery and take his or her place.** It is important to select a meeting place that is neutral and does not have any negative associations. The therapist has a clipboard and pad of paper on which to draw out the meeting place and where the client is located in the scene.
Therapist: As you imagine this scene, where do you see yourself in the riding ring? Find the right place where you'd imagine yourself sitting. When you're settled in, let me know. *(Client indicates that she visualizes herself sitting near the gate on a mounting block.)*	

Table 2.1 Case Example Transcript (Cont.)

Transcript	Analysis
If you invite all the different aspects or parts of yourself to enter into the riding ring and take their places, notice who or what shows up first. If they can't come into the ring, they might instead find their way into a corner, or somewhere beyond the fence or hiding in a run-in shelter in a nearby paddock.	**Step 7: Invite the emotional parts to enter the imagery.** As the client invites parts to the scene, the therapist adds these into the drawing, numbering them in order of appearance. It is important to use the wording "who or what," since parts may be experienced as inanimate objects, animals, spiritual entities, shadows, colors, demons, and so on, as opposed to just human.
Client: The first part I envision is the bully part. Part of me sees it like that horse that was being aggressive towards the other horses, but when I close my eyes I actually picture it like a pair of fists with a mean face looming over me. Is that ok?	The client identifies a persecutor part (a form of protector part) first. These are often introjects of people who have harmed the person in the past. These parts often exist to prevent other parts from behaving in ways that would have resulted in shame, harm, or rejection.
Therapist: Absolutely. There is no right or wrong way to envision or experience the parts of yourself. Where do you picture the inner bully in relation to you in the scene? *(The client indicates that the inner bully is located near her by the gate and the therapist adds it to the diagram.)* Thank you. As you imagine this scene, who or what shows up next?	
Client: That sentinel horse from earlier— I see him very clearly across from me on the other side of the paddock, keeping watch at a distance. I actually envision this part like the horse standing tall and looking around, on guard. It is always on the lookout for danger. *(The therapist adds in this part into the diagram.)*	The client identifies a helper part next, whose role has been to remain hypervigilant and on the lookout for threats to the rest of the system.
Therapist: Who or what shows up next?	
Client: There's a part of me that actually doesn't like therapy very much and doesn't like going along with things, even if they might be helpful. That part reminds me of a donkey on my uncle's farm growing up. He would always plant his feet and refuse to budge. I kind of picture that part like that old donkey. *(Client shares where she pictures the donkey in relation to the other parts, and the therapist adds it to the*	The client identifies another protector part, known as a fight part, whose role is to express resistance or to fight back against perceived threats.

(continued)

Table 2.1 Case Example Transcript (Cont.)

Transcript	Analysis
diagram. The client seems thoughtful for a little bit.) There's also this part of me that feels scared, like a little baby that is crying but sort of frozen at the same time. I'm not sure where I picture that part — maybe by itself alone on the other side of the fence. *(As the client observes the herd, another horse lies down and begins to roll on the ground. The client expresses a childlike glee at seeing this.)*	The client also names a child or young part. These parts often carry "feelings of longing, loneliness, dependency, and need for comfort, help, and safety, and also distrust and fear or rejection or abandonment" (Boon et al., 2011, p. 30).
Therapist: I wonder what you're noticing inside as you watch the horse roll around?	
Client: *(Giggles.)* That looks like a lot of fun. Go horsey! *(Suddenly, the client appears to switch again, and another childlike part appears with a more cautious tone and hunched body posture.)* We're not allowed to play like that or we might get punished.	Two more child parts appear, one that appears to be connected to a sense of childlike wonder and play, and another that experiences a sense of foreboding and shuts down joy to prevent harm.
Therapist: *(Speaking to the whole system through adult Emma.)* It makes complete sense that that part of you learned to follow the rules in order to avoid punishment or rejection. Can the grown-up part of you, the part of you that drove your car to the farm today, look at this part with kind, loving eyes? *(Emma nods.)* See if you can invite that part to look around through your eyes, and take in information about where you are now and who is here with you.	The therapist validates the self-protective strategies that were adopted by the system, and begins to help the parts to re-orient to evidence that it is the present time to help re-establish a sense of safety and connection with the adult ego state. In this example, accessing a kind, inner adult state was relatively easy to do; this is not always the case with structural dissociation, and work may need to be done first to develop inner resources (such as internalizing the qualities and traits of a kind, compassionate adult or friend) before identifying other parts in the system (Shapiro, 2016). This can be done with non-human role models as well, such as by observing a horse showing nurturing, affiliative behaviors to another horse and internalizing that horse and its response and qualities as a resource the client can draw from. "Wise being" archetypes (human, animal spirit guide, spiritual being, or otherwise) can also be useful in this regard.
Client: *(Orients slowly to her surroundings.)* Nothing bad is happening to that horse even though it's rolling on the ground. No one is hurting it for doing that. *(She exhales.)*	The client is able to orient to present time, and switches states less as she is able to differentiate present day from "trauma time."

This excerpt of a longer session shows an exercise that can set a foundation for an initial exploration of internal parts from a place of empathetic understanding, with the herd dynamics providing an adaptive reframing of the client's inner landscape. **Step 8**, which consists of **gathering clinical information**, can be elaborated upon over time. This can include obtaining the names of the parts (if any), their purpose or role, any sense of their ages (where applicable), the degree of time orientation of each of the parts, how much co-consciousness exists between the parts, and any alliances, phobias, or antagonistic relationships exist amongst them. Being able to have access to the parts makes working with them much easier moving forward, when wanting to determine which part(s) are hyper- or hypo-aroused, which parts are phobic of other parts, dealing with cognitive errors associated with outdated beliefs, and improving compassion, dialogue, and cooperation between the parts. For further information about how to work with the meeting place strategy to identify and subsequently work with parts safely, consult Boon et al. (2011), Martin (2012), and Shapiro (2016).

Case Example 2: Fostering Dual Awareness and Present Time Orientation

Diane (pseudonym) is a 53-year-old Caucasian female who experienced emotional and physical abuse by her mother and stepfather, along with emotional abuse and physical and sexual assault by her various partners in adulthood. She has difficulty with remaining connected with herself while in the presence of others, focusing externally and losing awareness of what is happening internally. She also experiences fragmentation of her personality and difficulty remaining oriented to evidence of her current age and circumstances. She was already aware of over a dozen EPs at the time of this session, and had done some parts work with a different therapist prior to coming to equine-assisted therapy. This excerpt from a session demonstrates how relationship building with a horse was leveraged to work on dual awareness and present time orientation. The session took place in a covered arena, with one horse on a lead rope to start, with a horse handler (Linda) present. The session began earlier with an approaching practice, with the client paying attention to the horse's body language as she began to move in the horse's direction, pausing when she noticed shifts in the horse like ears or head turning away. The transcript picks up once the client was standing next to the horse, considering the possibility of grooming with consent.

Transcript Analysis of Case Example Continued

The following transcript analysis is about a pseudonym client:

Table 2.2 Case Example Transcript Continued

Transcript	Analysis
Therapist: An important part of being in a relationship involves awareness of and consent from both members in the dynamic. Just like when you were approaching her, Ruby [horse] will also communicate how and where she likes to be touched, and you will get to determine the same for you. This requires the ability to be paying attention to what she is conveying nonverbally to you. It also requires you to be noticing what is happening inside you.	The therapist sets up the exercise in terms of what to expect. Transparency is important in working with trauma survivors in order to foster choice, voice, empowerment, and trust. Furthermore, ensuring that consent occurs for both the client and the horse is important so that the client's experience does not occur at the expense of the horse. Clients who have experienced trauma, especially those with fragmented EPs, can easily detect coercion and submission in vulnerable beings. Building trust with the EPs therefore involves acting in ways that respect and protect all involved. This also helps with repairing past relational ruptures.
Client: Ok, that sounds good. *(Client switches into one of her child parts.)* We like it that you let the horse say what it needs.	
Therapist: Your safety and the horse's safety are important to us. You have the option to try out any of the grooming tools, or simply use your hands if you like.	
Client: I'll try my hands. How should I do this? *(Client goes to touch Ruby's face, who moves her head away in response to the approaching hands.)*	Until this point, the exercise unfolds in a similar way to other grooming and relationship building exercises in equine-facilitated interventions, only with the awareness that the client is fragmented and more than one ego state is present. The therapist tracks the client as the switching occurs, recognizing when the client is reporting from her ANP or from her EPs.
Therapist: What did you notice happened just there?	
Client: She turned her head away when we tried to touch her cheek.	
Therapist: See what happens if you bring contact to another area of her body and how she responds to that location instead. You might also explore what kind of contact she prefers, like stroking or massage, with different amounts of pressure.	
Client: *(The client moves her hands along Ruby's neck to her shoulder, using a stroking motion.)*	

Table 2.2 Case Example Transcript Continued (Cont.)

Transcript	Analysis
Therapist: What are you noticing now?	
Client: She's dropped her head and she seems more relaxed. *(As she says this, Ruby cocks a leg.)*	
Therapist: What about you? What are you noticing in your own body as she settles into your contact?	The therapist invites the client to bring herself into the equation of the relational dynamic with the horse. Dual awareness of self while in relationship with other is a challenge for this client and a sign of how she had to survive in other important relationships in her life.
Client: I can't really sense my body at all right now when I focus on her.	
Therapist: See if you're able to expand your attention to noticing your feet on the ground as you stroke her shoulder.	
Client: *(Tries for a few moments.)* That's really hard. When I focus on my feet, I forget to focus on Ruby. But when I focus on Ruby, I lose awareness of the ground.	
Therapist: That's not unusual. It can be difficult to focus on both at the same time. Let's see if we can work on that a little more.	The therapist validates the client's experience in a reassuring tone. Remaining regulated and grounded is crucial so as to not increase fear, worry, or shame for the client about something that is already a challenge.
Client: I had no idea that I would lose contact with the ground like that so easily! I never noticed that before.	
Therapist: See what happens if you practice weaving your attention back and forth, between noticing the warmth of her fur beneath your hands, then noticing your feet on the ground inside your boots, wiggling your toes if necessary, then noticing her fur again. Take all the time you need to try this out.	An alternative version of this would be for the client to place her hands somewhere along the horse's ribcage and sense the horse's breathing, then bring her awareness to her own breath, then back to the horse's, eventually working up to the ability to notice how they breathe in synchrony or tandem.
Client: *(Gives it a try for a few moments.)* I can do it one after the other, but not at the same time.	
Therapist: That's ok—it might take some practice to be able to hold both in your awareness. Even being able to shift from one to the other and back again is a good start. Let's try something a little different. With your hand on the horse's shoulder, take your other hand	This exercise borrows from Levine (2008).

Table 2.2 Case Example Transcript Continued (Cont.)

Transcript	Analysis
and gently tap or touch the hand that is touching Ruby. Do this as many times as you need to get a sense of that part of your body. When you stop tapping, notice if there are any sensations that you become aware of. If tapping isn't comfortable, you might try rubbing or stroking that hand instead. As you do this, see what happens as you say the following words, either out loud or silently to yourself: "this is my hand, my hand belongs to me and is a part of me."	
Client: *(Engages in the exercise. However, not long after beginning, the client switches into another younger ego state, and appears frightened. Her body posture shifts, to be more hunched and childlike and she pulls her hands away from Ruby.)* We're not allowed to touch ourselves or we'll get in trouble.	As the client worked on building dual awareness of self and other, she lost dual awareness of present time while engaging in the exercise. Self-touch or experiencing pleasant sensations can often be over-coupled with terror or shame as a result of early trauma. The ego state switching shows a part stuck in "trauma time," not fully oriented to the safety inherent in the present moment. This strategy would have been necessary in the past to prevent potential harm or punishment.
Therapist: *(Speaking to the client's parts system in a gentle and reassuring tone.)* I want to remind every single part of self that you are responding to internal information right now. I understand that responding in this way was necessary under certain conditions. However, I want you to consider the possibility that those conditions are not happening right now. *(Diane nods.)* They might have happened in the past or might be happening in other places in your life, but not in this moment.	The therapist works on helping the parts caught in trauma time to orient to evidence of the present moment. Continuing with the dual awareness exercise of self and other is temporarily paused until the client is able to regain dual awareness of the present moment while triggered into past traumatic material. It is important to work on orienting the parts to present time as opposed to leading a grounding practice. Attempts at grounding a client while in a fragmented state sometimes backfire or are less effective when other parts are still caught in trauma time and focused on perceived threat, even if there is no threat occurring in the moment. This is not to say that teaching grounding exercises for stabilization is not important; these are still
Client: *(Adult self/ANP starts to come back online.)* I wasn't allowed to ask for hugs or do anything that might soothe me. They would get angry with me.	

Table 2.2 Case Example Transcript Continued (Cont.)

Transcript	Analysis
Therapist: How clever it was to make touching off limits and to stop sensing your own body. That was a really useful solution given the circumstances. I would never shame or harm you for making contact with yourself like this, or for needing to protect yourself under abusive conditions. If every single part of you looked through your eyes around you, you would see that there's only Ruby, Linda, and me. Your parents are not here and they will never come to this farm. It would be really helpful for all of you to see that they are not here and that no one else from your present or past life that have harmed you are here—only Ruby, Linda, and me.	a necessity, but in combination with present time orientation for either the whole system or the part(s) that became activated.
Client: *(Looks around tentatively, and exhales slowly. Ruby exhales as well and nudges the client.)*	
Therapist: Was this horse in your life as a child?	
Client: *(Visibly more settled.)* No, we only had a dog when we were little.	
Therapist: If Ruby wasn't in your life as a child, what year is this?	
Client: *(Smiles and names the year.)* That feels better.	
Therapist: What do you notice about Ruby right now?	The client is able to connect with her adult ego state/ANP again.
Client: That she's still here with me. She seems relaxed still and she's not angry at me. There's no danger right now, is there. Her body feels warm. *(Resumes stroking Ruby's shoulder and side.)*	
Therapist: Let's take a few moments to just hang out. If you like, you can continue grooming Ruby with your hands and move to a different spot on her body, seeing what she likes. Or we could try the hand-tapping exercise again and see what might be different this time around. How do the parts feel about that now?	Once the client is oriented to present time again, different options become available. The therapist again offers choice. It can take time to build dual awareness, so proceeding in small increments is important to build tolerance and capacity.

Case Example 3: Addressing a Perpetrator Loyal Part

Brian (pseudonym) is a 47-year-old Caucasian male who was subjected to ritualized sexual abuse from early childhood until his late teens. As identified transgender, his adult life is characterized by continuous sexually and emotionally abusive relationships. During his lifetime, he had been subjected to various psychiatric and psychological treatments and brought preexisting diagnoses of an eating disorder, reactive psychosis, schizophrenia, and various personality disorders with him. At the beginning of treatment, he presented himself with being aware of other voices in his head, only later becoming aware of a total of 27 personality parts. Much of the equine-assisted trauma treatment focused on stabilization, supporting the ANPs to become aware of the various emotional parts (EPs) that held memory of many of the severe traumatic events, and facilitating cooperation and acceptance between these parts that were experienced as separate entities and people. This client experienced severe flashbacks, intrusions, suicidal ideation, with overall high anxiety. As cooperation between the parts increased, one predominant complaint emerged concerning experienced nightly visits from an alleged perpetrator. This perpetrator reportedly performed severe abusive sexual acts. This client could not explain whether or not this visitor was a real person, nightmares, or a reenactment of prior experiences. Most disturbing to him was the evidence left behind after those visits: various items left in his body and bodily fluids such as blood and markings on his body alluded to the fact that these experiences were actually taking place. The following is an excerpt from a series of sessions where bilateral stimulation while being carried by a horse and the interactions with one of more horses was utilized. During one of the activities, the so-called perpetrator loyal part appeared for the first time.

Transcript Analysis of Case Example Continued

The following transcript analysis is about a pseudonym client:

Table 2.3 Case Example Transcript Continued

Transcript	Analysis
Therapist: While you are sitting on this horse, I invite you to focus on the sound the horses' hooves are making on the ground. We will walk across different footings—pay attention to what each surface sounds like and notice the differences.	**Introduction:** The therapist invites the client to remain focused on the here and now while allowing for the client to experience the rhythmic movement of the horse. Inviting the client to orient to sensory information in the environment (sound, texture) also supports present time orientation.

Table 2.3 Case Example Transcript Continued (Cont.)

Transcript	Analysis
Client: It feels good to be carried by someone — this horse is really strong.	The client is able to experience physical contact (as no saddle is being used) with another being. The experience of being "carried" by another being allows for the client to release some control.
Equine Specialist: What do you notice about the different hoof beats?	The equine specialist invites the client to engage in both sensory and cognitive awareness, further introducing trauma therapeutic grounding techniques (5–4–3–2–1 technique). Grounding is a technique that helps reorient a person to the here-and-now and in reality.
Client: I can hear the different sounds. *(Voice and body posture change in that the voice becomes higher and the body is more slumped, with legs moving more freely.)* It is nice to be sitting on this horsey!	An EP of a 4–5-year-old boy emerges and proceeds to speak more freely, sort of "chatters" and comments about the various things he is seeing, e.g., the road, the trees, a dog walking by. Several minutes pass, with various EPs switching in and out.
Therapist: I can see that too — is that so? — yes, that is nice ...	The therapist acknowledges the client's emotional experience without further supporting the changes, all the while maintaining close observation of the horse. Horses at this stage most often reflect changing EPs: observable changes often times can be noted through changes in gait, body posture, body tension, etc.
Client: I am starting to feel dizzy.	The client crouches on the horse, becomes rigid, then sits straight up. The therapist notices the ego state switching: Another part emerges, this one previously unknown to the therapist.
Therapist: *(Notes horse changing body tension and gait. Horse moves slowly toward a tree. Horse starts rubbing first its nose, then its neck, then its withers and back against the tree. Client, in the effort to avoid getting rubbed against the tree, slides off the horse, seemingly disoriented.)* *(The therapist instructs the client.)* Hold on to this lead line and watch out for the horse to not go grazing.	The client has dissociated and lost all perception in the here and now. By having the client take hold of the lead line with a non-threatening being (horse) attached, proprioceptive sensory input (horse moving toward grass and pulling the client on lead line along) facilitates the client's re-orientation in the here and now.

(continued)

Table 2.3 Case Example Transcript Continued (Cont.)

Transcript	Analysis
Client: I feel really dizzy now —I cannot hold this horse alone—will you help me?	
Therapist: I invite you to continue to focus on the horse—take note of how he breathes, and how he moves. *(Therapist and/or equine specialist also take hold of the second lead line attached to the horse and ensure that the client is in contact yet not overwhelmed by the horse. The client is close to the horse, who is grazing, continuously petting the horse.)*	The client has asked for help and has the opportunity to experience the therapist and equine specialist in a supportive function, while reorienting himself to the present through known techniques of focusing on and imitating the horses breathing.
Client: *(Very agitated.)* Now you see—that was HIM! Not even the horses like HIM, HE is dangerous!! I am never safe; HE can get me everywhere!	The client begins referring to the previously unknown perpetrator loyal part.
Equine Specialist: What did you see this horse do with HIM?	The client is invited to distance himself from his emotional experience by focusing on the horse's reaction to the alleged perpetrator loyal part.
Client: He got HIM off his back—he went to the tree and started rubbing against it so that he had to get off.	
Equine Specialist: There was a time when the horse moved slowly with a tree by its side—what was going on at that time?	A specific observation is pointed out to narrow down the focal point and invite the client to reflect further.
Client: I started to go away—there were a lot of us present, it was nice, we felt so comfortable—but then HE came because we are not allowed to feel good and safe and comfortable.	The client acknowledges punitive actions when feelings of safety and comfort are experienced.
Therapist: Is there anything else that happened at that time?	The therapist explores further.
Client: I felt very afraid and wanted to go away. He frightens me. He is really bad and evil and only wants to hurt me.	
Equine Specialist: We have observed the horses before—what have you seen them do when they did not like something or somebody?	By addressing knowledge based on past observations, the client is invited to further reflect and maintain an outside perspective
Client: The typically kick, run away, or bite.	

Table 2.3 Case Example Transcript Continued (Cont.)

Transcript	Analysis
Equine Specialist: And did you see the horse do anything like this today?	By focusing on the actual behavior of the horse with the alleged perpetrator loyal part, the equine specialist opens the opportunity for the client to realize the discrepancy between his emotional response and the actual event.
Client: No, he did not bite, kick, or run. He moved rather slowly, as if he did not want HIM on his back but wanted him off in a way that was possible for HIM to do safely. The horse did not act like he was frightened or didn't like HIM—he kind of was nice to him, as if to say "no" but not in a bad way …	
Therapist: (*Nodding.*) Based on what you have shared with us so far, you didn't feel safe very often—and when you did, you were often caught off guard by those who have done you harm. It seems like the horse did not perceive HIM as threatening. It may be interesting to learn more about what the horse reacted to, and why his reaction was so different than the one you anticipated.	

This experience allowed for the client to further explore the possibility of the perpetrator loyal part not being "evil" and also being part of himself. At a later stage, a trauma confrontation involving this particular perpetrator loyal part was conducted and the nightly visits ceased completely. However, one decisive factor was the client first perceiving the horse as "gentle" toward the part that was previously feared and split off. If the horse could accept the perpetrator loyal part, then perhaps the client could as well.

Parts work in cases of complex trauma and structural dissociation requires a nuanced approach, the ability to detect and work with the signs of dissociation, and build trust and collaboration among parts. At any point, should a client exceed their window of tolerance, in spite of the therapist's best efforts at tracking and titrating the process at tolerable thresholds, equine-assisted exercises should pause to focus on stabilization before continuing. Although it is possible to work as a solo cross-trained practitioner with a background in horsemanship and mental health, having an equine professional or horse handler present when working with clients with complex structural dissociation is especially beneficial so that the therapist can attend more closely to what is happening with the client's inner "herd" of parts, and the horse(s) and their needs can still receive the attention they deserve during the sessions.

Finally, although this chapter focuses mostly on ways parts work can be integrated into equine-based interventions, this does not mean that treating trauma-related dissociation cannot include other approaches that do not include equines, such as psychodynamic therapy, Somatic Experiencing®, Sensorimotor Psychotherapy, or EMDR. Indeed, each of these has also been combined with equine-assisted interventions and the structural dissociation model for the treatment of trauma, showing the versatility and potential for programs that offer healing with horses.

References

American Psychiatric Association (2013). Dissociative disorders. *Diagnostic and Statistical Manual of Mental Disorders* (5th ed.). Arlington, VA: American Psychiatric Publishing.

Boon, S., Steele, K., & van der Hart, O. (2011). *Coping with Trauma-Related Dissociation: Skills Training for Patients and Therapists*. New York: W.W. Norton & Company.

Bowlby, J. (1982). *Attachment*. New York: Basic Books.

Fonagy, P., Gergely, G., Jurist, E.L., & Target, M. (2008). *Affektregulierung, Mentalisierung und die Entwicklung des Selbst* (3. Aufl.). Stuttgart: Klett-Cotta.

Fraser, G.A. (1991). The dissociative table technique: A strategy for working with ego states in dissociative disorders and ego state therapy. *Dissociation*, 4(4), 205–213.

Handlin, L., Hydbring-Sandberg, E., Nilsson, A, et al. (2011). Short-term interaction between dogs and their owners: Effects on oxytocin, cortisol, insulin and heart rate—an exploratory study. *Anthrozoos*, 24(3), 301–315.

Herman, J. (1997). *Trauma and Recovery*. New York: Basic Books.

International Society for the Study of Trauma and Dissociation (2011). Guidelines for treating dissociative disorders in adults (3rd ed.). *Journal of Trauma & Dissociation*, 12(2), 115–187.

Julius, H., Beetz, A., Kotrschal, K., Turner, D.C., & Uvnäs-Moberg, K. (2014). *Bindung zu Tieren: Psychologische und neurobiologische Grundalgen tiergestützter Interventionen*. Göttingen: Hogrefe Verlag GmBH & Co. KG.

Kain, K.L. & Terrell, S.J. (2016). *Somatic Resilience and Regulation: Early Trauma* [training]. Victoria, BC: Somatic Practice.

Lanius, U.F., Paulsen, S.L., & Corrigan, F.M. (Eds.). (2014). *Neurobiology and Treatment of Traumatic Dissociation: Toward an Embodied Self*. New York: Springer Publishing Company.

Levine, P.A. (2008). *Healing Trauma: A Pioneering Program for Restoring the Wisdom of Your Body*. Boulder, CO: Sounds True Inc.

Levine, P.A. & Kline, M. (2007). *Trauma through a Child's Eyes*. Berkeley, CA: North Atlantic Books.

Martin, K.M. (2012). How to use Fraser's dissociative table technique to access and work with emotional parts of the personality. *Journal of EMDR Practice and Research*, 6(4), 179–186.

Martin, K.M. (2017). *Integrating Structural Dissociation Theory with EMDR Therapy* [training materials]. Rochester, NY: Author.

Odendaal, J.S.J. & Meintjes, R.A. (2003). Neurophysiological correlates of affiliative behavior between humans and dogs. *TheVeterinary Journal*, 165(3), 296–301.

Parent, I. (2016, September 22). *Becoming Trained in Equine Assisted Therapy and Learning*. Retrieved from www.facebook.com/notes/minds-n-motion-pferdeunterstützte equine-assisted-trauma-therapie/becoming-trained-in-equine-assisted-therapy-and-learning/10153954152666274.

Paulsen, S.L. & Lanius, U.F. (2014). Dissociation and psychotherapy. In U.F. Lanius, S.L. Paulsen, & F.M. Corrigan (Eds.), *Neurobiology and Treatment of Traumatic Dissociation: Toward an Embodied Self* (pp. 243–246). New York: Springer Publishing Company.

Pendry, P., Smith, A.N., & Roeter, S.M. (2014). Randomized trial examines effects of equine facilitated learning on adolescents' basal cortisol levels. *Human-Animal Interaction Bulletin*, 2(1), 80–95.

Shapiro, R. (2016). *Easy Ego State Interventions: Strategies for Working with Parts*. New York: W.W. Norton.

Sidran Traumatic Stress Institute (2010). *What Is a Dissociative Disorder?* Retrieved from www.sidran.org/resources/for-survivors-and-loved-ones/what-is-a-dissociative-disorder.

Steinberg, M. & Schnall, M. (2001). *The Stranger in the Mirror: Dissociation – The Hidden Epidemic*. New York: HarperCollins.

van der Hart, O., Nijenhuis, E.R.S., & Steele, K. (2006). *The Haunted Self: Structural Dissociation and the Treatment of Chronic Traumatization*. New York: W.W. Norton & Company.

van der Kolk, B. (1997). Traumatic memories. In P.S. Appelbaum, L.A. Uyehara, & M.R. Elin (Eds.), *Trauma and Memory: Clinical and Legal Controversies* (pp. 243–260). Oxford: Oxford University Press.

3 Increasing Tolerance for Calm in Clients with Complex Trauma and Dissociation

Sarah Jenkins

Introduction

More often than not our clients with trauma histories do not present with only single-incident trauma (Kessler, 2000) or simple posttraumatic stress disorder (PTSD). In contrast, the majority of our clients present with developmental and chronic traumatization, also known as "complex trauma." With extensive histories of interpersonal traumas at various developmental stages, and of various categories including, but not limited to, sexual, physical, emotional, maltreatment, and neglect (van der Kolk, 2005), this is a "complex form of posttraumatic disorder [that presents] in survivors of prolonged, repeated trauma" (Herman, 1992).

Coupled with the awareness that complex trauma is often the norm must be the awareness that these same clients' symptoms are also driven by EPs (emotional parts), i.e., defensive actions from the past (fight, flight, freeze, attachment cry, defending against attachment loss) (van der Hart et al., 2006). Trauma-based dissociation is structural in nature in that the client's entire internal system is organized around the client's attempt to focus on daily living, whilst also maintaining phobia to their internal experiences. Clients are attempting to solely do the "daily life" and the behaviors associated with day-to-day living, but experience an increase of the dissociative barriers to acknowledging and processing the traumatic material.

How structural dissociation shows up in the arena and office is that while clients tell us the "stories," their declarative memories, their internal systems are still actually *phobic* to that same traumatic material and the affect associated it. They experience the dance between feeling "too much" or "too little." Moment to moment in session, and outside, our clients' internal systems are seeking to maintain a balance between a state of hypo-arousal and hyper-arousal, a state of homeostasis between being in the now, fully 100% present in the knowledge of and *feeling* of the danger being truly over vs. over activation of the unhealed traumatic material. And, when our clients become "stuck," in hyper-arousal or hypo-arousal we are running up against the lower and upper reaches of his or her "window of tolerance" (Siegel, 1999). They are reliving. The defensive actions from the past are experienced as happening *now*, whilst the client is attempting to focus on daily living and experiences; *this* is structural dissociation.

For those with unhealed trauma histories when this dissociative process is the neurological norm, calm will actually feel *dangerous*. In fact, calm or even pleasant experiences can actually lead to a spike in anxiety or shutdown due to the client's fear of these feeling states.

As trauma-sensitive equine assisted psychotherapy/equine facilitated psychotherapy (EAP/EFP) practitioners, we know that we must always be observing out client, moment to moment, to ensure that they are in *their* window of tolerance. There is a "middle area" when learning and trauma healing can occur, and to expand this clients must have the ability shift into a calm state, to have an "emergency brake" besides dissociation. *A client's window of tolerance for any affect will not widen without calm being created and actively revisited, over and over, first and foremost and throughout treatment.*

The catch is that while we all can benefit from creating and maintaining a calming practice and skills, clients with unhealed traumas often hold the cognitive error that "calm is dangerous" and that "the other shoe will drop if I try to be calm." They struggle with practicing calming skills in between sessions and "forget" or "don't have time" and perhaps engage in process and substance addictions that encourage "shutdown" that they may even misconstrue as calm. For clients with unhealed trauma calm is uncomfortable, and may even be experienced as a threat. In fact, I often find that when therapists have a lack of tolerance for calm and struggle with the cognitive error that "calm is not okay" or is "dangerous" they will have a harder time identifying this issue in their clients.

Theoretical Approach Use to Conceptualize the Person and Problem

Protocol's Phase Two

Preparation phase work and the utilization of structural dissociation theory for the treatment of dissociation. This chapter offers the clinical rationale for, and examples of, utilizing equine-facilitated experiences to decrease the complex trauma client's phobia to calm. Equine professionals and equine therapists, regardless of what approach to equine-assisted/facilitated therapy is being utilized, can benefit from treating the client's *phobias* to calm at the very front end of treatment as a later springboard for reducing phobias to a wider range of affect.

Reason/Rationale Equine-Assisted/Facilitated Therapy Can Help Address This Problem

While numerous organizations provide foundational trainings in EAP/EFP, the utilization of a best practices based, staged, and titrated approach to equine-assisted trauma treatment is often overlooked, especially in the cases of complex trauma. As a result, the absence of incorporating principles and best practices in trauma therapy including increasing tolerance for calm, can lead to equine-assisted practitioners unintentionally reactivating clients' traumas, "pushing" the clients outside of their window of tolerance into re-living, and leading to an *increase in the* clients' dissociation, as opposed to a titrated and effective processing of clients' trauma histories. With dissociation present the traumatic memory cannot consolidate and the dissociation can actually grow, thus contributing to further posttraumatic decline.

Guidelines in Implementing with Consideration of Multicultural Issues and Ethics

With this in mind, and whether one chooses to utilize the EquiLateral™: Equine Assisted EMDR Protocol or another EAP/EFP modality, it behooves EAP/EFP practitioners to be cognizant that it is both *ethically and clinically necessary* to utilize a best practices model for trauma treatment.

While the EAP/EFP field affords us all a variety of unique and inspiring ways to approach trauma treatment it is still imperative that, as an EAP/EFP therapist, one considers the following: "If I wasn't in the arena, and was just in an office, would I know enough about trauma and dissociation? Am I confident, *no matter which EAP/EFP modality that I am utilizing*, of how to apply core ethics and principles surrounding the treatment trauma and dissociation? Do I know how to treat dissociation *before* considering trauma processing?" Similarly, if I am an equine specialist in partnership with an equine therapist, do I also feel that as a team we have that knowledge base, as well as how it applies to the equine(s) role in the EAP/EFP process? For the client's sake, our answer should be yes. We must especially be confident of this when working with complex trauma. Without doing so, we can actually cause harm and *increase* a client's dissociative process in response to going into the stories too quickly.

Goals and Objectives of the Specific Intervention

Just as our horsemanship asks that we pursue the emergency stop before we transition upwards, so it is in working with complex trauma. Our horsemanship teaches us not to build in the "emergency stop" *last*, but to do it *first*. And, while we hope it doesn't get to that place where we need it, we do have to have "brakes." It's the same with trauma work. Calm can be the brake. We must teach the client that dissociation is *not* the brake, but rather a very creative and brilliant strategy of distraction used at the time of the original danger(s) and in those original circumstances.

The goal of the experience described below is to support our complex trauma clients to create a system of regulation in place, a way to get themselves out of distress that is not dissociative in nature. For, unless there is calm, when there is distress activation into hyper-arousal or hypo-arousal will just be the client's norm and the phobia about the traumatic material and its associated affect will grow.

Step by Step Description of How to Implement the Intervention

In providing an exercise to treat clients' phobias to calm it is crucial for the reader to know that this example is a "process-based EAP/EFP experience" as opposed to an "activity-based" one. It is about the mindful intention of the equine-assisted experience. It is not about the "activity" with the horse generating something in and of itself, but rather the therapeutic team's ability to be attuned to the client and the horse in the interaction. The team must have the ability to *read the horse and the client's window of tolerance*, moment to moment, no matter what "activity" is utilized to increase tolerance for calm.

For this experience, the materials are quite flexible. Specifically, there is access to one or more horses, ideally, but not required, to be in a herd setting where the client can observe and interact with one horse at a time. The client is encouraged to pick from a variety of calming experiences with the horse, for example breathing with the horse, brushing the horse, or leading with the horse mindfully. The horse that the client works with ideally would be identified by the client when observing or interacting with the herd, or may self-select to work with the client. A halter and lead rope can be used, but is not required, thereby allowing the horse the freedom of choice, as well as provide the client the opportunity to create calm, even when the horse goes in and out of position with the client.

Case Example: Increasing Tolerance for Calm

The client in this example is a 41-year-old female with a history of complex developmental trauma, including, but not limited to, witnessing domestic violence between her birth parents between the ages of 4 and 10 years' old, her parents' ultimate divorce, and sexual abuse by her stepfather. In adulthood, she reports a series of emotionally abusive relationships with men, as well as presenting with dissociative symptoms, specifically an ongoing pattern of "shutting down" which is often preceded by hyperarousal and a "feeling like I can't handle it." She goes on to report, "If I feel how I feel, I won't be able to get out of it. It's like it will last forever."

Transcript Analysis of Case Study

The following transcript analysis is about a pseudonym client:

Table 3.1   Case Example Transcript

Transcript	Analysis
Counselor: Part of why we are working with horses today is because they have some really important lessons for us about healing from what distresses us.	The "why" we partner with the horse introduces the idea that the horse is co-therapist in trauma recovery We are also supporting activation of the client's social engagement system. Note that "what" is distressing from the past is not being activated. The goal is *not* processing here, or getting into the story, but first and foremost stabilization. Stay attuned. Keep them in the window of tolerance, no matter what stage of trauma treatment.
Client: I don't know anything about horses. What do I have to do? I'm really nervous.	The client is possibly teetering on the "edge" of their window of tolerance, regarding expectations. It is imperative that trauma clients repeatedly get the adaptive information, on a neurological level, that as adults they have choices, for as children they did not.
Counselor: That's no problem. I don't have the expectation that you do. In fact, it is really important that you know that you always have choices in this work. Today's experience is about giving your whole self the experience of learning about calm. You see, the horse knows calm. Horses know how to "dial it up" when they need to move out of harm's way, but they also know how to "dial things down" when the danger is over. They know how to be "relaxed and ready," whereas we humans, if we have unhealed distress, don't always trust that we can do that.	Clients with unhealed traumas can be concerned that they will not be "ready" and able to "handle" future dangers. Their internal experiences, their emotions, as well as external experiences, will be considered threats, resulting in either hyperarousal or shutdown, which is dissociation in response. If they do not have the ability to get to calm, they will dissociate because it is their system's "go to." The client could destabilize, and we can grow the phobia to their feelings, increasing their dissociation and time in treatment. This is especially true if we go into the traumatic stories without increasing their tolerance for calm first.
Counselor: In fact, sometimes folks I work with don't know that they have other skills, resources, and means to get themselves out of distress. They don't know, feel, or know how to use "calm" instead of going to "shut down" or actually staying in a state of being "always on."	We are checking for any cognitive errors about calm, trying to access the emotional parts of self that are likely phobic about it. We all have parts of self, but in the language of structural dissociation theory, primary, secondary, tertiary dissociation involves the emotional parts of self being

Table 3.1 Case Example Transcript (Cont.)

Transcript	Analysis
I have kind of a strange question for you. I'm wondering, if you were to check in with yourself, what percentage of yourself, from 0 to 100% would agree with the statement that it is "okay to be calm"? And, answer this from a place of what *feels* true, not just what you know logically.	stuck in trauma time and still defending from the past, as if it's happening, *now*. This question "gets to" the limbic system, where those emotional parts of self are likely defending against calm.
Client: Well, of course I know it's supposed to be okay to be calm. That makes sense, but when you put it that way, I would say only about 40% of me would agree that it is okay to be calm. I guess I would say that the majority of me doesn't trust calm. It's not okay to be calm. Something bad will happen. It feels like the other shoe is going to drop.	This is an expression of the lack of tolerance for calm. It is a cognitive error; the belief is that the state of calm has the ability to cause danger, that her internal state has the ability to cause something happening in the external environment. We have to *gently* increase the exposure to calm and introduce adaptive information that calm does not cause danger. Many clients, including therapists, miss this idea that calm does not *cause* danger. If calm was present before the danger happened, it does not mean danger will happen. It is actually that calm became a conditioned stimulus that the system has *associated* with danger.
Counselor: I can see that in your past, that belief was so important and an understandable perspective. Since the original danger is over, calm might be a different experience in your today. In our last session, we talked about how some of our work with the horses might include experiences like greeting them, breathing with them, brushing them, leading them, and essentially establishing a relationship with them. I am wondering if any of those experiences I had suggested might resonate with you right now?	We are joining with the cognitive error held by the system, and are now going to introduce adaptive information experientially. The client is given the choice of what activity resonates with them, also as a way to encourage the client to increase tolerance for an internal check-in, something that dissociation is designed *not* to do.
Client: I guess I could try breathing with a horse.	Proceed, but still monitor their window of tolerance. If the client had said "none" honor the choice to say "no." Then, gently ask "tell me more about that— what's important about not doing this experience?" "Notice that as an adult you do get to have the choice." Learn more about the beliefs surrounding calm and to identify any phobias to attachment, i.e., activation of the social engagement system.

(continued)

Table 3.1 Case Example Transcript (Cont.)

Transcript	Analysis
Counselor: Thanks for giving it a try. I am going to stand here and hold space for you as you do this. I'm wondering if there is a horse in this herd that you feel drawn to, that you would like to stand and breathe with?	In the ideal situation, the counselor is in an environment where the client can observe/interact with the herd, giving both the opportunity to self-select. Or this experience can be done by bringing the horse to the client on a line, or without a line at all, allowing "what happens to happen." Self-selection via client/horse is a profound opportunity for the client to learn about the horse's energy/responses to her internal states and external behaviors.
Client: Okay, I think I would like to be with that horse Pixie. So, you just want me to stand next to him and breathe with him. But, what am I supposed to *do*? I'm not doing anything and that's just not okay with me.	This in an opportunity to teach that we can have calm, peace vs. shutdown or hypervigilance. We can gently point out the cognitive error that I "have to keep doing" is a lack of tolerance for calm.
Counselor: Let's have you lean in, and notice that Pixie is here with you breathing while you stand next to him here. Or, you could even just hold the line and watch him breathing, and notice your breath as you do. Notice your feet on the ground, firmly planted in the present. That your whole self is here in this moment as an adult and not in those past circumstances. In fact, you standing next to Pixie, in this very moment, that his hooves are near to you, is a reminder to your whole self that you are no longer in those past circumstances. You can't be, you didn't know Pixie back then. You, and the horse, both, are in this present moment, and any of the dangers from the past are over.	The emphasis here is on time orienting the client's whole system; this is not just a grounding skill, but addressing the client's dissociative process and increasing the adaptive information that awareness of her internal experience, in being in a state of calm, is not dangerous and that the client's system is not in the past where it was conditioned to feel that calm was a danger. The emotional parts of self stuck in trauma time must get the adaptive information that being in the present does not mean being in the present from "back then." In fact, it means being present in a different "now" than those parts of self perceive it to be.
Client: Yeah that feels pretty good. I can feel my breath. I feel something changing.	While the client is making a positive statement, and we want to bring attention to that, be aware that this can actually increase anxiety if the client also has a phobia about the positive.
Counselor: What's that like?	Inviting the client to identify and label the experience. It is not a specific body-related question, which can be highly distressing for dissociative clients, especially at first.

Table 3.1 Case Example Transcript (Cont.)

Transcript	Analysis
Client: Well, Pixie is pretty chilled out. He doesn't look too worried about me.	Learning what calm "looks" and "feels" like as well as addressing the cognitive error that calm is not okay.
Counselor: Yes, Pixie does look pretty calm, huh? We've talked about what that looks in horses before. He's got calm breathing, his head is down, his eyes look soft, he's not shut down. What do you notice about you?	Teaching the client about calm and using horse psychology to demonstrate that it is "okay to be calm." Asking the client to observe the horse to encourage a tolerance for an internal exploration of calm.
Client: Yeah, that's pretty cool he's doing that. I think I'm calmer. I don't feel so revved up. I feel more here. I can breathe better and my heart rate is slowing down, but I don't feel like I'm cut off from how I feel.	The client is increasing tolerance and identifying *how* calm is experienced. It is important to get the description of the experience itself from the client.
Counselor: Now, I would like you to contrast that to other times when you say you got "calm." Like, the times you say you binge watch TV, numbing out, or those other kinds of things that you described as calming. So, is that the same state you are in right now with Pixie, or different?	Teaching the client the difference between a natural calm state vs. a shutdown state experientially with the horse, as opposed to a cerebral discussion of it.
Client: Yeah, I guess that is different. Like, when I watch TV, I just lose myself in the experience, it feels like I am in the show. It's not the same. I'm in this experience, now, but I still know and feel that I am here. I don't feel "sucked" into the experience and lose my connection to what is around me.	The client is learning the difference between calm and shutdown.
Counselor: Now when we began this I asked you that strange question "if you were to check in with yourself, what percentage of yourself, from 0 to 100%, would agree with the statement that it is "okay to be calm"? I'm curious, what would that percentage be now in this moment? What percentage of you, from 0 to 100% would agree that it is okay to be calm?"	The next question is designed to then get that adaptive information to the emotional parts of self stuck in trauma time.

(continued)

Table 3.1 Case Example Transcript (Cont.)

Transcript	Analysis
Client: Well, I think that's kind of weird, but it's increased a bit. I guess about 60% of me now knows it's okay to be calm. Because you have taught me about horses as prey animals, I know that if there really was a reason to be worried, that Pixie would have shown me that. He would know. Being calm in this moment didn't make anything bad happen.	There is adaptive information that is getting to the emotional parts of the self; the client's system is learning something about being in a state of calm does not "cause" danger to happen. The horse's behavior is also "proof" of this fact and helping to address the cognitive error that calm is dangerous.
Counselor: Now that your whole self has had this experience, I would like to invite you to actually take a mental snapshot of this moment in your mind, you can even take one of you and Pixie if you like, and use this 4 x 6 snapshot as a way to "get back" into that calm state whenever you need it. I am actually doing to ask you do to do this at least two times a day. Use it when you don't need it. Use it when you do. Calm is a like muscle, we have to keep using it, so then when we need it, it is available to us, and is readily available as a way we can get ourselves out of distress. Then, next week, I will be asking you how it went.	It is not enough to just teach a client calm, and to increase their tolerance for it. We must then ensure that they will *use* the skills in between sessions. In future sessions, we will continue to ask "what calming skills did you use?" or "how did you get yourself out of distress?" Also, in future sessions, we will continue to use the percent question about calm to check in on the phobia(s) to calm and to *gently* challenge the cognitive error that calm is not okay, is dangerous, or causes things to happen that are distressing.

Sample Client Session Note

50-minute session with emphasis on stabilization due to the treatment of dissociation being necessary before moving to trauma processing. Focused on increasing client's tolerance to calm and treating associated cognitive errors with goal of increasing client's window of tolerance for calm as alternative to hypo- or hyper-arousal. Provided additional adaptive information regarding calm including utilizing experiences with the equine to support time orientation, as well as to reduce phobias to calm and social engagement. Client reported increased tolerance for calm in session, and expressed a willingness to practice calming skills in between sessions. Utilized the resource of a 4 x 6 snapshot of today's equine-facilitated experience as an access point for calm for the client. Goal is to follow up with the client in future sessions regarding the client's use of calm whether in or out of distress and in between sessions.

References

Herman, J. L. (1992). Complex PTSD: A syndrome in survivors of prolonged and repeated trauma. *Journal of Traumatic Stress*, 5, 377–397.

Kessler, R. C. (2000). Posttraumatic stress disorder: The burden to the individual and to society. *Journal of Clinical Psychiatry*, 61 (Suppl. 5), 4–12.

Siegel, D. (1999). *The Developing Mind*. New York: Guilford.

van der Hart, O., Nijenhuis, E., & Steele, K. (2006). *The Haunted Self Structural Dissociation and the Treatment of Chronic Traumatization*. New York: Norton & Company.

van der Kolk, B. A. (2005). Developmental trauma disorder: Towards a rational diagnosis for children with complex trauma histories. *Psychiatric Annals*, 35(5), 401–408.

4 Natural Lifemanship's Trauma-Focused EAP for Reactive Attachment Disorder

Bettina Shultz-Jobe, Kate Naylor, and Tim Jobe

Introduction

Reactive attachment disorder (RAD) is a condition that typically affects children who have experienced severe abuse and/or neglect in their early childhood years, often in institutional or out-of-home settings. Children with this diagnosis have difficulty self-soothing and do not generally seek comfort from their caregivers when they are upset. These children may appear unhappy, irritable, sad, or scared more frequently than other children, or display a lack of emotions. The diagnosis is made if symptoms become chronic (AACAP, 2017). From Natural Lifemanship's perspective, at its most basic level, RAD is a connection and healthy relating issue, brought on by a client's inability to utilize their limbic system in a regulated, organized way. In the family unit, this causes significant conflict and distress. As the child grows into adolescence and adulthood, untreated RAD will continue to impact the individual's ability to form stable relationships—a fundamental building block to a healthy life.

Theoretical Approach

Natural Lifemanship's model of Trauma Focused Equine Assisted Psychotherapy (TF-EAP) is derived from various experts in the interpersonal neurobiology, attachment, and trauma fields. From this perspective, we understand that RAD arises from two specific causes—an unpredictable and unsafe environment, as well as a deprived environment of neglect. A lack of input (sensory and relational) results in a lack of neural connections, and unpredictable input results in disorganized neural connections. The disorganization begins in the brainstem (responsible for fight/flight/freeze and other automatic reflexes), moves up through the diencephalon and midbrain (responsible for motor regulation/movement), and into the limbic system, which is largely responsible for bonding and attachment. Disorganization and lack of connections in these lower regions will inevitably affect the neocortex (the site of concrete and abstract thought)—just as a shaky foundation impacts the roof and walls of a house. These differences can be seen in children diagnosed with RAD in the following ways: an inability to regulate fight/flight/freeze responses, a lack of interest or ability to form loving connections, a negative response to attempts at emotional or caring connection, and an inability to be soothed by caregivers.

Additionally, infants (indeed, all mammals) are born with an innate need to connect to their caregiver for nurture and for survival. The limbic system of an infant naturally *moves toward* his caregiver. When the caregiver is unresponsive, neglectful, or abusive, the survival parts of the brain *sound the alarm* and seek to *move away* from the caregiver. The limbic system is activated as the child seeks connection while in a state of fear or terror, driving the child more deeply into the survival parts of the brain. This is the beginning of compartmentalization in the brain and compromised cross-brain connections. The result is a child who feels no pleasure or extreme fear when connection occurs. This child seeks comfort (as the limbic system *moves toward*), but then can't accept the comfort they sought (as the brainstem *moves away*). Children with RAD find it very difficult to remain in a state of calm while requesting and experiencing a sense of connection with self and others.

Disorganization in the limbic system impedes the brain's ability to communicate across regions smoothly and effectively. With the location of the limbic system in the center of the brain and connecting the lower and upper regions— disorganization here disrupts the lower regions from communicating easily with the upper regions and vice versa, along with the general difficulty in relating and connecting found in a compromised limbic system itself. The result, then, is not only difficulty in building satisfying relationships, but also significant challenges in impulse control and emotion control. When a person or situation is deemed threatening the lower regions of the brain become active and fight/flight/freeze is activated. These impulses occur reflexively, in fractions of a second. In a well-organized brain, the message travels up through the limbic system and into the neocortex where the threat is evaluated. If the threat is deemed to be a mistake or ultimately non-threatening, the neocortex overrides the survival impulse and calms the nervous system—the body and brain can relax. However, if the limbic system—nested in between the survival brain and neocortex—is disorganized or shut down, the messages *to* the neocortex and *from* the neocortex are slow to be delivered, if at all. This often results in behavior that appears highly sensitive, over-reactive, and unable to be soothed in children with limbic disorganization.

Most importantly, from a neurobiological perspective, conceptualization of the child with limbic disorganization means we recognize the client does not *choose* to behave in these ways—the child behaves in a manner that has been learned from experience and would be appropriate in true survival situations. Natural Lifemanship sees these behaviors as learned but no longer of service to the child who is, hopefully, now in a safe living situation. This perspective is non-pathologizing and aims to address the root causes of the behavior, rather than attempting to eradicate the behavior alone. It becomes our job to help clients learn how to be in healthy relationships now that they are safe—our goal is to wake up and reorganize the brain systems, particularly the limbic system, in a safe manner, leading to long-lasting change from the inside out, not just behavior modification. As the brain develops based on experience, the best and only way to do this effectively is to support the client in engaging in safe, pre-dictable, and healthy relationships.

Reason/Rationale for Using TF-EAP to Treat RAD

TF-EAP attempts to re-engage the limbic system in a rhythmic manner (safe and predictable)—essentially, to develop the ability to be in a connected rela-tionship thanks to reorganization of the lower regions of the brain, and specif-ically the limbic system. A child with a RAD diagnosis will not only struggle to truly feel connected, safe, and calm while in the presence of a caregiver or other important relationships—but he will undoubtedly find it difficult to carry a sense of connection with him no matter where he is. Without an ability to have a felt *internal* sense of connection, the physical and emotional connections when close with others will lack security. Our larger goal, then, is to help the client feel a satisfying sense of connection with others—whether he is physically with the other or not. In Natural Lifemanship, we call this attachment (being with) and detachment (connected but exploring physical distance). Our use of the word attachment is intended to describe the behaviors that occur in a relationship that require closeness, such as coming together, touch, and general nurturing. We recognize that these behaviors can occur with or without healthy connection. The latter does not result in secure attachment. We teach that both attachment and detachment with connection are necessary for building an internal sense of connection.

Secure Attachment in TF-EAP

Attachment theory (Ainsworth and Bowlby, 1991) argues that a secure attachment allows individuals to feel safe and calm in relationship—with an ability to be flex-ible and balanced between nurture and structure. Dan Siegel (2012) clarifies that secure attachment comes from an integrated brain, or an organized brain that is capable of smoothly communicating across regions. An insecure attachment arises from disorganization or lack of neural connections in areas of the brain and results in anxiety, dependence, or a significant imbalance in nurture or structure. We partner with horses to offer clients a new experience in relating. Clients diagnosed with RAD already have neural pathways set in their brains about how human relationships should go. However, it is rare that the client has enough experience with a horse to have pathways established around horse–human relationships. A new relationship with a horse typically offers a blank slate on which to learn new ways of relating—and the client often experiences more willingness to learn in this relationship than in one with a human, where negative interaction is usually expected. Finally, the most important facet of the therapy is that the child be able to transfer his learning, his ability to form connections, outside of the work with his horse and into human relationships.

   As the client begins a relationship with his horse natural relationship challenges will arise. The client will experiment with connection and closeness

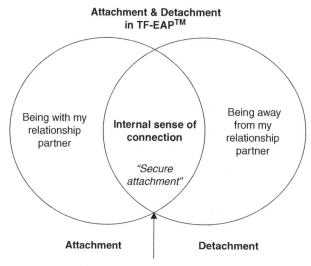

Attachment & Detachment in TF-EAP™

Both attachment AND detachment WITH connection are necessary for developing an *internal sense of connection.*

A healthy internal sense of connection is akin to a "secure attachment pattern" as described in attachment theory

Figure 4.1 Secure Attachment in TF-EAP

(attachment) and connection with distance (detachment). In order to find success with his horse, the client will have to search for connection within his own body ("what am I feeling?", "where am I feeling it?", and "how might I feel safe and calm?") as well as connection with his horse (what is my horse feeling, why, and how do I help them feel safe and calm?). This approach is entirely about repairing the wounds of past relationships by creating new experiences for the brain to learn and the body to feel. A horse's natural inclination is to respond positively to attuned connection—when a human is connected to their internal experience as well as that of the horse—and to be mistrustful of a disconnected, out of control human. Therefore, the client gets immediate feedback as to when he is disconnected, and when he is experiencing connection. This is often very different from human relationships, in which expectations, judgments, and projections interfere with authentic responding.

TF-EAP for a child with RAD addresses multiple aspects of healing. The client must develop skills for co-regulation and self-regulation if he is going to fully connect with his horse and sustain that connection; he will then have opportunities to practice regulation and connection (both while being together and apart) to solidify these growing neural pathways, with the horse responding in ways that validate and support his new learning. Through repetitive practice, the client's brain has begun to reorganize neural pathways related to relationship—making it much more likely the client will be able to transfer and sustain the changes made in session with his horse. The horse offers a gateway relationship for new, healthy ways of connecting that the therapist can then facilitate transferring to human relationships outside of therapy. Ultimately, the relationship with the horse is not what the client needs for long-term life satisfaction; what he needs is to be able to form secure connections with other people he chooses as he moves through life.

Ethical Issues in Animal-Assisted Therapy Programs

One ethical concern in this situation is the horse's welfare. Therapy horses should be monitored for signs of chronic stress, and not be required to participate in more sessions than is healthy for their unique temperament. Furthermore, when working with clients who struggle to connect with others in a healthy way, it is imperative that the therapy team (therapist, equine professional, or both) is able to provide calm connection with their therapy horses. If the horse cannot find connection with the client, he must be able to find it somewhere in the therapy team as to not be isolated and distressed during the session. The therapy team must be well versed in horse psychology so they are aware of the difference between compliance through submission, and connection through choice. If the therapy team models either permissiveness or dominance/control with their horse, negative relating patterns could be reinforced in the client.

Description of Technique: Goals and Objectives of TF-EAP

For the purposes of this chapter, we will discuss the process of building connection through an attachment activity (asking for connection with physical closeness), as well as detachment (connection with distance). Therapy goals include being able to calm the self (through co-regulation and eventually self-regulation and brain integration); increase ability to be connected with the self; ability to attach and detach with others while maintaining a connection; and decrease discomfort with appropriate physical touch.

Materials Needed

Natural Lifemanship relies mostly on the relationship itself for the therapy session. All that is required is a horse and a large enough space for the horse to move freely (i.e., a pasture or large round pen, preferably open-sided). Occasionally a halter and lead rope will be useful.

Step-by-Step Description

While techniques and a plan are important for good therapy work, Natural Lifemanship is a principle-based approach rather than a specific intervention or set of techniques. What follows is a sample of what could be done in session. Always consider what is in the best interest of the client and horse and allow for flexibility that stays true to therapy goals and relationship-first principles. If at any time the client displays (or horse communicates) dysregulation, bottom-up regulation becomes the priority, not the technique or task. The attachment activity we will describe in our case study is often possible a few sessions into the therapy process—however, it is not where therapy begins. In Natural Lifemanship, the intention is to begin therapy with a thorough intake and assessment process followed by meeting and choosing a horse partner. We briefly describe that process and then follow with the attachment technique.

Step-by-Step Description of TF-EAP Relationship Work

Table 4.1 Description of TF-EAP

Prior to the technique: How the client chooses a horse to build a relationship with A client begins therapy by choosing the horse she would like to work with, which involves meeting all the available horses. Some clients wish to know a horse's name, history, temperament, etc. If so, we offer any information we have. Others prefer to go based on feel or initial impressions. There is no wrong approach to choosing a horse. Many clients will project onto the horse, *"This horse doesn't like me"* or *"This horse is sad, like me."* While this projecting is an important aspect of learning more about the client, her story, and her functioning, projection in and of itself is not the goal. It is important to support the client in peeling back the layers of the projection through open-ended questions, such as *"What do you see in this horse that tells you he is sad?"*, *"Do you remember a time when you were sad?"*, *"How do you look when you are sad?"* or *"What do you feel in your own body when you are sad?"* It is important to the relationship building that a client learns to distinguish between what she is actually seeing in the horse, and what she is projecting onto the horse. For example, *"the horse has his head hung low and his ears are flopped out to the side"* is an observation. *"The horse is sad like me"* is a projection. If the client only relies on her projections and interpretations, she will struggle to truly connect with the horse that is right in front of her because all she is focusing on are her own feelings and sensations when near this horse. In RAD, choosing to be in a relationship is difficult in and of itself. The choosing of a horse partner may require multiple sessions. This is ok and entirely appropriate; therapy goals and objectives are still the focus. In the step-by-step description below, we assume the client has already chosen a horse and the horse is waiting for her alone in a small pasture with freedom to move, eat, and take care of himself.
1) Before entering the horse's space, help the client notice her horse. Ask her to notice what she sees in her horse's behavior. Often a client will project, guide the client through projecting as described in the opening paragraph.
2) Ask the client to notice anything inside herself as well—any sensations, feelings, or thoughts.
3) Ask the client how she would like to begin building a relationship with her horse. Process thinking to help client consider pros and cons of each option.

(continued)

Table 4.1 Description of TF-EAP (Cont.)

4)	The client enters the pen or pasture (depending on the client's awareness and ability to be calm—maybe accompanied by a therapist or equine professional). Some may not be ready to enter the pen—for our purposes we assume she does go in.
5)	Ask the client to observe the horse's behavior in response to her entering his space, and respond to any request the horse makes.
6)	Allow the client to initiate relationship in her own way (she may want to call the horse, approach, pet, groom, simply observe from a distance, etc.). Support the client in noticing the horse's responses to her attempts (perhaps the horse relaxes, or ignores her, or gets stressed and moves away, etc.).
7)	Ask the client to reflect on how the horse's responses to her attempts affect her—for example, when the horse moves away, what happens to her inside—what does she feel, physically and emotionally?
8)	If appropriate, help the client move from projection (this horse doesn't like me) to observation (this horse moved away when I got close).
9)	Explore possible reasons the horse made his choice (allow for typical horse behavior, the horse's internal experience, as well as the client's internal experience to have all been at play in some capacity). Ask the client to consider the quality of her connection with the horse—perhaps even scaling it from 0 to 10.
10)	Encourage the client to continue attempts at building the relationship. Concepts to explore might include: mutually beneficial relationships, "asking" vs. "making," offering choice. The therapy team is noticing any relational patterns that emerge.
11)	Throughout this dance of asking and responding, continue to help the client check in with her own internal experience—physical, mental, emotional, as well as observing the horse's experience—physical, mental, emotional. Pause when needed to help regulate the client through bottom-up regulation of the brain (i.e., sensory input and movement first).
12)	With practice, the client will learn how to control her internal energy to gain her horse's attention in a predictable and safe way. She will learn how to use appropriate pressure, watch her horse for a response, and adjust her pressure accordingly and predictably so her horse feels safe and knows what to do to connect with the client in that moment.
13)	Over time, the client and horse begin to communicate through body energy and nonverbal language, and attachment can progress from the horse paying attention to the client, to turning to face the client, to following the client, petting, grooming, etc. Detachment, or asking for space with connection, will naturally follow.
14)	When the client experiences moments of connection the therapist helps the client grow that sensation by exploring it (locating it in the body, naming it, giving it shape, color, etc.)—this creates an internal "object" which will help the client find an internal sense of connection to her horse when they are not together (detachment) and then transfer that feeling of connection to other relationships.

Table 4.1 Description of TF-EAP (Cont.)

15)	Alternatively, if the client is unable to create an internal "object" for their connection you can ask them to find an object on the property (a stick, rock, leaf, some horse hair, etc.) to choose and save to represent the connection. Have the client finish the sentence, "This object will remind me of _____, the moment I felt safe, calm, and connected with my horse." Ask the client to use the object to help her remember and connect to her horse at least one time each day between sessions. Eventually, she can start to transfer this sense of connection to other relationships when attached and when detached.
16)	Although this is unlikely to be possible immediately, the ultimate goal is for the client to practice carrying this sense of connection into other relationships—with parent or caregiver, hopefully. Family homework can support this effort.

Guidelines in Consideration of Multicultural Issues and Ethics

Multicultural issues/ethics in therapy require that we are flexible with our interpretations of behavior. This is why Natural Lifemanship is a principle-based approach, and process oriented. Practicing attuned connection supports the therapy team in respecting multicultural differences through noticing, acknowledging, and adjusting to always keep the relationship growing in a healthy way.

Case Example

Sarah (pseudonym) is an 11-year-old Ugandan female adopted into an American family at the age of 10 months. She lived in an international orphanage until her adoption, where she was severely neglected and abused. In the orphanage, Sarah was rarely touched and was forced into potty training through cruel methods. Immediately following her adoption, Sarah's parents placed her in occupational therapy for her sensory deprivation issues, which appeared to have helped with some brain reorganization as Sarah was very bright and performed well in school. However, Sarah was highly dissociative, unable to form relationships, and was very uncomfortable being touched or touching others. Previous attempts in other therapies were largely unsuccessful at helping Sarah in her relationships, and perhaps increased her dissociation related to touch due to an overemphasis on touching to build attachment. Sarah's resting heart rate was 125 bpm (reported by a primary care physician); however, she always appeared very calm and quiet and never displayed behavioral issues. Her internal experience was very different from what she displayed on the outside. Sarah's difficulties and disconnect from her own body suggested disorganization and shutdown in the lower regions of her brain, including the limbic system.

Transcript Analysis of Case Example

The following transcript analysis is about a pseudonym client:

Table 4.2 Case Example Transcript

Transcript	Analysis
Context: *It is important to note that in Sarah's first session in the small pasture with her horse, Hans, her presence caused him to run circles for minutes and minutes while displaying other signs of stress. While the therapist tried to help, Sarah breathe and calm herself, she was unable to do so and so stepped out of the pasture. When Sarah left the pasture, Hans stopped moving, took a deep breath, lowered his head, and began to lick and chew (all signs that he could relax). Hans' reaction suggested that more was going on under Sarah's surface; it seemed that her energy was dysregulating to Hans despite the fact that she appeared calm. Multiple sessions followed in which the therapist, Sarah, and Sarah's parent worked on noticing and tracking bodily sensations as well as finding safe ways to connect with others that did not require touch. This was also important in helping Sarah understand the connection between her body energy and the pressure she exerted on Hans, even when touch was not involved. As her capacity to be more regulated grew, Sarah was able to experiment with body energy and pressure in the pasture with Hans, as well. While it was recognized that touch would be an important part of building attachment and reorganizing her brain, to force or even encourage touch caused Sarah to further dissociate (check out and disconnect from herself and others). The following is a sample of a session after Sarah progressed further in her abilities to be co-regulated and was beginning to self-regulate at times. The therapist in these sessions with Sarah is dually certified as a clinician and equine professional — as you read the transcript you will see the therapist in both roles as needed.*	
Therapist: How would you like to begin your relationship with Hans [horse]?	The relationship is between the client and Hans — so it is her decision how to begin with him. Using his name supports his identity as an individual — not an object or tool.
Client: I don't know. I'm scared to go in there after last time.	The client is unsure in all relationships — the lower regions of her brain are dysregulated and allow for very little positive emotion when considering bonding with another.
Therapist: It was a little scary last time. Let's see if we can do something to feel calmer. Can you feel the sun on your face? See if you can really notice the sun's warmth on your face. Notice the clouds as they move in the sky.	The therapist validates and connects. Reminds client of a mindfulness technique they have used before. Employs visual rhythm to regulate the brainstem. Mindfulness, rhythmic sensory input, and validation support regulation in the lower regions of the brain and limbic system.
Client: That's a little better, but I still am not sure.	The client begins to regulate, but does not feel completely calm yet.
Therapist Is there something I or your mom could do to help you with this relationship?	The therapist encourages co-regulation and seeking relational support and connection, which requires more use of the limbic system.

Table 4.2 Case Example Transcript (Cont.)

Transcript	Analysis
Client: Will you go in with me?	The therapist offers co-regulation with the client—walking around the outside of the small pasture together (to regulate brainstem and diencephalon) and breathing together. When ready, they enter the pasture (the client's request shows relational progress).
Therapist: What do you notice with Hans?	The therapist encourages the client to be attuned to Hans' behavior (activating limbic system, building empathy), without interpreting/thinking for her.
Client: Hans is worried—he's running around the pasture.	The client makes an observation and an interpretation. The interpretation may or may not be correct, but it offers some insight into the client's experience.
Client: Hans looks on the outside the way I feel on the inside.	The client is connecting with Hans, relating to his current state. She is also offering insight to her own internal state by connecting with herself. She is accessing more of her limbic system. As the client identifies her own internal experience, Hans calms and slows his movements—as is common with horses, Hans feels safer now that the client is connected to herself and congruent.
Therapist: Wow, what happened when you noticed and then said that? **Client:** Hans stopped running. **Therapist:** Now that Hans is calmer, what would you like to be able to do with him?	The therapist is helping the client recognize her impact on Hans—her internal experience matters. This likely begins a new neural pathway for client—an engaged limbic system can be a positive thing. Some clients prefer to not ask anything of their horses, but this often results in a lack of mutual connection (and lack of progress in the relationship). The therapist must help the client tolerate discomfort to practice building a relationship. (This may take time. More bottom-up regulation is often necessary.)
Client: He's not running now, but he isn't really paying attention to me.	The client continues to be connected to Hans in a small way—noticing his behavior and where his attention is focused. Her limbic system continues to be activated while remaining in a state of calm—undoubtedly a new experience and neural pathway.

(*continued*)

Table 4.2 Case Example Transcript (Cont.)

Transcript	Analysis
Therapist: Why don't we ask for Hans' attention?	The therapist prompts the client to try something more challenging. Being calm is important, but new experiences are necessary for new neural pathways to build (eustress).
Client: I'm not sure." *(She looks down and away from therapist, her shoulders slumping slightly.)*	The client feels uncomfortable with the idea—starts to show signs of disconnect and dysregulation. The therapist begins to breathe deeply and swings the rope in her hand in a gentle, rhythmic way. She is helping to co-regulate client using own breath and rhythm.
Client: *(Sighs a deep breath.)* Will you do it with me?	The client feels connected to therapist and seeks support—even asking to link arms with the therapist—a big milestone in the therapy—touch becomes appropriate for her. The client and therapist mirror each other—moving together. Together they ask for Hans' attention. The therapist guides the client in rhythmic motion, staying with Hans as he moves.
Client: He's running!	The client's energy goes up quickly when Hans begins to move, unnerving the horse and causing him to run.
	The therapist guides the client in trying to not increase the pressure by being afraid or out of control, supports the client in keeping the pressure the same by slowly walking to maintain consistent distance from Hans or swaying from side to side (regulating most lower brain regions) and taking calming breaths together. (co-regulation)
Client: *(Breathing calmly.)* Look, Hans is slowing down.	As the client is able to regulate, Hans slows, and she is able to notice subtle changes in him—she is becoming more attuned to him as she is calmer and more connected (limbic connection).
	As Hans slows, he flicks his ear and eyes over to the client. In this attempt to connect, the client and therapist release all pressure (slow inhale/exhale and taking focus off of Hans' body). Hans feels the release of pressure and stops, turns his head and looks at client. The client and therapist back up a few steps, Hans begins to follow them, and they walk with Hans following behind.

Table 4.2 Case Example Transcript (Cont.)

Transcript	Analysis
Client: *(Smiles.)* I can feel him behind me.	The client has practiced noticing connection without touch; in this moment she is able to feel connected to Hans even though he is behind her and not touching her. She is developing the ability to feel connected in a relationship, *internally*. Her efforts to connect are rewarded, Hans is calm and following her. This reaffirms neural pathways in the brain for both the client and Hans—a positive experience with connection.
Therapist: When you notice and feel your horse behind you, where do you feel that connection to Hans the most in your body?	The therapist helps the client identify and grow the sensation of connection.
Client: It's in my chest, in my heart. I feel warm.	The client has enough regulation in her lower brain regions, and enough connection in her limbic system to identify a sensation that goes with connection.
Therapist: Does it have a shape or color?	The therapist will help the client name and describe internal experience (size, shape, color, movement)—thus building an "object" of sorts for the client to call upon again in the future.
Client: It's pink … it's gooey and dripping down into my stomach, making it warm there too.	The client's experience of connection grows and becomes more concrete.
Therapist: Let's say goodbye to Hans, and see if we can take this feeling out of the pasture.	The therapist is helping the client practice connection while exploring physical distance (detachment), and intending to help the client transfer experience out of the therapy session.
Therapist: Why don't you and your mom take a walk for the last few minutes of the session and try to keep that warm, gooey feeling in your chest and stomach.	Walking continues the bottom-up regulation, which helps the client solidify new neural pathways—specifically linked to the sensation of connection. Walking with her mother helps the client begin to transfer the sensation to her relationship with her mother. They link arms, practicing comforting touch as they walk.

Sample Client Session Note

Table 4.3 Sample Client Session Note

CONFIDENTIAL

Session Note	
Name: *Sarah*	**Date**: *mm/dd/yyyy*
Start Time: *9:30am* **End Time:** *10:30am*	**Diagnosis:** *Reactive Attachment Disorder (313.89)*
Service Type (CPT code if billing insurance)	
Average Heart Rate on EMWAVE (and observations) 125bpm (per PCP)	
Therapeutic Goals: Be able to calm self (through co-regulation and eventually self-regulation and brain integration). Increase ability to be connected with self. Be able to attach and detach with others while maintaining a connection. Decrease discomfort with appropriate physical touch.	
Check in with client (degree to which learning in session is transferring to other areas of life) Parent reports improvement in client's ability to self-soothe, using her skills learned in session. Parent and client have been engaging in mirror game and walks together to improve connection (attachment).	
Intervention/s used: Bottom-up regulation including: rhythmic sensory input, therapist regulation (breathing, heart rate, voice), walking. Identify internal experience. Observe experiences of others. Practice self-regulation skills (breathing, mindfulness). Support in transferring learning to relationship with parent.	
Client's response to intervention/s: Client arrived somewhat dysregulated to session—but willingly engaged in walking and mindfulness techniques, resulting in improved regulation. Client showed improvement in relationships: demonstrated in her ability to seek out relational support and practice self-observing, as well as experiencing and naming the sensation of connection.	
Future Plan: Continue sessions, 1X weekly. HW: Parent and client draw own pictures of sensation of connection together.	

The following scale is scored by the clinician, and is representative of the client's regulation during the session (first order outcome).

0	1	2	3	4
No self-regulation; client gave up/refused to continue or was unable to change state	Client able to self-regulate with considerable intervention from therapist (e.g., co-regulation or giving step by step instructions)	Client able to self-regulate with some prompting from therapist (modeling, recalling techniques learned for breathing, muscle relaxation, mindfulness, etc.)	Client able to self-regulate with minimal prompting from therapist (e.g., asking child to recall what worked for them the last time x happened)	Client able to self-regulate with no prompting from therapist

_____

Therapist Signature/Credentials

Blank Session Note

Please refer to Table 4.4 at the end of the chapter for Blank Session Note.

References

Ainsworth, M. D. S., & Bowlby, J. (1991). An ethological approach to personality development. *American Psychologist*, 46, 331–341.

American Academy of Child & Adolescent Psychiatry (AACAP, 2017). Attachment Disorders. Retrieved from www.aacap.org/AACAP/Families_and_Youth/Facts_for_Families/FFF-Guide/Attachment-Disorders-085.aspx on June 25, 2017.

Siegel, D. J. (2012). *The Developing Mind: How Relationships and the Brain Interact to Shape Who We Are* (2nd ed.). New York: Guilford.

Trauma Dissociation.com (RAD, 2017). Reactive Attachment Disorder. Retrieved from http://traumadissociation.com/rad on June 25, 2017.

Table 4.4 Blank Session Note

CONFIDENTIAL

Session Note	
Name:	Date:
Start Time: End Time:	Diagnosis:
Service Type (CPT code if billing insurance)	
Average Heart Rate on EMWAVE (and observations)	
Therapeutic Goals:	
Check in with client (degree to which learning in session is transferring to other areas of life)	
Intervention/s used:	
Client's response to intervention/s:	
Future Plan:	

The following scale is scored by the clinician, and is representative of the client's regulation during the session (first order outcome).

0	1	2	3	4
No self-regulation; client gave up/refused to continue or was unable to change state	Client able to self-regulate with considerable intervention from therapist (e.g., co-regulation or giving step by step instructions)	Client able to self-regulate with some prompting from therapist (modeling, recalling techniques learned for breathing, muscle relaxation, mindfulness, etc.)	Client able to self-regulate with minimal prompting from therapist (e.g., asking child to recall what worked for them the last time x happened)	Client able to self-regulate with no prompting from therapist

Copyright © Laura McFarland

_____

Therapist Signature/Credentials

5 Working with Relational Trauma

Limbic Restructuring through Equine-Facilitated Psychotherapy

Philippa Williams

Introduction

The experience of enduring relational trauma such as sexual, physical, and/ or emotional abuse can be terrifying, debilitating, and confusing to the person who struggles to survive. Survival in abusive environments leads to maladaptive understanding of what primary care givers or close others should be and maladaptive acceptance of their traumatic behavior. Responses to threatening events are reappraised as being normal and OK. For example, "My partner shows me she loves me by shutting me in a cupboard in the dark when I talk too much," or "My grandpa says I'm special and he loves me the most, and that's why we have sex." As a result, neural pathways change to accommodate their learned response to an unsafe environment.

To survive in abusive environments, individuals figuratively turn off the alarm system in the brain that is sending signals to the nervous system to fight, flight, or freeze. This method of disengagement is known as dissociation, which allows the individual to detach from experiencing both the immediate physical environment and internal emotional experiences. Unfortunately, dissociation can result in individuals putting themselves in further risky situations. In addition, the sympathetic nervous system can be on a constant hypo-arousal state of fight or flight. The connection between body and mind becomes extinct, and coping strategies to not feel are adopted. Furthermore, a loss of sense of self is experienced. Commonly, trauma survivors seek relief from their turbulent environment and feelings through self-harm, anorexia, binge eating, isolation, anger, drug, or alcohol use, or addiction to gaming or TV.

Talking Cognitive Therapy vs. Equine Facilitated Psychotherapy

Talking cognitive therapies are commonly used to address trauma in individuals seeking help from mainstream government services. In the UK, the National Institute for Clinical Excellence (NICE) (2005) recommends cognitive behavioral therapy as the intervention of choice for post-traumatic stress disorder (PTSD). However, from the perspective of an experienced equine-facilitated psychotherapist (EFP) and researcher of body–mind processes of trauma, there are some challenges to the recommended cognitive therapies for trauma survivors.

Cognitive models of PTSD, such as Ehlers and Clarke's approach (2000), focus solely on the cognitive functions of memory and attention bias, and are based on the premise that intrusive memories and deficits of attention bias are maintaining factors of the presenting trauma symptoms. Yet, van der Kolk's (1998, 2003) neuropsychological and biological research contradicts the cognitive therapy theories by focusing on the multifaceted dimensions of trauma. Van Der Kolk (2017) proposes that Broca's area of the brain that controls language can shut down in trauma survivors who are experiencing dissociation as a result of PTSD. Given that Broca's area is involved with verbal working memory (van der Kolk, 1998), and since the premise of cognitive therapy is to work on traumatic memories (Would et al., 2017), van der Kolk's research suggests that to solely rely on cognitive therapy is illogical. Furthermore, cognitive therapy focuses on a top-down brain methodology to treat attention biases and traumatic memory, rather than a bottom-up methodology that is needed for trauma survivors (Woud et al., 2017).

Culbertson (1995) advocates that many trauma survivors have fallen victim to external events within their environment, which have been out of their control. Therefore, placing the responsibility and emphasis on the individual's cognitive processes as the reason for maintaining their trauma symptoms minimizes the impact of their environment and the multiple bodily processes adjoining the experience of self (Orlans & Levy, 2014). As mentioned above, trauma survivors commonly lose their sense of self during and after the process of relational trauma, so the notion of solely relying on cognitive processes to aid healing from trauma seems paradoxical. Chahal (2013) also points out that survivors of relational trauma have already been subjected to blame, shame, and the misbelief that the trauma was their fault. That considered, it could be argued that the cognitive top-down therapies are in danger of re-traumatizing the abuse survivor by solely using a cognitive model with minimal emphasis on environment, bodily processes, and bottom-up methodology (Gómez et al., 2016).

The LEAP Model

Leading Equine Assisted Practitioners (LEAP) (2014) work with individuals in a person-centred, pluralistic way. This entails drawing on a number of evidence-based interventions, and applying them to the LEAP model, while keeping an overall body mind approach. Working in this way allows for multifaceted processes that affect an individual who has survived relational trauma, without losing out on the individual's subjective experience. The LEAP model was designed primarily with a focus on working with trauma and moves away from the traditional room-based talking therapy. Within room-based therapy, a top-down, cognitive process relies on being able to verbalize and access parts of the brain that may have shut down during the trauma, and are now either inaccessible, or too painful to articulate. The LEAP model therefore takes into consideration the need to offer therapy in a non-verbal way. It draws on practices such as body-based awareness and emotional regulation, and encourages the process of reconnecting body and mind. Facilitators are trained to execute specific exercises of working with horses so clients can respond to new situations with a non-traumatic response, thus encouraging new limbic pathways to be formed. The bottom-up approach also encourages clients to engage with unconscious neurobiological memories that are stored in the body (van der Kolk, 2017) making equine therapy a powerful tool for intervention.

Why Horses?

Horses are social mammals that live in groups and small communities similar to humans. They communicate in a non-verbal way that is controlled by the limbic region of the brain. McCraty & Zayas (2014) suggest that all mammals, not least of all humans, are able to communicate in this non-verbal way due to the electromagnetic signals that are given out via the heart. Neuroscientific research has confirmed that people have neural networks (brains) not only in their heads, but in their guts, too (Cooper, 2000). When people talk about a "gut feeling," they are suggesting that they can feel and communicate through energy fields. The main neurophysiological difference between humans and horses is the proportionate size of the head, heart and gut brains. The human head brain is extremely large in comparison to the horse, and consequently humans spend a lot more time being cognitive and thinking than horses. Humans have also evolved to use language, which complicates and sometimes overpowers their ability to use their gut brain and limbic system. This results in humans spending a lot of time in their heads, and commonly leads to mental disorders such as anxiety and depression amongst others. In other words, humans have a tendency to overuse cognitions, and lose touch with gut feelings, which maintains dissociation.

Benefits of Equine-Facilitated Psychotherapy

Horses sense the intention of predators, such as mountain lions or wolves, to determine whether predators are simply resting nearby or about to strike. Horses will then either stay relaxed to continue grazing, or be triggered into fight or flight, allowing the herd to flee if they are in danger before the predator is even in sight. For trauma survivors, these sensing mechanisms that allow for rest get switched off so they can survive and endure constant threats of actual danger within their environment.

The notion of sensing danger is frequently demonstrated during an EFP session. Upon entering a paddock of horses, the client often has a high arousal level. This is particularly common in those who have experienced trauma, as

Promotes – communication, empathy, disclosure, problem solving, assertiveness, concentration and focus, co-operation, boundaries and awareness of personal space etc.

Emotionally congruent animals – Respond to what is happening in the moment and mirror what human body language is telling them.

Emotionally intelligent animals – very sensitive, sociable, powerful but gentle.

Prey animals – therefore very aware of behaviour of human (as a predator).

Provides – safe, non-sexual, non-violent, healthy, physical contact, coupled with an 'in-body' experience (less cognition)

Range of applications – children, adults, different client groups, individuals, families, team building.

Figure 5.1 Reasons Equines Are Helpful in Healing Trauma
Equine Enlightenment 2016 ©

commonly they are permanently in a state of hypo-arousal (e.g., Szalavitz & Perry, 2010). It can be immediately recognized that horses sense clients' hyper-arousal, which is then reflected by movement within the herd. Once the client's arousal level lowers, through tools facilitated by the EFP practitioner, the horses become still, and begin to accurately mirror and reflect the true feelings of the client, without masking them. This dynamic makes horses exceptionally honest teachers for clients who are not aware of what they are radiating, and possibly being incongruent. This process is largely important for clients who may have become dissociative, incongruent, and non-verbal. Through EFP, clients can learn to use the whole of their body when communicating, thus getting in touch with their true feelings and promoting an embodied experience of healing (Solomon & Heide, 2005).

Furthermore, clients do not have to enter into a verbal dialogue with the therapist, which may in some cases re-traumatize them (Evans & Gray, 2011). This non-verbal processing provides credence to van der Kolk's (2003) hypothesis that action is more important than verbalization, and is crucial for healing to take place. EFP therefore teaches clients to use their bodies as a sensing tool, and develops the use of mindfulness. Clients become grounded (moving from their heads into their bodies), less stressed and anxious (Morrison, 2007), and have a better understanding of how they relate to others, and why others relate to them the way they do. In turn this improves both intrapersonal and interpersonal relationships at home, school/work and with close others, thereby promoting a healthy sense of self (Kruger & Serpell, 2006).

Limbic Restructuring

Both humans and horses have a well-developed limbic system. The limbic system is responsible for emotion and its regulation (Fulton, 1953), and incudes the formation of new memories to past experiences. Limbic neural pathways develop early, before the capacity for verbal and logical reasoning takes place, thus forming the foundation for attachment and belonging throughout life (Szalavitz & Perry, 2010). Trauma, family dysfunction, and violence can set the limbic brain and autonomic nervous system on a permanent state of fight or flight mode (an automatic reaction to danger), leaving an imprint on the mind–body system with a constant hyper or hypo state of arousal (Szalavitz & Perry, 2010). This inhibits healthy development and formation of the reasoning part of the brain (the cortex), and is particularly impacted by interpersonal violence/trauma, when humans who should be providing safety are the abusers (Lewis et al., 2000).

Lewis et al. (2000) propose that in order to move a person from trauma to healing requires the neural pathways to be restructured. The only way for this to happen is for the individual to experience new responses and activities, which soothe or regulate the limbic region of the brain. This neurological "re-wiring" will occur when the following three stages are met.

1. Limbic resonance: shared empathy in which two mammals attune to each other's inner states.
2. Limbic regulation: two mammals reading each other's emotional cues, adjusting to each other and physiologically soothing or regulating the other.
3. Limbic revision: the adaptation to a healthier template for future relationships.

Diagram of the Limbic System within the Human Brain

Neural restructuring via Lewis et al.'s (2000) three stages is achieved through the powerful and effective therapeutic intervention of EFP, as an alternative to

The Limbic System

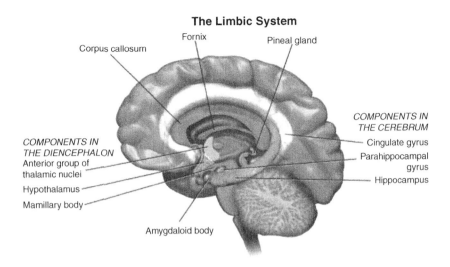

Figure 5.2 Diagram of the Limbic System within the Human Brain
(Blausen.com staff (2014). "Medical gallery of Blausen Medical 2014". *WikiJournal of Medicine*1 (2): 10. doi:10.15347/wjm/2014.010. ISSN 2002 4436.)

talking therapy. With the assistance of exercises facilitated by a qualified mental health professional, specifically an EFP practitioner, horses can facilitate the three stages in the following way:

1. Horses are naturally non-verbal and have a heart that is ten times the size of a human's heart. Simply being amongst a herd of horses naturally creates limbic resonance by becoming part of the magnetic energy fields, and leads to resonating with and tuning into the horses (McCraty & Zayas, 2014).
2. Human arousal levels are required to become regulated in order to become accepted by and to engage with any horse(s). Therefore, the individual begins to learn healthy adjustment and control of his/her limbic regulation (Panksepp, 2011).
3. Limbic revision is achieved through specific exercises or tasks assigned to the client by the therapist, which necessitates the individual to regulate themselves and respond to cues from the horse with a new emotion. This allows for restructuring of neural pathways that move away from the initial traumatic response. Since horses are socially supportive and able to give love and unconditional acceptance, humans experience a template for future relationships (Trotter et al., 2008).

Exercises that Encourage Limbic Restructuring

These limbic restructuring exercises from the LEAP model are shared with permission by the directors Mike Delaney and Ella Jones with further information available at www.leapequine.com. It is important to stress that these exercises could be dangerous if carried out by a practitioner who has not had mental health or equine training specific to working with trauma survivors.

Body Awareness Scan LEAP©

At the beginning of every session, grounding exercises are used to ensure it is safe for the client to be amongst the herd. It also encourages reconnection to the body. This includes a guided body awareness scan at the check in stage. It encourages the client to get in touch with how they are feeling in their body— something that can be quite alien to some clients. It is also an active exercise that the client can engage in without having to become verbal. It is important to note that some clients will not be able to tolerate entering into their bodies for long periods of time, as it may trigger the alarm system in their brain that was originally set off from trauma. This is something the practitioner will need to monitor carefully, and it is mandatory that the practitioner carrying out the exercise has had full training to use this technique with this specific population group. The body awareness scan exercise prepares the client for communication with and being amongst the herd for the next exercise that is performed each session.

Meet the Herd LEAP©

This non-verbal exercise attempts to move the client from a place of cognition (where clients will spend too much time thinking) into their bodies. Weekly practice of this exercise allows dissociation to dissolve over time. It is carried out without touch at this stage, for a number of reasons, not least of all because physical touch can be a trigger for some trauma survivors and could disinhibit their process early on. This point in the session allows the practitioner to assess and formulate what is going on for the client, without having to enter into an intense verbal conversation. The herd members are able to accurately reflect what is going on for the client through mirror neurons in the brain being activated and arousal levels being shared. As shown in Figure 5.3, the client's body is initially tense, causing the horse to be distant. As shown in Figure 5.4, as the client's body relaxes, through limbic resonance, the horse senses enough safety to approach the client. During or after this exercise, if the client chooses, they can also engage in conversation, write, or draw about their feelings in relation to each horse. It is important that throughout this exercise the practitioner holds and maintains a safe, silent space within the herd, taking into consideration, and monitoring any safe guarding issues. The practitioner aims to keep a reasonable distance between self and the client, ensuring they are in view at all

Figure 5.3 Tense Client with Horse

times. How close the practitioner stands to the client is dependent on how safe the client feels. Clients new to EFP sometimes request for the practitioner to be quite close at the beginning of the exercise.

Reflective Grooming LEAP©

The Reflective Grooming LEAP© exercise teaches the client to self-soothe non-verbally, while creating an opportunity for new limbic pathways to be structured, and thus encouraging healing. Over time, this will reflect a calmer sympathetic nervous system, and assist the client in moving out of being in a constant hypo-arousal state. Reflective grooming is about the client intentionally setting out to relax the horse, either by using their hand through

Figure 5.4 Relaxed Client with Horse

touch, directly or just above the skin, or by using a brush of their choice. Sometimes horses surrounding the horse being groomed begin to lie down, one by one, which eventually leads the horse being groomed to join them. This phenomenon is a result of limbic resonance, in which the herd members and client all share the same calm energy. It is a powerful experience for the trauma survivor, and solidifies the healing that can be taken and practiced in everyday life.

Active Round Pen LEAP©

The final exercise offered as an intervention for working with clients is the Active Round Pen LEAP©. It begins with the client choosing a horse they would like to work with, and of course the horse's willingness to agree to participate. Once a partnership is established, the client and horse enter the round pen, with the practitioner on the outside, by the gate. Prior to this the practitioner will have demonstrated the exercise, and debriefed the client on the safety aspects. The idea of this exercise is for clients to raise their arousal levels sufficiently to influence the horse into moving, and then to be able to lower their arousal levels to influence the horse into slowing down or stopping. This exercise is incredibly powerful for clients who struggle to regulate their emotions, or who experience severe levels of anxiety or depression. Through the action of being task orientated, the client engages with the cortex (rational part of the brain) as well as the limbic system, which begins to create new neural pathways and targets neurobiological memories held in the body.

This exercise illustrates how the multidimensional process of EFP can be a powerful alternative to cognitive talking therapy. The exercise solidifies a new response that will enable clients to picture, practice, and integrate the experience they have had in the round pen into everyday life. For example, if clients feel overwhelmed, triggered, and unable to get out of bed, they can work with the new body memory and neural pathway that was created in the round pen, through visualization, to re-experience control of their arousal levels through raising them, regaining function, and getting out of bed. In summary, this exercise creates limbic revision by allowing clients to respond to external triggers in a different way, thus creating new neural pathways.

It is unlikely that all the exercises mentioned here would be used in a single session. They are each powerful in their own right, and can set off neurobiological processes in the client's body that may not be physically seen or felt immediately. Therefore, less is more so as not to overwhelm the client and to ensure proper exploration. EFP is high-impact, slow-release work. The processing can continue for hours, days, and weeks after a session. It is therefore ethically crucial for practitioners to ensure they have debriefed their clients about this, and ensured the clients have safety structures such as dialectical behavioral therapy (DBT) techniques (Linehan, 2014) in place outside of the sessions to manage whatever comes up for them.

Case Example: Description of Client

Louise (pseudonym), age 23, has a mother who has been emotionally and physically abusive throughout her life, an absent father, and is a survivor of childhood sexual abuse. She has continued a pattern of seeking out abusive romantic partners, and has also experienced being raped in her adult years. She presents with high levels of anxiety, has regular panic attacks, self-harms in order not to engage with her emotions, and restricts her food intake, saying she struggles to want to eat because of how anxious she feels. This may also be an attempt to regain a level of control in her life, as the abusive events have felt regularly out of her control, and she now experiences this with her arousal levels too. She carries a lot of shame due to her abuser's behavior, and internalizes this as being her own. Along with feeling anxious, she also struggles with debilitating episodes of low mood, and finds it difficult to regulate her emotions.

Transcript Analysis of Case Example

The following transcript analysis is about a pseudonym client:

Table 5.1 Active Round Pen LEAP© Dialogue

Transcript	Analysis
Counselor: OK, now I have demonstrated how the exercise works, would you like to have a go?	Introduction to the exercise with counselor demonstrating how to raise energy levels and then lower them, and how these affect the horse.
Client: OK, I'll give it a go, but you made it look so easy, I don't know if I'll be able to do it.	The client is experiencing uncertainty about whether she has the ability to raise and lower her arousal levels.
Counselor: Are you worried about a particular aspect of this exercise?	The counselor explores whether there is a specific element to this exercise that the client is worried about, in order to support and guide her. It may also help the client
	to reflect and become aware of what she perceives her difficulty is. This may be a core element that forms part of her existence in her internal everyday world.
Client: I don't think I have the energy to get the horse to move.	The client is sensing that she will find it hard to raise her arousal levels enough to impact the horse moving forwards.
Counselor: Is struggling to raise your energy levels something you struggle with on an everyday basis?	Exploring and encouraging the client to reflect on how she feels in her body outside of the session.
Client: Yea, I think so. Sometimes I find it hard to even get out of bed … although … at other times I can feel so anxious I don't know how to calm myself down. It just feels … so … out of control.	The client is describing periods of low mood and anxiety, and that, at times it feels like she loses control over her embodied, lived experience.

(continued)

Table 5.1 Active Round Pen LEAP© Dialogue (Cont.)

Transcript	Analysis
Counselor: OK, that sounds overwhelming. Would it be helpful to you for us to try the exercise together to begin with until you get the hang of it?	Offering the client the opportunity to take part in the exercise, attempting to provide a containing, supportive space for the client to continue to explore how she experiences her arousal levels, at her own pace.
Client: Yes please. So, will you come in the pen with me?	The client seems to feel assured and more confident to attempt the exercise for the first time, and because the counselor has not pressured her, the therapeutic alliance did not shut down.
Counselor: Yes, are you ready? Let's enter the pen together.	The counselor leads the way to begin the exercise, and client follows.
Counselor: In a moment I am going to raise my arousal levels and see if I can get the horse to move. I'd like for you to join me in this- are you ready to give it a go?! Sometimes I find it useful to think of myself growing inside like a great big lion roaring.	The counselor describes how to begin, and invites the client to join in. The client manages to mirror the counselor and to her surprise raises her arousal levels to successfully move the horse.
Client: I did it! I did it! For the first time, I felt like I had control of my energy!	The client seems elated that she has discovered she has the internal resources to be able to raise her arousal levels, having previously felt powerless over them.
Counselor: Fantastic! Keep going, I'm going to take a step out of the pen. In a moment, I will ask you to lower your energy and think of making yourself small and timid. You may even like to physically shrink yourself lower to the ground.	The counselor affirms the client and encourages her to continue the exercise whilst she steps back. It is important that the client experiences this exercise without the help of the counselor, as there's a risk of disempowerment occurring, and the client regressing back to a position of feeling like she does not have the internal resources to change how she feels.
Client: OK … like this? … Oh, yea, he's slowing down … this is amazing.	The client has engaged in the exercise and managed to both raise and lower her arousal levels sufficiently to evoke movement and stillness in the horse. She has learnt that although she has previously felt powerless over her embodied experience; she does in fact have the ability to affect how she feels.

Table 5.1 Active Round Pen LEAP© Dialogue (Cont.)

Transcript	Analysis
Counselor: Well done! You managed to both raise your arousal levels, and lower them to the point of affecting the horse's energy! What a fantastic achievement. What are your reflections from this exercise?	The counselor is reflecting back the client's achievement and success of engaging in this exercise. The validation and affirmative stance the counselor takes is a powerful tool to encourage the client to begin to recognize herself, how well she is doing, and begin to
	validate her own experience. It also forms part of the secure base the counselor is attempting to provide the client, in order to safely and confidently explore vulnerable parts of herself.
Client: I can't remember the last time I felt so much energy. Although it was hard work, I feel as though I've reminded myself that I can change how I feel. I'm also going to hold onto this experience and think of Rob [horse] next time I can't get out of bed … and maybe pretend I'm a lion [laughs].	The client is validating her own experience and acknowledging for herself, the re-discovery that she has the ability to change how she feels. By visualizing Rob, she is creating a tool for her everyday experiences outside of the session, which will encourage her to repeat her experience of active round pen. This is an important progression, and illustrates how the client is moving into a position of feeling confident in her internal construct of self.

Conclusion

Relational trauma can cause individuals to cope through hypo-arousal and dis-sociation between the body and mind. Cognitive talk therapies that use a top-down brain approach fall short in the multidimensional impact of relational trauma. The LEAP model provides a person-centred, bottom-up approach of working with horses and trauma survivors. It increases body-based awareness and emotion regulation, and encourages the process of reconnecting body and mind. Horses aid in the process because they are sensitive to physiological arousal, and are safe and social animals. EFP practitioners offer a platform in which individuals can learn to use their bodies as a sensing tool, like the horses do, and to better understand how they relate to others. LEAP exercises implemented by trained practitioners facilitate neurological rewiring via limbic resonance, regulation, and revision so that those who have experienced trauma can learn to engage safely and comfortably with other people as they have done with the horses.

References

Blaussen Medical (2014). Scientific and medical animations. Retrieved from http://blausen.com/home.

Chahal, P. K. (2013). A trainee counseling psychologist's considerations in CBT informed practice with adult survivors of childhood sexual abuse. Counseling Psychology Review, 28(3), 30–42.

Cooper, R. K. (2000). A new neuroscience of leadership: Bringing out more of the best in people. *Strategy & Leadership*, 28(6), 11–15.

Culbertson, R. (1995). Embodied memory, transcendence, and telling: Recounting trauma, re-establishing the self. *New Literary History*, 26(1), 169–195.

Ehlers, A. & Clark, D. M. (2000). A cognitive model of posttraumatic stress disorder. *Behaviour research and therapy*, 38(4), 319–345.

Evans, N. & Gray, C. (2011). The practice and ethics of animal-assisted therapy with children and young people: Is it enough that we don't eat our co-workers? *British Journal of Social Work*, bcr091.

Fulton, J. F. (1953). The limbic system. *The Yale Journal of Biology and Medicine*, 26(2), 107.

Gómez, J. M., Lewis, J. K., Noll, L. K., Smidt, A. M., & Birrell, P. J. (2016). Shifting the focus: Nonpathologizing approaches to healing from betrayal trauma through an emphasis on relational care. *Journal of Trauma & Dissociation*, 17(2), 165–185.

Kruger, K. A. & Serpell, J. A. (2006). Animal-assisted interventions in mental health: Definitions and theoretical foundations. *Handbook on animal-assisted therapy: Theoretical foundations and guidelines for practice*, 2, 21–38.

Leading Equine Assisted Practitioners (2014). Retrieved from www.leapequine.com.

Lewis, T., Amini, F., & Lannon, R. (2000). A general theory of love (12–15). New York: Random House.

Linehan, M. (2014). *DBT skills training manual*. New York: Guilford Publications.

McCraty, R., & Zayas, M. A. (2014). Cardiac coherence, self-regulation, autonomic stability, and psychosocial well-being. *Frontiers in Psychology*, 5, 1090.

Morrison, M. L. (2007). Health benefits of animal-assisted interventions. *Complementary Health Practice Review*, 12(1), 51–62.

National Institute for Health Care Excellence (NICE) (March, 2005). Post-Traumatic Stress Disorder: Management. *Clinical Guidance* (1.9). Retrieved from: www.nice.org.uk/guidance/cg26/chapter/1-guidance.

Orlans, M. & Levy, T. M. (2014). *Attachment, trauma, and healing: Understanding and treating attachment disorder in children, families and adults*. London: Jessica Kingsley Publishers.

Panksepp, J. (2011). Cross-species affective neuroscience decoding of the primal affective experiences of humans and related animals. *PloS one*, 6(9), e21236.

Solomon, E. P. & Heide, K. M. (2005). The biology of trauma: Implications for treatment. *Journal of Interpersonal Violence*, 20(1), 51–60.

Szalavitz, M. & Perry, B. D. (2010). *Born for love: Why empathy is essential – and endangered*. New York: William Morrow.

Trotter, K. S., Chandler, C. K., Goodwin-Bond, D., & Casey, J. (2008). A comparative study of the efficacy of group equine assisted counseling with at-risk children and adolescents. *Journal of Creativity in Mental Health*, 3(3), 254–284.

van der Kolk, B. A (2017, March 9). How trauma lodges in the body. On Being. Retrieved from: https://onbeing.org/programs/bessel-van-der-kolk-how-trauma-lodges-in-the-body/.

van der Kolk, B. A. (1998). Trauma and memory. *Psychiatry and Clinical Neurosciences*, 52(S1).

van der Kolk, B. A. (2003). *Psychological trauma*. Washington, DC: American Psychiatric Publishing.

Woud, M. L., Verwoerd, J., & Krans, J. (2017). Review: Modification of cognitive biases related to posttraumatic stress: A systematic review and research agenda. *Clinical Psychology Review*, 54, 81–95.

6   Equine-Assisted Group Therapy for Adolescent Sexual Trauma Survivors

Development, Implementation, and Outcomes

Kirby Wycoff and Virginia Murphy

Introduction

Childhood trauma, abuse, and adversity represent a significant public health crisis in our country. In the United States, child sexual abuse alone impacts as many as one in three girls and one in seven boys (Briere & Elliot, 2003). The Crimes Against Children Research Center at the University of New Hampshire indicated that, based on self-reports, 20% of adult females and between 5 and 10% of adult males have a recollection of childhood sexual abuse encounter (Finkelhor, 2008). In the United States, over the course of one year 16% of all youth between the ages of 14 and 17 had reported a sexual abuse incident and 28% of youth between the ages of 14 and 17 in the United States had been sexually victimized over the course of their lifetime (Finkelhor, 2008). The United States Department of Health and Human Services reported on *Child Maltreatment* that "9.2% of victimized children had been sexually assaulted" (US Department of Health, 2011, p. 24). The 2003 National Institute of Justice report indicated "three out of four adolescents who had been sexually assaulted, were victimized by someone they knew well" (Kilpatrick et al., 2003, p. 5). The report further indicated that victims of sexual assault were three to five times more likely than non-victims to have negative outcomes as a result of their trauma. Perhaps even more concerning and alarming is that most sexual assaults (86%) had not been reported to authorities (Kilpatrick et al., 2003). Adverse childhood experiences and childhood sexual trauma is a serious public health issue in our country.

Adverse Childhood Experiences Study and Sexual Trauma

The Adverse Childhood Experiences (ACE) Study is one of the most robust, longitudinal studies of its kind to document the deleterious impact of early adversity and trauma on later physical and mental health in adults. Adverse childhood experiences refer to myriad negative incidents, including child sexual abuse, child physical abuse, neglect, parental substance abuse, and a number of other traumatic stressors that occur to an individual under the age of 18. Felitti and Anda conducted a study of individuals who were exposed to chronic, toxic stress, and adversity in childhood. These individuals had poorer health outcomes in adulthood compared with those who did not experience multiple adversities in childhood (Anda et al., 2006; Felitti & Anda, 2010; Felitti et al., 1998). With a sample size of more than 25,000 individuals, the team generated an adversity screening tool that assessed the number of categories of exposures an individual had to different adversities, prior to age 18 (Anda et. al., 2006; Felitti & Anda, 2010; Felitti et al., 1998). It is important to note that this inventory did not calculate the total number of exposures, just categories of exposure. For example, contact sexual abuse, even if it happened three different times, was calculated as one category. The outcomes indicated that a scant one-third of the sample population had an ACE score of 0. That is, the other two-thirds of the sample had at least one adversity exposure in childhood (Anda et al., 2006; Felitti & Anda, 2010; Felitti et al., 1998). If someone had an ACE score of 1, there was an 87% likelihood that there was (at a minimum) one other ACE category present. One out of every six people in the study reported an ACE score of four or more while one out of nine had an ACE score of five or more. Women were 50% more likely than men to have been exposed to five or more categories of childhood adversity (Anda et al., 2006; Felitti & Anda, 2010; Felitti et al., 1998). According to Felitti and Anda (2010), the categories on the ACE inventory, including prevalence rates, are noted below:

Abuse (Felitti et. al., 1998)

1. Emotional—recurrent threats, humiliation (11%)
2. Physical—beating, not spanking (28%)
3. Contact sexual abuse (28% women, 16% men, 22% overall)

Household Dysfunction (Felitti et al., 1998)

1. Mother treated violently (13%)
2. Household member alcoholic or drug user (27%)
3. Household member imprisoned (6%)
4. Household member chronically depressed, suicidal, mentally ill, or in psychiatric hospital (17%)
5. Not raised by both biological parents (23%)

Neglect (Felitti et al., 1998)

1. Physical (10%)
2. Emotional (15%)

Essentially, a graded risk model was built. The more exposure you had to adversity under the age of 18, the higher risk you are at for a whole series of other problems later in life. "There is a long-lasting, strongly proportionate, and often profound relationship between adverse childhood experiences and important categories of emotional state, health risks, disease burden, sexual behavior, disability and healthcare costs" (Felitti & Anda, 2010, p. 4). Childhood exposure of any kind has a negative impact on neuro-regulatory systems that mediate physical illness as well as behavior and mental health (Anda & Felitti, 2006). The risk of emotional health challenges, somatic complaints, substance abuse, and other factors all increased as the ACE scores went up (Anda & Felitti, 2006).

Further, "high perceived stress, difficulty controlling anger, and the risk of perpetrating intimate partner violence (IPV) were increased 2.2-, 4.0-, and 5.5-fold, respectively, for persons with ≥ 4 ACEs" (Anda & Felitti, 2006, p. 7).

Particularly relevant to this chapter is that individuals with an ACE score of 4 or more are six times more likely to have had sex before the age of 15, potentially placing these individuals at an even higher rate of re-victimization. Targeted interventions that address both the posttraumatic symptoms of childhood sexual abuse as well as work to protect re-victimization are of value to clinicians and researchers alike.

Pregnancy Risk (Hillis et al., 2004)

- 0 ACES = 16% risk of becoming pregnant as a teenager
- 1 ACE = 21% increased risk of becoming pregnant as a teenager
- 2 ACES = 26% increased risk of becoming pregnant as a teenager
- 3 ACES = 29% increased risk of becoming pregnant as a teenager
- 4 ACES = 32% increased risk of becoming pregnant as a teenager
- 5 ACES = 40% increased risk of becoming pregnant as a teenager
- 6 ACES = 43% increased risk of becoming pregnant as a teenager
- 7–8 ACES = 53% increased risk of becoming pregnant as a teenager

Over the past two decades, the Felitti and Anda team (with data now replicated by countless other researchers) have demonstrated that exposure to adversity in childhood can contribute to a number of significant negative health outcomes in later life. Adverse childhood experiences are likely one of the United States' most significant public health threats and the treatment that is documented in this chapter is one possible intervention that may address this threat.

Trauma-Focused Cognitive Behavioral Therapy (CBT)

Childhood sexual trauma casts a high burden on survivors, families, and the community at large, and there is vested interest in interventions that can assist in treating this population. While some child survivors of sexual abuse meet criteria for posttraumatic stress disorder (PTSD) as articulated in the *Diagnostic and Statistical Manual of Mental Disorders* (2013), many others suffer from debilitating symptoms related to their sexual abuse, without meeting full criteria for the disorder. This challenge can largely be attributed to the fact that children's symptoms often present differently when compared with older adolescents and adults (van der Kolk, 2014). Broadly speaking, both children and adults have symptoms that include physiological changes (such as a state of hyperarousal), intrusive thoughts or memories of the abuse, re-experiencing of the traumatic events (either through flashbacks, nightmares, or fragments of flashbacks), and a desire to avoid trauma triggers. How these broad symptoms manifest themselves, however, can be vastly different from person to person, and among children versus adults (Substance Abuse and Mental Health Services Administration [SAMHSA] (2014).

The treatment of child sexual abuse can, and has, taken many forms and approaches, and the type of treatment chosen is often dictated by the treatment provider's training and theoretical orientation. However, the treatment approach with the most extensively researched, evidence-based body of literature is cognitive behavioral therapy (CBT). Broadly, CBT approaches clients' problems from the perspective that how people (both children and adults) view their problems directly influence how they react emotionally to their problems, which in turn affects how they react behaviorally to those problems or situations (Beck, 1979). CBT is a goal-oriented and problem-focused approach, designed to help people identify and alter maladaptive, unhelpful, or false beliefs they may carry about themselves, the world, or their future. Since its inception, CBT has a strong literature base demonstrating its efficacy in treating a wide range of problems and diagnoses in both adults and children, including depressive disorders, anxiety disorders, behavioral disorders, substance abuse disorders, and personality disorders.

As national and international attention has turned to trauma responses in both children and adolescents, several cognitive behavioral treatment approaches have been developed to address PTSD symptoms in children and adolescents. Among those available, the authors relied on tenets from trauma-focused CBT (TF-CBT), developed by Cohen et al. (2012). This approach, specifically developed for use with traumatized children, incorporates exposure therapy and habituation, key elements to any cognitive approach to anxiety reduction.

TF-CBT includes the following components in treatment:

- Psychoeducation with the child/adolescent and caregiver regarding the nature of PTSD, and a clear rationale for treatment
- Exposure to trauma cues under safe conditions (including the tenets of habituation and counter-conditioning)
- Revision of trauma-related schema (beliefs that are unhelpful or untrue, related to sexual trauma)
- Coping skills training (affect regulation, relaxation training, cognitive coping skills)
- A focus on decreasing avoidant coping strategies and increasing cognitive coping strategies (seeking help, confronting symptoms, and learning to "talk back" to unhelpful thoughts)
- The development of a trauma narrative, the story of the sexual abuse, including thoughts and feelings that are presenting as obstacles to recovery

Since TF-CBT has a strong base of efficacy in clinical trials as well as clinicians' offices, it seemed important to infuse TF-CBT into our equine-assisted therapy group. Specifically, the components of addressing and reframing unhelpful beliefs about trauma, the trauma narrative (exposure work), boundary-setting, and cognitive coping were integrated as experiential activities with the horses.

Equine-Assisted Therapy and Trauma

The clinical team integrated a trauma-focused cognitive behavioral therapy approach with equine-assisted therapy to address the posttraumatic stress symptoms of a group of adolescent female students in a residential school setting who had been experienced sexual trauma. The rationale for the development of this program was built on the strong literature base for both TF-CBT and equine-assisted modalities in working with similar populations.

Bachi et al. (2012) noted that equine-facilitated psychotherapy (EFP) is one modality that can be useful in treating high-risk adolescents who live in residential settings. They noted, over the course of weekly sessions throughout a seven-month period, 14 teens in a residential treatment facility (compared with 15 students in a control group who received no intervention) demonstrated positive changes in self-image, self-control, trust, and overall life satisfaction (Bachi et al., 2012). These authors defined EFP as a form of animal-assisted intervention that occurs in the natural surroundings of a stable and integrates the use of horses. Bachi et al. (2012) noted that the intervention focused on self-image, self-control, and trust as they are often particularly problematic for the at-risk adolescent population (Bachi et al., 2011; Cawley et al., 1994; Emory, 1992; MacDonald & Cappo, 2003). The therapeutic alliance in any modality is important, and in the EFP, the relationship and alliance include the horse. Drawing on references to Bowen (1978) structural family therapy model, Bachi et al. (2011) noted that the inclusion of the horse can be compared to Bowen's therapeutic triangle and can be useful in enhancing the traditional therapeutic alliance between client and provider (Bachi et al., 2011). This therapeutic relationship offered an opportunity to the client to engage in a healthy attachment experience. Drawing on Bowlby's work (1973) Bachi et al. (2011) stated, "Creating a therapeutic alliance that will support, contain and offer a potential healing experience for negative early life experiences of the client is critical for building trust with the 'other' and establishing interpersonal adaptation skills" (p. 3). Wycoff and Murphy used the grounded theoretical model offered by Bachi as a foundation for the trauma-focused equine-assisted intervention used in their work.

Group work for sexually traumatized youth has been well established in the literature (Lowenstein & Freeman, 2012), and cognitive therapy groups, in particular, are efficacious in working with sexually abused children (Cohen et al., 2004; Deblinger et al., 2001). Reichert (1994) noted Yalom's work in reporting a number of therapeutic benefits that occur when working with sexually abused children in group therapy. Reichert (1994) noted: "Therapeutic elements include: The child's discovery that she is not alone in her victimization; the acquisition of a cohesiveness is often absent from the lives of these children; and the opportunity for catharsis about the victimization experience" (p. 55).

In individual counseling, animals have been found to be useful in working with sexually traumatized children. Reichert (1998) notes that in working with animals, children can project their feelings about themselves onto the animals. Animals, in the context of a safe, supportive, and healthy relationship, can engage with humans in nonjudgmental ways. Further, understanding and observing how the individual relates to the animals provides an understanding of how the individual might relate to others in his or her world and provides the clinician with insight into the client's experience outside of the therapy setting. Early research (Peacock, 1984) indicated that animal-assisted therapy may help clients engage in more self-disclosure in the therapeutic process. For the group discussed in this chapter, the adolescent females that were chosen for the group had demonstrated some treatment resistance before this group. They were considered high utilizers of services and still experiencing symptoms of their trauma, and had not fully benefitted from traditional therapies in the past.

The research and clinical interest in animal-assisted work with traumatized youth continues to grow and gain national attention. In a recent publication of case studies, Naste et al. (2017) examined the efficacy of equine-facilitated therapy for complex trauma (EFT-CT) with three children exposed to multiple traumas. It is important to note that the intervention model outlined in this work is for individual (not group) intervention, and involved therapeutic riding (rather than more novel interactions with the horses). Their findings, while pre-liminary, support the use of equine-assisted trauma work with children suffering from complex trauma, and further advance our collective understanding of equine-assisted trauma interventions.

In examining the specific outcomes of working with sexual assault survivors who have a PTSD diagnosis, the use of animals in the therapeutic setting can be an asset. The presence of animals lowers physiological arousal, improves the therapeutic alliance, and decreases anxiety, particularly during the pro-cessing of traumatic memories (Lefkowitz et al., 2005). Lefkowitz et al. noted that most treatments addressing trauma include exposure to feared memories or reprocessing of those traumatic memories. Additionally, many therapeutic approaches to trauma work include a high attrition rate (Hembree et al., 2003). Clients, at times, find the treatment itself somewhat distressing and may ter-minate therapy prematurely or disengage in the therapeutic process. As noted in Lefkowitz et al. (2005), Altschuler's (1999) approach called for a model of animal-assisted prolonged exposure (AAPE) that integrated animals with trauma work. Integrating animals into existing treatment models for PTSD could potentially "encourage hesitant survivors to participate in, and complete, the treatment by making more tolerable demands and could positively alter survivors' perceptions of themselves and the world" (Lefkowitz et al., 2005, p. 276).

Altschuler's model (1999) suggested the use of animal-assisted interventions in working with PTSD largely due to anecdotal feedback from his clients.

Observing that some PTSD clients were resistant to treatment, he noted that they appeared less anxious when around animals. Re-experiencing the traumatic event can be quite distressing to many trauma survivors, and most therapeutic approaches involve the survivor re-experiencing the trauma in the therapy room (Hensley, 2002; Weinstein & Rosen, 1988). This in and of itself can create a barrier for trauma patients seeking treatment. Lefkowitz et al. (2005) noted that the therapist's ability to connect with the sexually abused survivor quickly and build trust will likely affect the client's willingness and ability to continue in treatment. It is with this in mind that clinicians Wycoff and Murphy developed a trauma-focused equine-assisted therapy group for adolescent females who had experienced sexual trauma.

Program Context: Trauma-Focused Equine-Assisted Therapy

In order to provide soundly developed programming to a specific target population, it is critical that the program developer understand the context in which the program is embedded (Maher, 1981; Maher, 2012; Maher & Bennett, 1984; Wycoff, 2011). This clarity is critical, both to the consultation and to the organization's ability to provide valuable programming. "Lack of clarity about a presenting situation—particularly about a target population, its needs, and relevant context within which those needs are embedded—fosters limited perspectives on how to add value in a programmatic way" (Maher, 2012, p. 7). Lack of clarity undermines a program and prevents relevant stakeholders from having a true understanding of what their program is, who it serves, and what its potential is for sustainability (Maher, 2012). In contrast, having clarity about a program allows relevant stakeholders to make well-informed decisions regarding the program (Maher, 1981; Maher, 2012; Maher & Bennett, 1984; Wycoff, 2011).

This clinician (Wycoff) led the organization in a multi-year consultation process to integrate animal-assisted interventions into the organization's therapeutic approach. The team needed to have a complete understanding (based on reliable and valid data) of who the target population was, what their needs were, how an animal-assisted therapy program could meet those needs, and the relevant context within which the needs were embedded. Using Maher's (2012) approach to program planning and evaluation (PP&E), a number of activities were used to develop and implement programming that actually targeted a need in the population, evaluated efficacy of the intervention, and could be sustainable over time. The following description outlines the phases of the PP&E processed and how it was used to provide equine-assisted therapy services for sexually traumatized adolescent females.

The identity of the residential school in which this programming was developed has been altered to protect the confidentiality of the clients within the organization. Consent and assent was received from both the minor clients and their guardians to collect data on the program and use that data for program development and educational programming purposes. The target population was a group of students at a residential school in the Midwestern portion of the United States. Based on a permanent product review of admissions data and the eligibility requirements of the school itself, the followwming characteristics defined the target population: At the time of the programming, there were 1,798 students enrolled at the school. All student families met a minimum income level that was below the poverty line. At the time that the programming was developed, a family of four could generate no more than $21,000 annually to be considered for enrollment. Students' intellectual profile were generally within the average range (standard scores on IQ screener, no lower than 80). Finally, approximately 70–80% of students had a significant trauma history and had experienced many of the stressors that are associated with intergenerational poverty and adverse childhood experiences.

The phase that is documented in this chapter was the final (of three) phases of program implementation and roll-out. The first phase (developed and implemented over the course of one year) included an animal-assisted therapy (AAT) group in the elementary school, the second phase (also one year long in development and implementation) included an AAT group in the high school, and the third phase (also one year long in development and implementation, presented here) included an AAT group in the middle school. A slow, methodical roll-out system was specifically built to allow time for thoughtful and informed program development, implementation, and evaluation. At each phase of roll-out the previous year's group continued to be offered. At the conclusion of the three-year roll-out, there was an AAT therapy group being offered at the elementary, middle and high school levels.

The broad target population (1,798 students enrolled at the residential school in the Midwest) was further segmented to focus the scope of the programming. This third segmentation included "All students in middle school." Once the parameters of the target population were identified, a needs assessment was conducted. In partnership with relevant stakeholders including the head psychologist (Murphy) and other clinicians, a group of students were identified that might benefit from this programming. This initially included "Any female sexual abuse survivor, with a PTSD diagnosis in the seventh and eighth grades." This was further segmented to include eight specific female sexual abuse survivors who had been in treatment in the past and were additionally identified as "treatment resistant." Treatment resistance was operationalized to include a student who had been in individual services to treat her PTSD symptoms but did not have a significant reduction in symptoms at the conclusion of the intervention.

In many psychological service settings, group modalities are an effective way of managing increasing caseloads, while also providing valuable services to clients. As it relates this program development, this was part of the rationale for developing the intervention. In guiding the needs assessment, the team considered: What *need* does the target population have and what *service* does our program offer to help meet that need. Specific clarity on the needs of the target population allowed these two clinicians, Wycoff and Murphy, to develop group programming that was specific, measurable, attainable, relevant, and timely. Once the target population was further specified (through the referral process), the specific needs of those students were to be assessed. The entire program was built around the needs of the clients. A *need* is defined as *a discrepancy between a current state of affairs having to do with the psychological or educational functioning of the target population and a desired state of affairs* (Wycoff, 2011). More specifically, a human service need can be said to exist when these two conditions are present:

1. A *current state of affairs* represents a psychological or educational state of the target population, which has been identified and judged by the client, other stakeholders, or by the consultant, as being amenable to change or that is not satisfactory in some way (Maher, 2012; Wycoff, 2011).
2. A *desired state of affairs* represents a psychological or educational state of the target population, which has been identified and judged by the client, other stakeholders, or by the consultant, as being a desired outcome of a goal attainment of a specific parameter (Maher, 2012; Wycoff, 2011).

A need is not a solution (i.e., the need for a particular program). Rather, a human service need has to do with the psychological or educational state of the target population. As such, the need has to do with a human performance domain (i.e., skill level, cognitive ability, social skills, communication skills, physical skill development, etc.) (Wycoff, 2011).

Relative to the students functioning, the current state of affairs (CSA) and desired state of affairs (DSA) were determined. The discrepancy between those two reflects the actual need of the student. The need can be thought of regarding the knowledge, skills, abilities (KSA) that we want the target population to gain from participation in the program. The KSA will be the "value added" for program participants (Maher, 2012; Wycoff, 2011). Again, the need is not the program itself as a solution, but the need is the discrepancy between where students are at and where we want them to be (on some educational or psychological domain). The program is then designed to meet those specific needs (needs first, then program). This does not occur in reverse order, which is, unfortunately, often the case in human services programs, where an "off the shelf" program or curriculum is chosen, and it is assumed to meet some unarticulated need (Maher, 2012; Wycoff, 2011). This equine-assisted therapy group for adolescent females was developed with this heuristic guiding the process.

Based on the needs of the target population, the identified group of clients (which had already been screened for suitability using inclusion and exclusion criteria) completed pre-intervention measures which included the Behavioral and Emotional Rating Scale, 2nd Edition (BERS-2; Epstein, 2004) and the Multidimensional Anxiety Scale for Children, 2nd Edition (MASC-2; March, 2013). This group met once weekly for eight weeks between May and June. It is important to note that the organization already had a therapeutic riding program in place and the director of the program was equine-assisted growth and learning association (EAGALA) trained. That program director was an invaluable partner in the development and delivery of this group. There was a barn facility that included multiple indoor stalls, large turnout areas, and a riding ring. The barn (an old bank barn) also had a sizable hay loft which served as the primary meeting space for this group. The two clinicians leading the group were a licensed psychologist with expertise in TF-CBT and a postdoctoral resident with expertise in AAT and equine-assisted therapy (EAT). Each group session followed a predictable pattern including starting together as a group in the hay loft to discuss highs and lows (Wycoff & Teske, 2012), provide psycho-education (on pre-selected themes), and set up the experiential horse activity for the second half session. All sessions ended with a debriefing, connecting new learning to previous learning and a ritualized group closing as well as a weekly Critical Incident Questionnaire (Brookfield, 1995) that provided feedback to the clinicians and allowed for adjustments as needed. Additionally, both clinicians completed session notes and Psycho-Social Session Rating Forms (Trotter et al., 2008) for every client after every session. Session outlines included:

Opening Session

- Check-ins
- Review ground rules

Session Goals

- Introduction of weekly theme
- Discussion of goals
- Connect last week's content to this week's content

Session Activities

- Psycho-education (thematically based psycho-education)
- Experiential (experiential therapy encounter with the equine)

Reflection

- Process activity and debrief
- Connect new learning to old learning
- Reflect on goals (group and individual)

The group also started with an individualized goal sheet for each participant to articulate their own goals for the group experience, an example of which can be found below.

Individualized Goal Sheet for Trauma-Focused Equine-Assisted Therapy Group

Name:_____

You have been selected for this group because you have experienced some very difficult things, often called *traumatic experiences*—these can be abuse, neglect, or tough family circumstances. This group is designed to work with horses to help you overcome some of the effects those traumatic experiences may have had on you.

We would like each student to develop an individual goal or goals for the group. To help you develop this, please think about and answer the following questions:

1. Do your past experiences get in your way now? If so, how? Some examples of how our past gets in our way include: anger problems, communication problems, trust difficulties, boundaries issues, among many others.
2. At the end of our group experience what would you like to be doing, thinking, or feeling differently? Another way to think about this question is: How would you like yourself or your life to be different, by the end of this group?

These clinicians used the work of van Fleet (2010) (problem-resolution, self-regulation, attachment/relationship, empathy) Knapp's Horse Sense Skills Cards (2011) (self-respect, boundaries, assertiveness, learning zones, anger, knowing my body), and others to guide the development of a thematic approach to each of the eight weeks, with a particular focus on addressing areas of need that were specific to traumatized individuals. The knowledge, training, and experience of the EAGALA-certified equine specialist as well as these two authors, in combination with the Horse Sense Skills Cards, were used in selecting specific activities for clients to engage in with the horses. The final eight weekly themes were offered sequentially to build safety and trust over time and were manualized for use within the organization. Using the manualized approach developed by these authors, the program continues to remain in existence and now has multiple years of implementation data to support its efficacy from a case study perspective. The tenets of TF-CBT (including connections of thoughts, feelings, behaviors, and psycho-education on the impact of trauma) were woven throughout the entire eight-week group to specifically address processing of the traumatic event and re-victimization prevention. The eight weekly themes included:

1. Safety
2. Trust
3. Respect
4. Communication

5. Empathy
6. Boundaries
7. Relationships
8. Closing

Each of these themes were broken down into a weekly session, and before every session both clinicians and the EAGALA-certified equine specialist reviewed the session plan. In addition to the resources noted above, *Teaching Empathy: Animal Assisted Therapy Programs for Children and Families Exposed to Violence* (Loar & Colman, 2004) was an excellent resource that was used in to develop this group programming. It is important to note that the experiential activities with the horses were based on multiple sources of information and a wide knowledge base and adapted to meet the needs of these specific clients. These activities in and of themselves are not particularly unique or innovative, but they were specifically modified to meet the needs of this target population. An example of two different session outlines and plans can, be found below.

Session Example #1 – *Weekly Theme: Communication*

Session Goal

Teach and experience the concept of communication; how we express feelings, needs, and wants and recognize these in others, as well as how we communicate respect and how communication keeps can keep us safe.

Session Activities

- Students had a snack while reviewing individual highs and lows
- Briefly, review the previous topic of respect and build upon that in session.
- Set the stage by sharing with students the general plan for the session.

Note: REVIEW—themes of SAFETY and RESPECT from last week. Debrief last week's activity, including discussing the experiential activity. Lessons learned? How did this activity connect to RESPECT and SAFETY? How do those things show up in our life? How do our themes from the first two weeks, connect with our theme for this week, COMMUNICATION.

Psychoeducation

Discuss the topic of communication in general terms. Facilitate discussion on the following:

- What are the things that we communicate with others?
- What are the ways that we communicate?
- How do we communicate respect for ourselves and others?
- How do we communicate when we are feeling safe or unsafe?
- How do we communicate with ourselves?

Listening as communication:

- We communicate a lot through how we listen
- What are some of the ways we communicate that we are a good listener?
- How do we adapt our communication style based on someone else's listening?

Discuss topic of communication in the context of trauma:

- Communicating with yourself includes recognizing and identifying feelings, physical sensations, needs, and wants
- When we communicate these things, it is easier for other people to help us and give us what we need
- The way that we communicate with others can tell a lot about how vulnerable we may be

Often times, abuse can include limitations on communication:

- We may be asked to keep secrets
- We may not feel safe communicating how we are feeling or what we need to others
- We may communicate in very subtle ways

Abuse can also lead to shutting down communication with ourselves or communicating negative messages to ourselves. Communication with ourselves and others about our feelings, needs, and wants can help us identify dangerous situations and get help:

- How do we recognize danger and communicate it to ourselves? To others?
- How can we communicate that we need help or support?

Experiential Learning Opportunity (with Animals)

Animals communicate a lot of information nonverbally. What are we saying about ourselves nonverbally? What are the animals around us communicating? How do we know what they might feel a need or want? How do we communicate respect for them?

You will work in pairs with one other group member. The horses will be at liberty (no tack or equipment can be used) in their two different paddocks. This week we will meet our horses and learn more about them. We will focus on our ability to observe what the horses are telling us about themselves and their relationships with one another. Consider that before we can ever ask our horse partners to do something for us or with us, we need to get to know them. Consider how you feel if someone asks you to do something without getting to know you first.

Work with your human partner to get to know one specific horse in the paddock. Notice what the chosen horses are doing or not doing. Notice where he/she chooses to stand or move. Do they like being with other horses or by themselves? All of this should be done at a distance, before ever approaching the horse. Consider how you can respect your horse's boundaries around space (personal bubble). Is it bigger or smaller than yours or other horses? How did you balance your desire or fear to be close to the horse (want to pet him, touch him) or your fear (don't want to get too close) with what your horse was telling you? Focus on your horse's body language, facial expressions, posture, use of ears, feel, tail, eyes, and how your horse moves in space. Did your horse feel safe with you around, did you feel safe with your horses around?

Reflection

Questions/prompts for consideration (*In small groups and then in larger group*)

- What did you learn today?
- Tell us about your horse?
- How does what you learned from your horse today related to your own trauma?
- How are your thoughts, feelings, and behaviors connected?
- How are safety, respect, and communication related?
- How do we connect what we learned in previous weeks with new learning?

Closing Ritual

Students engage in a team song that they created in the first week of group and encourage each other to have a good week.

Session Example #12—*Weekly Theme: Trust*

Session Goal

Teach and experience the concept of trust and its role in relationships. This includes trusting oneself (inner voice) as well as trusting others. We will also weave this into the preceding concepts (safety, respect, communication). Write previous sessions themes on poster paper, so we are all on the same page with regards to topics we have discussed, etc.

Session Activities

- Students had a snack while reviewing individual highs and lows
- Review group rules, facility information.
- Set the stage by sharing with students general plan for the session.

Psychoeducation

Start with a general discussion of trust. When we say, "I trust you," what do we mean? Who are we referring to? Do we trust them with our lives? Our deepest secrets? To complete a task for us? There are levels of trust, and they correspond to the evolution of relationships. Do you have one person with whom you enjoy a very high level of trust? Person or animal (or one of each)? What makes him/her trustworthy? (Use flip chart to draw trust circles.) Who is at the center of the circles? (Explore self-trust—trusting one's inner voice.) *(Note: movement across circles, horses, and us starting relationships together, and reflect on last time with the horses, how we were just entering into relationship and thus on the outer circles.)*

Sometimes, after abuse or neglect, we are not good at trusting ourselves. We may have been told, "You were dreaming, that didn't really happen"; "I wasn't drunk"; "I just pushed you—I didn't hit you"; "I love you—I would never hurt you." Allow group remembers to share experiences. Explore: HOW DOES TRUST RELATE TO MIXED MESSAGES (incongruent messages)?

When we are told something that is different from our experience and reality, we begin to doubt our ability—we do not trust ourselves. Learning to trust ourselves and each other takes time and patience. It doesn't happen overnight and requires us to take small steps in our relationships. It also requires us to "check in" with others about what we experience—to test that we are judging reality correctly. Over time, we learn to trust our inner voice again, and we no longer need to "check in" with others—we just know.

Experiential Learning Opportunity (with Animals)

Each student will pair with another group member and a horse. The activity involves taking small steps to build a relationship with the horse you are working with. Your goal is to earn the trust of the horse, using the communication skills that we reviewed in the previous session.

Students should "check in" with their human partner—i.e., what do you think the horse is feeling now? What did behavior X mean? This will give you the opportunity to practice "small steps" in building relationships. In the end, the group will process what it meant to test reality with their partner. Was it helpful—were they always in agreement? Were they able to pay close attention to the trust level in the relationship with the horse? Did the exercise increase their trust between each other (the humans)? Where would you put this horse and/or human partner in your trust circle? Why or why not?

Reflection

Questions/prompts for consideration *(In small groups and then in larger group)*

- What did you learn today?
- Tell us about your horse?
- Tell us about your human partner?
- How does what you learned today to connect to my traumatic experience?
- How are my thoughts, feelings, and behaviors connected?
- What new learning did you have today?
- How do we connect what we learned in an earlier session with new learning?

Closing Ritual

Students engage in a team song that they created in the first week of group and encourage each other to have a good week. Both of these group sessions reflect different ways of integrating thematic concepts into the work of trauma-focused equine-assisted interventions. These can be adapted to a wide range of settings and therapeutic goals.

Case Example

With the consent of the participants and their guardians, all therapy sessions were videotaped for later analysis. This case example is derived from that video analysis. During one of the weekly groups, one particular student was attempting to enter the gate to the paddock. Upon hearing the student at the gate, a black gelding named Midnight trotted to the gate. The gate was not open, and the horse stopped at the gate. When the student attempted to open the gate, the horse crowded her space and was not respectful of her entering the paddock. He did not back up when he felt the pressure of the gate on his chest. The student quickly closed the gate and stepped backward. The transcript of the interaction between the client and clinician (Wycoff) is reported below.

Transcript Analysis of Case Example

The following transcript analysis is about a pseudonym client:

Table 6.1 Case Example Transcript

Transcript	Analysis
Clinician: I noticed Midnight trotted right to the gate when you walked up to open it.	Observation and tracking comments by the clinician on what is noticed brings information into the client's awareness.
Client: Yeah, he rushed right up and crowded my space.	The client is noticing and experiencing that her space was invaded by the horse rushing the gate.
Clinician: How did that make you feel when he rushed right up and crowded your space?	The clinician reflects the client's experience back to the client and gives the client space to explore feelings related to this.
Client: It was kind of pushy. Like he was rude. It felt like he might run me over	The client expresses feelings related to personal space being compromised.

(continued)

Table 6.1 Case Example Transcript (Cont.)

Transcript	Analysis
Clinician: I hear you saying that it felt like Midnight was being pushy and might even run you over.	The clinician reflects the client's experience back to the client and give the client space to explore feelings related to this.
Client: Yea, like he was just push me out of the way or bump into me.	The client expands on feelings related to personal space being compromised and expresses that her body might be compromised as well.
Clinician: How did that make you feel?	The clinician reflects the client's experience back to the client and give the client space to explore feelings related to this.
Client: Like that wasn't a good spot to stand. I should have moved, and I shouldn't have been there in the first place. Like it wasn't safe there, maybe? And like it was my fault, I shouldn't have been standing there. Like, duh, don't stand there.	The client expresses anxiety around not feeling safe and second guessing her choice about where to stand. The client is also reflecting some possible themes of guilt and shame around "it" being her fault.
Clinician: So, you felt unsafe when Midnight trotted up to the gate where you were standing? And perhaps like it was your fault that you were there in the first place?	The clinician reflects the client's experience back to the client and give the client space to explore feelings related to this.
Client: Yea. Because I didn't know how to tell him to stop, or to not run be over, or just, like, respect my boundaries.	The client further expresses anxiety regarding the situation and how to keep herself safe and how to put clear boundaries into place.
Clinician: Hmm, I think I am hearing that you felt unsure about how to protect your space and you felt like he didn't respect your boundaries. Am I getting that right? I am wondering if there is anywhere else your life where you have felt similar feelings or had similar thoughts?	The clinician reflects the client's experience back to the client and gives the client space to explore feelings related to this. The clinician also attempts to draw similarities to this current experience with Midnight and any other places this client has felt this way in the past.
Clients: I don't know [pause]. Kind of like the stuff happened last year, maybe. I'm not sure.	The client offers (after some hesitation) that she may have felt this way before. The client goes on to expand on sexual abuse experience from a year before.

The experience with the horse named Midnight allows this particular client to access and share information from a traumatic experience that she had not been able to talk about previously. After some processing, this is expanded into problem-solving around ways that she could increase her feelings of safety around Midnight and set up clear and fair boundaries. Discussion ensued around the fact that you can have a healthy relationship with an individual (horses and humans) that have clear boundaries and are safe. This also leads to significant clinical growth around the issues of guilt and shame as this client had a number of core beliefs that the sexual assault was her fault. This was a pivotal growth point for the client in this case.

Program Outcomes

Every single client in the therapeutic group endorsed some degree of positive goal attainment on their goal sheets that were developed at the outset of the group. Using Trotter and Chandler's Psycho-Social Session Ratings Forms (with permission) as well as the BERS-2, MASC-2 and Clinical Interviews, clients were assessed pre- and post-intervention as well as on a weekly basis. These measures allowed clinicians the opportunity to begin to assess goal attainment and symptom reduction throughout the group. All sessions were videotaped in their entirety and were used to evaluate individual student growth and program effectiveness. All student participants had a significant reduction in self-reported trauma related symptoms as indicated in post-intervention data collection and exit interviews. On the Psycho-Social Session Rating, negative symptoms decreased, and positive symptoms increased throughout the course of the group. Negative symptoms include things like students presenting as guarded, passive, withdrawn, and physically or verbally aggressive. Positive symptoms included things like expresses feelings, expresses thoughts, expresses a need, was assertive, cooperative, and was engaged (Trotter et al., 2008). This tool was used with the authors' permission and converted into an electronic algorithm that computed all scores across time. Scores from this qualitative, clinician-scored measure are summarized below. It is important to note that while this tool has a great deal of clinical utility, future research could include ratings by an independent researcher/clinician who was not directly involved in the therapeutic process to reduce rater bias. In general, students who were reportedly treatment resistant and had difficulty engaging with clinicians in the past appeared better able to participate in the group work with the horses present. Of course, it is important to note that this is one single-case study design, so outcomes cannot be generalized across other settings or populations. Given the setting of this pilot study, wait-list control groups were not ethically or clinically feasible as students in distress needed timely interventions. As such, there was no control group and the sample size was small. The primary mode for evaluating effectiveness was driven by the client's clinical presentation before, during and after the group intervention. Given that this was a purely clinical setting, the rigor of research was compromised in favor of clinical need. Despite

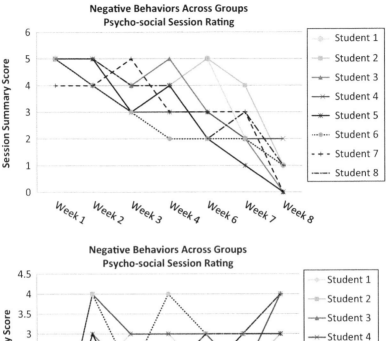

Figure 6.1 Program Outcome Year 1

this, the data that was collected provided strong qualitative feedback to these clinicians and administrators and provided a necessary rationale for continuing with the equine-assisted therapy offerings within the organization.

Beyond Year One

The animal-assisted trauma group was replicated in subsequent years, with minor alterations. The group continued to serve previously treatment-resistant adolescent female sexual abuse survivors, who were screened for suitability for this type of group therapy. We decided to replace the MASC-2

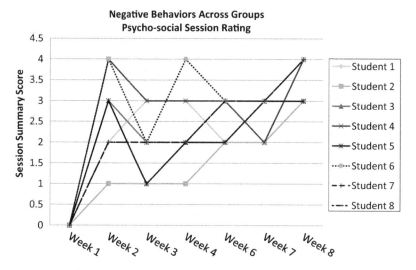

Figure 6.2 Program Outcome Year 2

as a pre-/post-measure with the UCLA PTSD Reaction Index (Pynoos et al., 2014), in order to more specifically examine the extent to which this intervention impacted trauma symptoms. We retained the use of the BERS-2 and the Psychosocial Summaries, as well as clinical interviews pre- and post-group. Not surprisingly, clients served in this group consistently showed robust improvement, as measured by the pre-/post-measures and clinical interviews, in terms of their ability to understand and articulate their trauma experiences, regulate their own emotions, and respond adaptively to intrusive trauma memories.

Summary

With the ever-growing number of children and teenagers who have been exposed to violence, adversity, trauma, and abuse, equine-assisted therapies may offer one treatment modality to address these deleterious symptoms. Child abuse and childhood exposure to adversity are one of the primary causes that lead to adult health risk behaviors, physical disease, and premature death (Felitti et al., 1998). Providing psychoeducation and experiential therapeutic interventions to these individuals may alter the pathway to later adoption of risk behaviors and increase the likelihood that these individuals can experience productive, healthy, and safe lives. Qualitative indicators appear to support the use of this modality, but further research will be needed to assess the efficacy of integrating trauma-focused and cognitive behavioral interventions with equine-assisted interventions to treat childhood sexual trauma.

References

Altschuler, E. L. (1999). Pet-facilitated therapy for posttraumatic stress disorder. *Annals of Clinical Psychiatry*, 11 (1), 29–30.

Anda, R. F., Felitti, V. J., Bremner, J. D., Walker, J. D., Whitfield, C. H., Perry, B. D., Dube, S. R., & Giles, W. H. (2006). The enduring effects of abuse and related adverse experiences in childhood. *European Archives of Psychiatry and Clinical Neuroscience*, 256(3), 174–186.

Bachi, K., Terkel, J., & Teichman, M. (2012). Equine-facilitated psychotherapy for at-risk adolescents: The influence on self-image, self-control and trust. *Clinical Child Psychology and Psychiatry*, 17(2), 298–312.

Beck, A. (1979). *Cognitive therapy for depression*. New York: Guilford Press.

Briere, J., & Elliott, D. M. (2003). Prevalence and psychological sequelae of self-reported childhood physical and sexual abuse in a general population sample of men and women. *Child Abuse and Neglect*, 27, 1205–1222. doi:10.1016/j.chiabu.2003.09.008.

Bowen, M. (1978). *Family Therapy in Clinical Practice*. New York: Jason & Aronson.

Bowlby, J. (1973). *Attachment and Loss*. London: Hogarth Press.

Brookfield, S. D. (1995). *Becoming a Critically Reflective Teacher*. San Francisco: Jossey Bass.

Cawley, R., Cawley, D., & Retter, K. (1994). Therapeutic horseback riding and self-concept in adolescents with special educational needs. *Anthrozoos*, 7(2), 129–134.

Cohen, J. A., Mannarino, A. P., & Deblinger, E. (2012). *Trauma-Focused CBT for Children and Adolescents*. New York: Guilford Press.

Cohen, J. A., Deblinger, E., Mannarino, A. P., & Steer, R. A. (2004). A multisite, randomized controlled trial for children with sexual abuse–related PTSD symptoms. *Journal of the American Academy of Child & Adolescent Psychiatry*, 43(4), 393–402.

Deblinger, E., Stauffer, L. B., & Steer, R. A. (2001). Comparative efficacies of supportive and cognitive behavioral group therapies for young children who have been sexually abused and their nonoffending mothers. *Child Maltreatment*, 6(4), 332–343.

Diagnostic and Statistical Manual of Mental Disorders, 5th Edition (2013). Washington, DC: American Psychiatric Association.

Emory, D. K. (1992). Effects of therapeutic horsemanship on the self-concept and behavior of asocial adolescents. Unpublished doctoral dissertation, University of Maine, Orono.

Epstein, M. H. (2004). Behavioral and Emotional Rating Scale – 2nd Edition: A strengths-based approach to assessment. Austin, TX: PRO-ED.

Felitti, V., & Anda, R. (2010). The Relationship of Adverse Childhood Experiences to Adult Health, Well Being, Social Function and Health Care. In *The Hidden Epidemic: The Impact of Early Life Trauma on Health and Disease*. (pp. 77–87) Cambridge: Cambridge University Press.

Felitti, V. J., Anda, R. F., Nordenberg, D., Williamson, D. F., Spitz, A. M., Edwards, V., Koss, M.P., & Marks, J. S. (1998). Relationship of childhood abuse and household dysfunction to many of the leading causes of death in adults: The Adverse Childhood Experiences (ACE) Study. *American Journal of Preventive Medicine*, 14(4), 245–258.

Finkelhor, D. (2008). *Childhood Victimization: Violence, Crime, and Abuse in the Lives of Young People*. Oxford: Oxford University Press.

Hensley, L. G. (2002). Treatment for survivors of rape: Issues and interventions. *Journal of Mental Health Counseling*, 2 (4), 331–348.

Hembree, E. A., Foa, E. B., Dorfan, N. M., Street, G. P., Kowalski, J., & Tu, X. (2003). Do patients drop out prematurely from exposure therapy for PTSD? *Journal of Traumatic Stress*, 16(6), 555–562.

Hillis, S. D., Anda, R. F., Dube, S. R., Felitti, V. J., Marchbanks, P. A., & Marks, J. S. (2004). The association between adverse childhood experiences and adolescent pregnancy, long- term psychosocial consequences, and fetal death. *Pediatrics*, 113(2), 320–327.

Horse Sense of the Carolinas, Inc. (2011). Horse Sense Skills Cards. http://horse sensebusiness.com/skill-cards/.

Kilpatrick, D., Saunders, B., & Smith, D. (2003). Youth Victimization: Prevalence and Implications. Washington, DC: U.S. Department of Justice, National Institute of Justice.

Lefkowitz, C., Prout, M., Bleiberg, J., Paharia, I., & Debiak, D. (2005). Animal-assisted prolonged exposure: A treatment for survivors of sexual assault suffering post-traumatic stress disorder. *Society & Animals*, 13(4), 275–296.

Loar, L., & Colman, L. L. (2004). *Teaching Empathy: Animal-Assisted Therapy Programs for Children and Families Exposed to Violence*. Alameda, CA: Latham Foundation for the Promotion of Humane Education.

Lowenstein, L., & Freeman, R. C. (2012). Group therapy with sexually abused children. In P. Goodyear-Brown (Ed.), *Handbook of Child Sexual Abuse: Identification, Assessment, and Treatment* (pp. 355–375). Hoboken, NJ: John Wiley.

MacDonald, P.M., & Cappo, J. (2003). Equine-facilitated mental health with at risk youth: Does it work? *NARHA Strides*, 9(3), 30–31.

Maher, C. (2012). *Planning and Evaluating Human Services Programs: A Resource Guide for Practitioners*. Bloomington, IN: Authorhouse.

Maher, C. A. (1981). Training of managers in program planning and evaluation: Comparison of two approaches. *Journal of Organizational Behavior Management*, 3(1), 45–56.

Maher, C. A., & Bennett, R. E. (1984). *Planning and Evaluating Special Education Services*. Englewood Cliffs, NJ: Prentice Hall.

Naste, T. M., Price, M., Karol, J., Martin, L., Murphy, K., Miguel, J., & Spinazzola, J. (2017). Equine Facilitated Therapy for Complex Trauma (EFT-CT). *Journal of Child & Adolescent Trauma*, 1–15.

Peacock, C. (1984). The role of the therapist's pet in initial psychotherapy sessions with adolescents: An exploratory study. Dissertation, Boston College, Graduate School of Arts and Sciences.

Reichert, E. (1998). Individual counseling for sexually abused children: A role for animals and storytelling. *Child and Adolescent Social Work Journal*, 15(3), 177–185.

Reichert, E. (1994). Play and animal-assisted therapy: A group-treatment model for sexually abused girls ages 9–13. *Family Therapy*, 21(1), 55–62.

Substance Abuse and Mental Health Services Administration (2014). SAMSHA's Concept of Trauma and Guidance for a Trauma-Informed Approach. Washington, DC: Department of Health and Human Services.

Trotter, K. S., Chandler, C. K., Goodwin-Bond, D., & Casey, J. (2008). A comparative study of the efficacy of group equine-assisted counseling with at-risk children and adolescents. *Journal of Creativity in Mental Health*, 3(3), 254–284.

Thompson, K. L., & Gullone, E. (2008). Prosocial and antisocial behaviors in adolescents: An investigation into associations with attachment and empathy. *Anthrozoos*, 21(2), 123–137.

U.S. Department of Health and Human Services, Administration for Children and Families, Administration on Children, Youth and Families, Children's Bureau. (2011). *Child Maltreatment 2010*. Washington, DC: Author. Available from www.acf. hhs.gov/cb/resource/child-maltreatment-2010-data-tables.

van der Kolk, B. (2014). *The Body Keeps the Score: Brain, Mind, and Body in the Healing of Trauma*. New York: Penguin.

VanFleet, R., & Faa-Thompson, T. (2010). The case for using animal assisted play therapy. *British Journal of Play Therapy*, 6, 4–18.

Weinstein, E., & Rosen, E. (1988). Counseling victims of sexual assault. In E. Weinstein & E. Rosen (Eds.), *Sexuality counseling: Issues and implications* (pp. 201–223). Belmont, CA: Brooks/Cole Publishing.

Wycoff, K. L. (2011). A case study of the process of formulating a strategic plan for a non-profit organization serving student-athletes in urban communities. Rutgers, The State University of New Jersey, Graduate School of Applied and Professional Psychology.

Zilcha-Mano, S., Mikulincer, M., & Shaver, P. R. (2011). Pet in the therapy room: An attachment perspective on animal-assisted therapy. *Attachment & Human Development*, 13(6), 541–561.

7 Experiential Equine-Assisted Focal Psychodynamic Psychotherapy

Addressing Personality and Attachment in Clients with Chronic Childhood Trauma

Géza Kovács

Introduction

Chronic early traumatization (CET) is the harmful psychological, biological, and social consequences resulting from persistent childhood traumatic events such as prolonged abuse (emotional, physical, sexual); prolonged neglect (psychic, pedagogical, physical); witnessing prolonged violence in the family; being in war conditions and/or having to flee; painful medical procedures for a prolonged time; or multiple traumatic loss in the family (Rensen, 2017). CET is a prevalent social problem that occurs across cultures. In the Netherlands, more than 3% of the Dutch population between 0 and 18 years old experience chronic trauma (Alink et al., 2011). In addition, 50–70% of the mental health clients in the Netherlands have a background of childhood trauma (Trimbos, 2007). In the USA, over 45% of the children and adolescents served by the National Traumatic Stress Network (N = 10,991) experienced domestic violence for an average of 4.5 years (Pynoos et al., 2014).

CET may lead to a variety of psychological, physical, and social problems that negatively impact personal life until late adulthood, the immediate environment, and society (Trimbos, 2007; Putnam et al., 2013). Since CET generally occurs within an interpersonal context, it can result in a continuous disruption of the quality of attachment and bonding relationships. Therefore, a strong relationship between CET, continuous disturbance of attachment with a disorganized attachment representation, and psychiatric problems in adulthood are apparent.

Attachment, Psychotherapy, and Neurobiology

More and more evidence is emerging on the integration and mutual underpinning of attachment theories, psychotherapy, and neurobiology (e.g., Siegel 2001, Fuchs; 2004; Perry, 2006; van der Kolk, 2014; Solms, 2015). A general conclusion is that the brain and nerve circuitry are much more plastic, or open to continuing influences from the environment, throughout life than previously supposed. The capacity for attachment classifications to change beyond the early years of life may be related to this ability of the brain (Siegel, 2006). Attachment plays a central role in the emergence of different mental and mood states. These serve as a defense of feelings of fear, give shape to the accessibility of autobiographical memory, the ability to coherent thinking, and the ability to view new experiences and thoughts in a new light, i.e., the ability to metacognition and mentalization (Siegel, 2001; Nicolai, 2016). This means that one should take in consideration when treating adults with CET the duration of traumatization, the amount of early traumatization, in which developmental stage it occurred and the quality of safe interpersonal relations. Psychotherapists can create an intersubjective attachment relationship in psychotherapy, which results in optimal affect regulation in the presence of a reflective another (Wallin, 2007). In this relationship one must find space to tune into the nonverbal expressions of nonverbal experiences of the client (Beebe et al., 2003).

The problem with traditional, exclusively verbal (cognitive) psychotherapy is that the emotional core of the self probably cannot be accessed by linguistics (Siegel, 2001; Wallin, 2007; Schore & Schore, 2008; van der Kolk, 2014). This barrier exists for the following reasons:

1. Attachment models and regulations originate before the acquisition of speech.
2. Threats to the attachment will be dissociated.
3. The brain areas for speech and autobiographical memory start functioning between 18–36 months.
4. Acute and/or relational traumas suppress the activity and development of these neuronal structures.
5. The formation of internal working models reflects implicitly procedural knowing rather than explicit linguistic facts or memories.

Consequently, psychotherapy with CET clients needs to restructure neural networks in the subcortical-limbic system, which is responsible for unconscious emotional motivations and dispositions. "Insight" or "appeal" reach only corticohippocampal structures, which correspond to conscious memory and cognition, but have very limited effects on the motivational system (Fuchs, 2004). Schore and Schore (2008) therefore suggest "a right brain" receptive focus for therapy because it increases "implicit relational knowledge" stored in the nonverbal domain. Psychotherapy with CET clients should be offered in a way that matches the hierarchical (bottom-up) vertical (left–right) brain structure (Perry, 2006). Equine-assisted psychotherapy (EAP) fulfills this suggestion in a number of ways.

First, EAP occurs in nature, which allows for conscious and unconscious stimulation of senses that instigates reintegration and recovery of basic trust (van der Kolk, 2014; Ottosson, 2007). Second, during EAP, observation of horses enhances self-regulation abilities (Adriaens & De Block, 2011). Third, horses might serve as an access point into the client's emotional world, according to Mormann's et al. (2012) neurological study showing that animals have an emotional effect on humans, more than other stimuli. Fourth, horses encourage people to take responsibility and to express affection towards them by means of stroking, petting, and brushing.

Fifth, horses may function as transitional objects and provide the opportunity to experience safe attachment, thanks to their tendency to display unconditional acceptance and opportunity for nurturance (Zilcha-Mano et al., 2012; Fine, 2015). Julius et al. (2013) explain that close human–horse relationships can be conceptualized as attachment or caregiving relationships—allowing switching of roles, from receiving social support from the horse to providing care for the horse. EAP helps provide close bodily interactions with horses that "sculpt" the mentalization process of the mother–child relationship, with awareness of mental distinctions between "subject–object," "self–other," and even "pleasure–pain." (Brown, 2007; Fotopoulou & Tsakiris, 2017). Nonverbal, preverbal layers of development are reached through touch, warmth, closeness, with horses. The affective connection between horse and client creates a projective identification as a body-to-body communication or a somatic countertransference (Wallin, 2007).

Finally, dealing with horses helps the client be in the here-and-now. Seen through the lens of neuroscience, it is necessary to work with the here-and-now because the limbic system needs calm states to foster left–right brain connections. When working with horses and a therapist, the client has the possibility to connect his causal explanations to his emotional and sensory experiences in order to find insight and understanding (Siegel, 2001; Morgan, 2015; Smith et al., 2016).

Experiential/Equine-Assisted Focal Psychodynamic Psychotherapy for CET

Taking the above into consideration, Kovács and Umbgrove (2014) constructed an animal-assisted psychotherapy, experiential/equine-assisted focal psycho-dynamic psychotherapy (EFPP), in which the horse has a special place. EFPP is in line with Bachi's (2013) concepts of attachment-based psychotherapy, including a secure base and haven of safety through the provision of a holding environment, affect mirroring, mentalizing and reflective functioning, and non-verbal communication and body experience.

EFPP offers important attachment-based healing components of rhythmic movement (Trevarthen, 1998); being carried and rocked; touching and being touched; and affect attunement. In horseback riding, it is important for the rider to flow with the movements of the horse in order to find a joint rhythm while being mindful of his/her breathing and balance. When this balance is found, the interaction between human and horse can be experienced as a natural pro-cess. Clients can influence the ongoing attachment process with the horse even after mistakes because the therapist helps them repair the relationship through mentalization and mindfulness.

Horseback riding has positive effects on motor function as well as on para-sympathetic activation, the stress-reducing system (Håkanson, 2008). The autonomic nervous system and affective subcortical centers are not separate from the somatic, musculoskeletal nervous system. The bilateral, rhythmic, patterned movement of the horse's gait provides bottom-up regulation, which is critical for clients who are dysregulated and unable to benefit immediately from primarily cognitive approaches to therapy (McFarland, 2016). Self-regulation skills (mindfulness, breathing exercises, etc.) can be taught to clients with the horse providing both eustress and biofeedback (Merkies et al., 2014), which could combine mechanism for learning and generalizing these skills. At the same time, mounted work (due to the bilateral, rhythmic, patterned repetitive movement) helps clients become passively regulated and organizes the lower regions of the brain. The horse's positive response to the client's successful attempts at self-regulation is rewarding and therefore reinforcing for the client. The more this is practiced, the greater the neural pathways necessary for self-regulation are reinforced (McFarland, 2016).

In EFPP it is the horse, rather than the psychotherapist, that becomes the object of transference, which elicits the resisted fear and represents the social relationships of the client with (significant) others (Kovács & Umbgrove, 2014; McCullough, 1997). The psychotherapist clarifies and positively processes this transference from the client to the horse. The psychotherapist's goal is to reach beneath the defense and fear to the client's hidden feeling, and to relate this feeling existing in the present to its origin in the past, usually in relation to the parents.

EFPP uses horse(s) (and other animals like dogs) and a team of therapists, specifically the psychotherapist and clinical psychologist (both trained by animal-behavioral experts) (Kovács & Umbgrove, 2014). From a neuropsychoanalytic view (Ouss-Ryngaert & Golse, 2010), the role of one clinician is to engage with the client and the role of the other is to hold the technical clinical awareness. As such, one clinician processes the right brain (attuned, empathic, emotional communication) while the other clinician processes the left brain (cognitive). During the intake, it is made clear to clients that the therapist works under the direction of the clinical psychologist and is accountable to and is in frequent contact with him or her. The client engages predominantly with the therapist and animals during EFPP. The clinical psychologist, who positions himself/herself not explicitly visible in the background, determines the focus and selects tailored exercises. It is made clear to the client that when there is confrontation, clarification, empathic validation, or psychoeducation by the therapist, it is guided by the clinical psychologist.

Schematically, the various phases of the therapy with its interpretation are shown below. Due to comorbidity and the transdiagnostic approach in CET (van der Hart et al., 2006), I do not want to argue for a particular protocol regarding a particular DSM-disorder, but I want to emphasize and justify ingredients that are important for this group of clients. It is up to the creativity of the treatment team to work with the client to come to a fertile course of treatment from a trial-and-error principle, similar to daily life. This approach requires a proper safe environment in which ruptures in the therapeutic relationship are quickly repaired. The treatment phases for CET—stabilization and symptom reduction, treatment of traumatic memories, and personality(re)integration (van der Hart et al., 1989)—are often alternated or seamlessly interwoven after an initial period of stabilization, depending on the needs of the client.

Transcript Analysis of Case Example

The following transcript analysis is about a pseudonym client:

Table 7.1 Case Example Transcript

Diagnostic Phase		
Client	**Therapist**	**Clinical psychologist**
Is introduced to and encouraged to use senses, rhythm, balance, being in contact with horse.	Acts as a participating observer and holds a "not-knowing-stance," equivalent. Provides safety and holding. Explains equine needs and tells stories/background of the horses.	
Projections on horse and herd.	In relation to equine activities he focuses on: collaboration, reflective dialogue, repair, coherent narratives, emotional communication (Siegel, 2001).	
Observational tasks on herd; leading horse and riding.	To stress self-direction, clients are approached with four basic questions formulated by Van Os (2014) which are challenged during the activities within the different phases of the treatment: 1. *What happened to you (which circumstances have led to the current situation)?* 2.*What are your resiliencies and vulnerabilities?* 3.*What is your goal?* 4.*What do you need?*	
Core-Conflict or Focal Phase		
Client	**Therapist**	**Clinical Psychologist**
Exercises in round pen, parcourse. Horseback riding. Taking care of the animals and creating a relationship with animal that is characterized by (reciprocal) attunement, trust, respect, and self-control.	Focus is discussed and explained to client. Exercises and tasks with horses, both mounted and ground work are constructed in relation to the focus. Challenging the client's dysfunctional belief system by learning to take appropriate responsibility for their actions, practice self-control, and respect their relationship partner (the horse) as an autonomous being capable of making its own choices. The relationship process	Observations of the therapist coupled with facts on and when the fracture(s)/trauma in development occurred and how (affect) defenses are constructed, s/he sets the focus of the treatment derived from schema focused therapy (Young, 1999).

(continued)

Table 7.1 Case Example Transcript (Cont.)

Diagnostic Phase		
Setting and expanding boundaries in order to find grip on his/her vulnerability and resilience.	supported by the animal and the therapy team therefore creates a shift in the client's relational schema, or what they believe and have come to expect in relationships. Continuously clients are encouraged to find attunement in interaction with the animal. S/he helps the client to foster a sense of competence.	

Consolidation Phase		
Client	**Therapist**	**Clinical Psychologist**
Important experiences contributing to resilience and insights are strengthened with mounted and ground work.		The clinical psychologist explains the origins of the client's dysfunction (disorder) from a psychodynamic and neurobiological view; the client could experience a de-stigmatization ("unblaming") of his/her dysfunction. However, the clinical psychologist is also able to point to the client's responsibility of his/her suffering. The client and clinical psychologist elaborate on positive animal–client–therapist experiences.

Termination Phase		
Client	**Therapist**	**Clinical Psychologist**
Creating transitional object. Creative expression of what one leaves behind and what positive experience is taken with. Interaction with horse who symbolizes the above.		

Case Example

Mary (pseudonym) had a history of severe sexual abuse by multiple people including her father beginning at a very young age. Since her mother knew about this but did nothing to change it, Mary learned to stop asking for help. She stated she survived via dissociation. Because of the abuse, Mary had five pregnancies but all the children died. Somehow Mary managed to be a contributing member of society. Mary worked with several traditional therapists but she stated they did not give her what she needed to trust them enough to start working with them. The first therapist with whom Mary was able to open up to and have enough confidence to start working with was at the Rainbow Ranch (an animal-assisted psychotherapy EFPP facility in the Netherlands). Mary described her experience with EFPP during a presentation at the European Society of Trauma and Dissociation Congress in 2016:

Working with the horses was very special. They are big, bigger than me. At the same time they are flight animals so they will run before they attack. You can stand in front of the horse and take control. You can stand beside them and make yourself equivalent to the horse. You can put yourself between the horse and the environment and feel safe. And of course you can ride the horse which was and is the most special experience. You are literally carried. My whole childhood I was the only one bearing the immense burden of my experiences. It was too heavy but leaving it behind me was impossible. There was no one who wanted to help me carry my burden let alone someone who wanted to take it. And then you ride a horse with your big load and for the first time it was not too much, too difficult, it could be there without having to answer questions or come up with reasons and explanations. That was a whole new experience to me.

Beside the burden of my experience I had a lot of resistance to my body. My body and I were no friends at all because I felt so betrayed by my body. And then you ride a horse and you don't have to do all the physical and emotional work of literally carrying yourself. You are greater than all the people around you. You look down on them and at the same time you know that it's not your height, but borrowed height of the horse. So you can't really look down on anybody. I loved to ride a horse and let the horse carry me and my burden. The horse did not get overwhelmed when I told about what was bothering me, what happened to me, when I told about my deceased children or when I could no longer cope. The horse did not judge, they did not leave me, it was never too much ... I was never too much. That was and is a wonderful experience.

A new experience was also that the horses are always in the present, something I'm not so good at. I discovered during the sessions I was absent much more then I was aware. I knew I was sometimes absent but I thought it was something everyone had and that I just exaggerated. I just had to pay more attention I told myself. I was just too busy with myself.

And when I lost people because of this it was of course my fault. Until I came here and realized that I was suffering from dissociation. I realized that maybe it was not all my fault.

Dissociation was once my salvation, but now it was more and more an obstacle in my life. But how do you control something when you lose touch with yourself? Just paying more attention was not enough. The horses have helped me very well. When I was absent it was often not noticed by my surroundings. I often keep talking, I do what needs to be done and sometimes I'm just absent just like other people sometimes are. I was not aware when I got slowly dissociated, I quietly went further and further away from myself. And when I dissociate because of a trigger I did not know that. Sometimes I knew when I came back I missed something … and sometimes not. It felt really bad when I came back and felt totally disorientated. The trick is to pretend you know what you're doing and what happened and find the appropriate action to get out of the embarrassing situation. Ending in blaming myself for not paying attention again and trying to find a way to prevent this from happening.

With the horses, it became obvious to my therapist when I dissociated. Horses respond in fact very well: a sudden stop during walking and/or they take a different route and aren't corrected. The question of the therapist "what happens now" was a great question. I could return to the present at my own pace. Of course, I generally had no answer to the question, and when I thought I had, it is debatable whether that was indeed the answer. It was a great opportunity to learn more and better when these things happened.

The solution for not dissociating was being more aware of my body, feeling my body, feeling the horse, walking, sitting conscious, feeling my muscles, my breathing and all those annoying physical things that I did not want to feel. It was hard for me but step by step I was able to connect more with my body in a relatively safe way with the horses.

The horses were able to physically come very near in contrast to my therapist who, at one point, I sent 50 meters away in the forest as a safe place to be. I love to touch and be touched but with people I'm often not able to do so. But a horse is safe to touch. Horses have exactly the right size so that you do not have to be very careful. You do not easily hurt them and yet they are warm, round, and subtle. You can follow them in their movements when they walk, you can follow their breathing, you can feel their muscles move and they are completely safe. I could more easily feel my movements, my breathing, and the rest of my body with a horse nearby.

A very nice moment was when I was riding a horse and just with my body had to indicate which direction we were heading. This was the first time in my life I felt that I could determine anything with my body. To me, my body had betrayed me during the abuse and now I was able to let a big horse do what I want him to do with just my body. It was a super experience. And what made it even better was that my therapist was genuinely happy for me. I realized that he really understood what it meant to me. He made me really commit to this therapy no matter how scary it sometimes got. Off course I haven't made it easy for him but he withstood my testing him very well.

At this moment I can say that this whole experience has brought me a lot. I became more aware of my dissociation and I'm more able to deal with it. I recognize it faster and can adjust more quickly.

I am less critical of myself and I am finally accepting that I don't have to solve everything, that some things will remain no matter what. I knew I am as good as anyone else but now these words are not just words anymore, it has become a feeling inside.

It has given me enough confidence in myself that once again I tried to get pregnant. After my pregnancies during the abuse and death of my babies it was my biggest wish to be able to have a child and being able to care and provide for him. I had made earlier attempts but was unfortunately unsuccessful. Together with my therapist I dared to take on the challenge again.

I became pregnant and have been able to fully experience my pregnancy because I dared to feel my changing body. I had enough self-confidence to take on the challenge of the obstacles in the hospital. Things like accepting help and care from doctors and nurses and meanwhile setting my boundaries when they wanted to define things for me I didn't want or need. I was able to properly communicate my wishes and needs, I was able to hear their needs without losing myself and crossing my boundaries. Not everything went as I wished it would but in the end I always got the feeling that they heard and respected me. It was a very stressful time but I look back with satisfaction. I've always seen my pregnancy and childbirth as the ultimate test that you can overcome anything and you can always make dreams come true. I feel I passed this test with flying colors.

Therapeutic Analysis of Case Example

Initially, the client's life-story left doubt with the therapist whether the story could be believed, while the client had a strong desire for being heard. Repetition of old relationships, as often seen in a psychotherapeutic relationship, was obvious from the beginning. Immediately the therapist was tested: *"Does the therapist believe my story or not?"* However, it was not important that her story about her traumatization was "true"; instead her thoughts and how she felt about it now was important. The joint interaction with the horse(s) brought both therapist and client in the here-and-now which, as it turned out was very important, failing sensationalism or denial about her story.

The quickly gained trust by this client was striking, which may be caused by the different treatment setting than usual: *"The horse did not judge, they did not leave me, it was never too much, I was never too much."* In addition, it was helpful that the primary focus was on a joint equestrian activity, so that attention could be paid to feelings and what they meant to the client in small steps. In contrast, disregarding clients' pace and going too fast with this group of clients is disruptive and activates survival strategies. Yet, in EFPP, attention can be maintained at a bodily level, naturally, instead of a cognitive level.

For clients who have disorganized attachment and are hypervigilant, it is necessary to encourage thinking-about/mentalization instead of encouraging emotional outpourings. This is illustrated when the client described her traditional therapy as *"guiding me in a direction I did not want to go."* In contrast, EFPP provides space for self-direction so an autonomous animal mentalization could be promoted. A sense of self-direction was also physically manifested by the task of directing the horse with her body. Self-direction was encouraged by asking the client what she needs. It was also helpful to frame the feeling *"I felt that I could determine anything with my body"* and what it meant for the client, which was a sense of agency and competence.

Connection and separation can be considered as key targets from a psychoanalytic perspective (Nicolai, 2016). Clients have a physical feeling of what is theirs and what is the horse's. It is helpful to ask the client to lead the horse and pay attention to the physicality of the horse and herself, the rhythm of the steps, breathing, heart rate, and other sensory sensations. Subsequently, emotional meanings could be explored and the marked mirroring (Fonagy, 2001) by the horse could be put into words with the help of the therapist. For the client described above, this process helped her feel safe and more comfortable with her body.

A strong internalized shame and anger, common in clients with disorganized attachment and sexual abuse, was masked when the client made jokes, resulting in disruption in the therapaeutic collaboration between the client and the horse. In the context of transference and countertransference between client and therapist, this kind of joking could elicit the idea that things are going well and that her suffering is less severe. Yet, the horse is not sensitive to jokes (or other verbalizations or silence) but to the intentions on the affective level. Paying attention to the horse's response helped the therapist focus on the underlying intent of the client's jokes, which functioned as a survival mechanism.

The client had a tendency to apologize during the various activities—*"I'm always awkward, I always forget everything, It's just my luck, etc."*—as if she was just a bothering person. In psychological terms, she expressed an internalized offender, that she is someone who actually had to adapt constantly, never meeting the requirements, resulting in passing her limits, and causing an inner rage, which in turn she had to dissociate. Again, by constantly questioning the actual activity about what happens and what the horse needs and she needs, she could start to mentalize on her actions, feelings, and thoughts. In the above case, the client describes how the horse suddenly stopped horseback riding. Through a not-knowing curious stance of the therapist, the client was aware that the horse stopped and that she could be aware of the action of stopping in an earlier stage. It helped her to identify if the motivation of this action was hers or that of the horse. She was prompted to tune into the horse and herself so that they could correct the relationship and proceed their route. Her intentions became clear again for the horse, visible in the working relationship between them.

Maintaining the relation with the therapist was harder for her: *"The horses were able to physically come very near in contrast to my therapist who at one point I had to send 50 meters away in the forest as a safe place to be."* As she was able to experiment with correcting the relationship with the horse, she could do the same with the therapist. The order of learning how to regulate (Nicolai, 2016) becomes clear on a small level:

1. Get to know your own biological rhythm.
2. Give attention to what your body feels.
3. Regulate/comfort yourself, i.e., to let arousal fade away.
4. Think about your own feelings and those of the other (initially the horse, later that of the therapist).

Obviously a sense of resilience was apparent outside the therapy sessions regarding her pregnancy: *"I've always seen my pregnancy and childbirth as the ultimate test of that you can overcome anything."* It seemed that she could apply her EFPP experiences to her daily life.

Conclusion

The presented case shows how certain ingredients of EFPP stimulated her recovery. In particular, the inter-subjective relationship with the horse, but also with the therapist appeared to be important for the client, possibly reinforcing the neural pathways necessary for self-regulation. The shared experience between therapist and client during EFPP stimulates Fonagy and Campbell's (2015) epistemic trust. The client's feedback supports earlier studies on EFPP's efficacy, which showed the following experiences typical of clients with early traumatization undergoing EFPP (Kovács, 2011, 2016a, 2016b):

- being carried (by the horse)
- being in the here-and-now
- the experienced safety of the animal and the therapist
- getting in touch with competencies (to direct the horse with her body)
- being seen by and being in connection with animal and therapist
- connecting to daily life
- rhythmic and other physical experiences

Aspects from an attachment theory perspective are clearly visible. The horse serves as a transitional object on which client projections can take place and the horse ensures a safe and appropriate working relationship with the therapist like a supportive ego. There is a so-called physical transfer between client and horse, which, helped by the therapist team, can be more easily experienced and understood, allowing corrective emotional experiences, i.e., affect regulation. The embodied experiences due to the interaction with the horse connect the client with the self interoceptively. In other words, as van der Kolk (2014) explains, selfhood depends on the ability to make a coherent whole of our memories, which needs an adequate connection between the conscious mind and the self-system of the body, a connection often damaged through trauma.

The experiential, nonverbal characteristic of EFPP resembles Tronick's mutual regulation model (Tronick, 2007). In this model, the therapist helps regulate the affect that threatens the client's willingness to risk change while at the same time co-creating dyadic states of consciousness, in which client and therapist can make new, more complex and coherent meanings. EFPP possibly affects the lower regions of the brain because of the embodied experience of the horse. The above case supports Fotopoulou and Tsakiris' (2017) argued fundamental dimension of embodied experience (both interoceptively and exteroceptively) in selfhood that the sense of agency is not just the experience of having a body but also of controlling one's body in order to cause desired effects in the environment.

Unlike many conventional therapeutic settings, within EFPP the client is offered a unique context in which she is to formulate her own answers in the here-and-now, because dealing with animals asks for making own choices and decisions due to its relative unpredictability. It enhances self-direction and self-responsibility about the client's own process of change. Thus, EFPP provides a context with the opportunity to experiment in a playful manner making the client aware of her resilience, similar to how one would grant such an experience for a growing child.

Due to the presence of different transference objects, there is not one truth and the desired and sought reality by the client becomes visible through the unfolding narrative of the client with the help of the stories and history of the animals allowing space for integrating traumatic memories. It is not only the client who is subject to the relative unpredictability, but also the therapist team. The horse, therapists, and client are thrown into the world of the given actuality exchanging experiences in a "non-psychotherapeutic" manner. With the help of the horse, the therapist team is forced to provide creative, tuned-in interventions to increase collaboration and positive transference.

Acknowledgment

The author would like to thank Martijne Rensen (2017), developer of Multidsiciplinair Integral Tauma Treatment, founder and president CELEVT/STRAKX foundation, the Netherlands, for her contribution on CET numbers and facts.

References

Adriaens, P. & De Block A. (Eds.) (2011). *Maladapting Minds: Philosophy, Psychiatry and Evolutionary Theory (International Perspectives in Philosophy and Psychiatry)*. New York: Oxford University Press.

Alink, L., IJzendoorn, R. van, & Bakermans, M. (2011). *Kindermishandeling in Nederland Anno 2010; de Tweede Nationale Prevalentiestudie Mishandeling van kinderen.* Leiden: Casimir.

Bachi, K. (2013). Application of attachment theory to equine-facilitated psychotherapy. *Journal of Contemporary Psychotherapy*, 43, 187–196.

Beebe, B., Knoblauch, S, Rustin, J., & Sorter, D. (2003). A comparison of Meltzoff, Trevarthen, and Stern. *Psychoanalytic Dialogues*, 13(6), 809–836.

Brown, S. (2007). Companion animals as self-objects. *Anthrozoos*, 20(4), 329–343.

Fine, A. (Ed.) (2015). *Handbook on Animal-Assisted Therapy, Foundations and Guidelines for Animal-Assisted Interventions.* San Diego: Academic Press.

Fonagy, P. (2001). *Attachment Theory and Psychoanalysis.* New York: Other Press.

Fonagy, P. & Campbell, C. (2015). Bad blood revisited: Attachment and psychoanalysis, 2015. *British Journal of Psychotherapy*, 31, 2, 229–250.

Fotopoulou, A. & Tsakiris, M. (2017). Mentalizing homeostasis: The social origins of interoceptive inference. *Neuropsychoanalysis*, 19, 1, 3–28.

Fuchs, T. (2004). Neurobiology and psychotherapy: an emerging dialogue. *Current Opinion in Psychiatry*, 17, 479–485.

Håkanson, M. (2008). Equine assisted therapy in physiotherapy. PhD thesis, University of Gothenburg.

Julius, H., Beetz, A., Kotrschal, K., Turner, D. & Uvnas-Moberg, K. (2013). *Attachment to Pets: An IntegrativeView of Human Animal Relationships with Implication for Therapeutic Practice.* Gottingen: Hogrefe.

Kovács, G. (2011). Corrective emotional experiences through horse–human interactions in short-term psychodynamic psychotherapy. Oral presentation at European Congress of Psychology, Istanbul.

Kovács, G. (2016a). Psychological benefits of an animal assisted psychotherapy, EFPP, in comparison to a psychodynamic group psychotherapy for adolescents. Oral presentation at the 2nd International Neurosequential Model Symposium: Advances in Implementation and Innovation in Practice, Program Development and Policy, Banff.

Kovács, G. (2016b). Psychological benefits within the framework of attachment of an animal assisted psychotherapy, Equine assisted Focal Psychodynamic Psychotherapy (EFPP). Oral presentation at international ESTD 2016 Conference Trauma, dissociation and affect dysregulation across the life-span, Amsterdam.

Kovács, G. & Umbgrove, I. (2014). *Psychotherapie in beweging: Dieren en natuur bij psychodynamische therapie.* Antwerpen: Garant Uitgeverij.

McCullough, L. (1997). *Changing Character: Short-Term Anxiety-Regulating Psychotherapy for Restructuring Defenses, Affects and Attachment.* New York: Basic Books.

McFarland, L. (2016). Natural lifemanship: The science and art of connected relationships. Available at www.naturallifemanship.com.

Merkies, K., Sievers, A., Zakrajsek, E., MacGregor, H., Bergeron, R., & König von Borstel, U. (2014). Preliminary results suggest an influence of psychological and physiological stress in humans on horse heart rate and behavior. *Journal of Veterinary Behavior*, 9(5), 242–247.

Morgan, M. (2015). Neuroscience and psychotherapy. Napier: Hakomi Institute. Available at www.hakomiinstitute.com/Forum/Issue16-17/2_NeurosciTherap-Format.pdf.

Mormann, F., Dubois, J., Kornblith, S., Milosavljevic, M., Cerf, M., Ison, M., Tsuchiya, N., Kraskov, A., Quiroga, R.Q., Adolphs, R., Fried, I., & Koch, C.

(2012). Category-specific response to animals in the right human amygdala. *Nature Neuroscience*, 14(10), 1247–1249.

Nicolai N. (2016). *Emotieregulatie als basis van het menslijk bestaan: De kunst van het evenwicht*. Leusden: Diagnosis uitgevers.

Ottosson, J. (2007). The importance of nature in coping-creating increased understanding of the importance of pure experiences of nature to human health. Alnarp: Department of Work Science, Business Economics and Environmental Psychology, Swedish University of Agricultural Sciences.

Ouss-Ryngaert, L. & Golse, B. (2010). Linking neuroscience and psychoanalysis from a developmental perspective: Why and how? *Journal of Physiology – Paris*, 104, 303–380.

Perry, B. (2006). Applying principles of neurodevelopment to clinical work with maltreated and traumatized children. In N. B. Webb (Ed.), *Working with Traumatized Youth in Child Welfare*. New York: Guilford Press.

Putnam, K., Harris, W., & Putnam, F. (2013). Synergistic childhood adversities and complex adult psychopathology. *Journal of Traumatic Stress*, 26(4), 435–442.

Pynoos, R., Steinberg, A., Layne, C., Liang, L., Vivrette, R., Briggs, E., Kisiel, C., Habib, M., Belin, T., & Fairbank, J. (2014). Modeling constellations of trauma exposure in the national child traumatic stress network core data set. *Psychological Trauma: Theory, Research, Practice, and Policy*, 6(S1), S9–S17.

Rensen, G. (2017). *Multidisciplinaire Integrale Traumabehandeling, onderzoek en innovatie;* Amsterdam: Stichting STRAKX.

Schore, J. & Schore, A. (2008). Modern attachment theory: The central role of affect regulation in development and treatment. *Clinical Social Work Journal*, 36(1), 9–20.

Siegel, D. (2006). An interpersonal neurobiology approach to psychotherapy. *Psychiatric Annals*, 36(4), 248–258.

Siegel, D. (2001). Toward an interpersonal neurobiology of the developing mind: attachment relationships, "mindsight", and neural integration. *Infant Mental Health Journal*, 22(1–2), 67–94.

Smith, A., Proops, L., Grounds, Wathan, J., & McComb, K. (2016). Functionally relevant responses to human facial expressions of emotion in the domestic horse. *Biology Letters*, 12(2), 20150907.

Solms, M. (2015). *The Feeling Brain: Selected Papers on Neuropsychoanalysis*. London: Karnac.

Trevarthen, C. (1998). The concept and foundations of infant intersubjectivity. In S. Braten (Ed.), *Intersubjective Communication and Emotion in Early Ontogeny*. Cambridge: Cambridge University Press.

Trimbos (2007). *Psychische gevolgen van kindermishandeling op volwassen leeftijd: resultaten van de 'Netherlands Mental Health Survey and Incidence study* (NEMESIS), edited by J., Verdurmen, M. en Havet, R. de Graaf, S. van Dorsselaer, H. van 't Land, & W. Vollenbergh. Utrecht: Trimbos instituut.

Tronick, E. (2007). *The Neurobehavioral and Social-Emotional Development of Infants and Children*. New York: W.W. Norton & Company.

van der Hart, O., Brown, P., Van der Kolk, B. (1989). Pierre Janet's treatment of post-traumatic stress. *Journal of Traumatic Stress*, 2, 4, 379–395.

van der Hart, O., Nijenhuis, E.R.S., & Steele, K. (2006). *The Haunted Self: Structural Dissociation and the Treatment of Chronic Traumatization*. New York: W.W. Norton & Company.

van der Kolk, B. (2014). *The Body Keeps the Score-Brain, Mind, and Body in the Healing of Trauma*. New York: Penguin Books.

van Os, J. (2014). *De DSM-5 voorbij! Persoonlijke diagnostiek in een nieuwe GGZ.* Leusden: Diagnosis Uitgevers.

Wallin, D. (2007). *Attachment in Psychotherapy.* New York: The Guilford Press.

Young, J. (1999). *Cognitive Therapy for Personality Disorders: A Schema-Focused Approach.* Sarasota: Professional Resource Press.

Zilcha-Mano, S., Mikulincer, M., & Shaver, P. R. (2012). Pets as safe havens and secure bases: The moderating role of pet attachment orientations. *Journal of Research in Personality*, 46(5), 571–580.

Section Two

Trauma Occurring during Adulthood

8 Equine-Assisted Therapy for Trauma – Accidents

Nina Ekholm Fry

Introduction

Brief Description of Issue

In 2013, there were a reported 28.1 million visits to US emergency rooms with unintentional injury (accident) as the reason of visit (Rui et al., 2013). Categories included: falls, motor vehicle crashes, being struck by objects or persons, poisoning, and traffic-related injuries. Motor vehicle accidents are the most researched in the context of trauma, with prevalence estimates varying from 7% to 39% of individuals receiving a diagnosis of post-traumatic stress disorder (PTSD) after the accident (Heron-Delaneya et al., 2013).

While accident-related PTSD is not a separate category in the DSM-5 (American Psychiatric Association, 2013), accidents typically involve some kind of physical injury (to self with potentially associated complications and treatments, or injury or death to others, including animals, with potentially associated grief) and there are usually considerations related to the cause of accident (Was it due to negligence? Were there litigation and assigning of fault post-accident? What is the public perception of the accident?). A number of factors have been identified as potentially predictive when it comes to developing PTSD after an accident, including prior history of trauma and related risk factors, peritraumatic dissociation, and post-event litigation (Heron-Delaneya et al., 2013; Gandubert et al.,2016). The importance of recognizing different paths of post-traumatic psychopathology post-accident is emphasized by Lanius et al. (2003) and Lanius and Hopper (2004). Helping the client identify different aspects of the accident and explore which ones carries the most weight for them can make the therapeutic process more effective, as is recognizing that the client might be connecting to multiple, past traumas. Here the therapeutic technique of containment is beneficial (Shapiro, 2001).

In order to meet diagnosis of PTSD as defined by the DSM-5, symptoms must have been present for a month (or have appeared by six months with delayed specification) and the client, through being exposed to actual or threatened death or serious injury (also indirectly), must be experiencing symptoms from the following four clusters: intrusion (re-experiencing); avoidance; negative alternations in cognitions and mood; and arousal (disturbances in arousal and reactivity such as hyperarousal or hypoarousal) (American Psychiatric Association, 2013).

This chapter contains theory and rationale for equine-assisted therapy in the treatment of trauma arising from an accident through use of a case example. For the purposes of this chapter, the term equine-assisted therapy (EAT), also referred to as equine-assisted mental health (EAMH), is used to describe a treatment strategy employed by mental health professionals appropriately credentialed to legally practice psychotherapy or counseling in their state or country. In addition, the mental health professional has received education, training, and supervision in equine-assisted therapy in order to practice ethically and effectively, and is appropriately integrating their theoretical framework and clinical skills in the process. Throughout the chapter, the term therapist references a mental health professional such as a counselor, clinical psychologist, clinical social worker, marriage and family therapist, or psychiatric nurse practitioner.

Theoretical Approach: Trauma Treatment

Viewing trauma in the context of basic features of mental health can be helpful in understanding and conceptualizing its treatment. As a result of trauma, disturbances in arousal and reactivity lead to decreased response flexibility and relate to *regulation*, re-experiencing and avoidance relate to lack of *integration*, and alterations in cognition and mood relate to *meaning making* (Figure 8.1). The tri-phasic model of trauma treatment (Figure 8.2) originally proposed by Judith Herman (1992), provides a useful framework for treatment sequence and associated tasks. Please consult your professional mental health association for the latest recommendations regarding evidence for specific approaches (American Psychological Association, 2017).

Aspects of a Healthy Mind (source: Siegel, 2012)

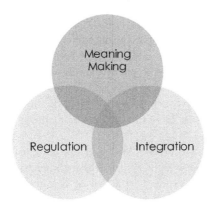

Figure 8.1 Aspects of a healthy mind (source: Siegel, 2012)

Tri-Phasic Trauma Treatment Model

Advances in the field of neuroscience (Siegel, 2012; van der Kolk, 2014) support the notion that effective trauma treatment includes both somatically and cognitively focused components. Helping the client understand the nature of trauma and the functionality of their responses within the context of an overwhelming experience, including orienting and defenses, along with building skills to stabilize and guide both the mind and the body, are central tasks in phase I of the tri-phasic model. The core mechanism of a traumatic memory is a missing "time stamp," which allows it to be re-lived, as opposed to re-visited in a fragmented and disorganized way. The lack of involvement of parts of the brain responsible for time and perspective as well as lack of creation of a coherent story line at the time of the overwhelming experience, is the reason for this. In phase II, the client is assisted in integrating a traumatic event with all necessary parts active. This is facilitated by reducing arousal in relation to the traumatic memories, the excess of which created the lack of integration in the first place, and allowing for a coherent narrative to emerge. In phase III, the key tasks revolve around connection, trust, and compassion for self and others. The phases are neither linear nor sequential; however, there needs to be sufficient mastery of tasks in phase I in order for therapist and client to move to phase II without risk of re-traumatization.

In the technique described in this chapter, the client is in phase I of treatment and working on understanding their body's defenses (Kozlowska et al., 2015) and orienting patterns (Ogden et al., 2006). Further, the client is working on

---

Phase I: Stabilization and Moving Toward Sense of Safety
Establishing a therapeutic relationship and a roadmap for treatment
Psychoeducation
Creating body access and awareness
Developing mind skills
Putting words to feelings and distress
Understanding orienting, appraisal and evolutionary automatic defenses

Phase II: Integration of Traumatic Memories and Events
Integrating traumatic memories
Constructing and integrating a narrative

Phase III: (Re)Connection
Connecting with self
Connecting with others
Connecting with community

Tri-Phasic Trauma Treatment Model (source: Herman, 1992).

Figure 8.2 Tri-phasic trauma treatment model

being able to pay attention to internal information and external information, a form of dual attention (Shapiro, 2001), while regulating the arousal state of their body.

Rationale for Equine-Assisted Therapy in the Treatment of Trauma

Finding ways to help individuals seek treatment, to remain in treatment, and for practitioners to optimize treatment can be especially challenging when addressing trauma (Sayer et al., 2009; Najavits, 2015). By utilizing the simultaneously experiential, somatic (mind–body focused), and relational aspects of equine-assisted therapy, therapists can enhance evidence-based trauma treatment in a setting that can be less threatening for many: together with other animals outside the confines of a traditional office. Within the tri-phasic model of trauma treatment (Figure 1.2), equine-assisted therapy can, for instance, create an opportunity to: practice skill in an experiential but less threatening setting, co-regulate with a horse in order to increase body awareness, use the calm presence of the horse as an anchor point, and discover relational aspects of the self through touch and movement with another species. Ekholm Fry (in press) provides a lengthy presentation of horses in the treatment of trauma.

To experientially practice skills related to regulation and orienting within the therapy session, without yet directly integrating traumatic memories, which is the goal of the technique described below, provides an opportunity to build skill in a sequential and sustainable way. It also provides an opportunity for the client to experience hope, which Briere and Scott (2006) notes as a crucial therapeutic action, as well as a sense of courage and trust resulting from putting their acquired skills to use in the therapeutic setting.

Finally, examples of client precautions and contraindications specific to equine-assisted therapy are: severe allergies, phobias (such as extreme fear of horses), inability to follow directions, medical conditions that limit safe involvement in the equine environment, and lack of interest in equine interactions. The risk of re-traumatization, which is present in any therapeutic treatment model, is discussed in the context of equine-assisted work by Ekholm Fry (in press).

Ethical Issues in Equine-Assisted Therapy Programs

Therapist Training

If a therapist is intending to treat trauma they must have appropriate education, training, and supervision in trauma work (American Counseling Association [ACA], 2014). If a therapist is intending to provide equine-assisted therapy, the same naturally applies: education, training, and supervision is needed for counselors in how to merge their theoretical framework and clinical skills with the nature of equine-assisted therapy and the facilitation thereof. Since there does not yet exist national educational standards or regulation for organizations providing training to therapists in equine-assisted therapy, there are existing organizations that certify providers after less than a week total of training. In order to practice ethically and effectively within their scope, it is advisable that therapists seek independent, national board certification through the Certification Board of Equine Interaction Professionals (2017) after appropriate education, training, and supervision in equine-assisted therapy. The competencies document for animal-assisted therapy in counseling provided by the ACA (2016) is a helpful guide to the content of education and training.

Horses in Equine-Assisted Therapy

Therapist knowledge, skills, and attitudes have the biggest impacts on the welfare of horses who are part of equine-assisted therapy. Therapists who are not dually trained in equine behavior might not be able to recognize subtle cues that horses communicate when distressed or might not know how to create and sustain a therapeutic environment that includes consideration for the horse. This involves helping the client accurately understand the behavior of the horse and intervening soon enough, and in a therapeutic manner, in situations where the client creates inescapable pressure or flight in the horse or does not respond to the horse's signals of discomfort. In addition, inadequate or non-existent work role preparation creates confusion and unwanted behaviors in horses, especially when paired with inappropriate management practices such as confinement, restricted access to hay or grass (only being given "meals"), and lack of access to other horses (McGreevy, 2012).

There have only been a handful of studies measuring the effect of a tense or anxious human on horses (Hama et al., 1996; Keeling et al., 2009; Gehrke et al., 2011; Merkies et al., 2014), and the results are inconclusive. Only one pilot study to date involved measuring horses' response to individuals diagnosed with PTSD (Merkies, 2016). Behavioral and physiological responses of horses to humans were more pronounced based on the human's experience with horses and was not linked to a PTSD diagnosis. It is likely that horses, similar to humans, have different thresholds of tolerance for tension in others due to a variety of factors.

Therapist attitudes such as "my horse loves doing trauma work" or "horses are called to heal trauma" might cause the therapist to misunderstand and overlook basic needs, post-session maintenance, and signs of distress in horses. Similarly, attitudes such as "the horse can take care of themselves" or "a traumatized horse will heal a traumatized client if I get out of the way" discount the responsibility that the therapist has for the equine-assisted session and all parts of the therapeutic environment.

A larger ethical issue in the equine-assisted therapy field not frequently discussed relates to social justice and rights, which are central to mental health fields such as psychology, counseling, social work, and marriage and family therapy. Are therapists who include horses in their practice sufficiently considering privilege, power, and oppression, also in relation to other species, such as the horse, and the position horses have, on a systemic level, in society? The therapeutic environment, which includes therapist, client, horse and environment, cannot be fully therapeutic if the perceived position of power that the therapist has is overlooked, and the same goes for the position of power vis-à-vis the horse. When clients who experience marginalization in their daily lives also sense it in the therapeutic environment, the therapeutic relationship, which, in equine-assisted therapy is expanded to include the horse, is not beneficial.

The ACA competencies document for animal-assisted therapy in counseling (2016) mentions consideration for animal rights. There is a need to move beyond basic frameworks such as the Five Freedoms (Farm Animal Welfare Council, n. d), developed for production animals, and for therapists to consider the challenges and possibilities that come from having horses as part of human mental health services from a privilege and power perspective. Is it okay to keep a horse in solitary confinement in a stall for most of the day? Is it okay that horses are exposed to training methods that have been abandoned in human phobia and trauma practice (such as flooding)? More discussion is needed around this issue; otherwise the field of animals in human health, and specifically horses in mental health, simply creates another way that humans exploit other animals.

Description of Intervention and Case Example

Goals and Objectives

The goal of the technique described here is for the client to practice regulation skills in an experiential, functional setting. The opportunity to practice comes in the context of a functional and typical activity in the equine setting which tends to elicit some initial discomfort for clients: walking around the hindquarters of the horse. Outcomes include: increased awareness of body sensations; tangible experience of the body's orienting and evaluation patterns and how they are connected to body defenses; ability to pay attention to internal and external information simultaneously; and experience in guiding internal arousal in a functional setting. From the experience that guiding their inner state is possible, even in a setting that involves some client-perceived risk, a sense of trust in the body and the mind's ability to guide it can emerge.

Setting and Materials Needed

A therapist and a client will interact with a single horse. In addition to being comfortable standing tied, the horse's work role requirements include: being comfortable with humans touching their body, and being comfortable with humans touching their hindquarters (no recent injuries or concerns should be present). The horse should be tied with a halter and lead rope using a safety clasp/quick release knot and tied at a length that allows movement of the head and no tension on the halter (general tying guideline). It is also possible for the horse to be held in hand by an assistant. Excepting severe weather or client preference, an outdoor setting is preferred. There should be plenty of space to navigate around the horse, making a stall or a barn isle unsuitable.

Case Example: Brief Description of Client

The client is 32 years old, identifies as male and Latino, and resides in an urban area. After two in-patient treatment stays for co-occurring disorders (PTSD with episodic poly-drug addiction), lasting a total of 11 months, the client is regularly taking part in support groups, has enrolled in college, and is maintaining a part-time job. The client was recently involved in a two-car accident where the other driver was determined to be at fault. No serious injuries were sustained. The client is experiencing frequent anxiety, hypervigilance, disrupted sleep, concentration issues, irritability, and feelings of hopelessness, and is avoiding driving altogether after the accident. During in-patient treatment, the client heard from peers how much they benefitted from equine-assisted therapy and wanted to experience what it was like. The client expresses an interest in horses but does not have much experience with them.

The client has had two previous sessions, both taking place in the therapist's office, which is adjacent to the equine facility where the therapist provides services. For part of the second visit, the client interacted with several horses, learned a few things about their behavior, communication, and needs, and brushed one horse, Prime.

Step-by-Step Description of Intervention with Transcript and Analysis

The therapist can choose whether to make the goal of this equine interaction/technique explicit, meaning that the connection to the client's trauma treatment goals is facilitated throughout the experience, or they can emphasize the reason for the experience only in relation to the functional interaction with the horse and afterwards help the client see the connection to their trauma work. The former process is described below.

Starting Point

The client and therapist are standing by Prime, the horse that the client has chosen to interact with. Prime is standing tied (see "Setting and Materials" section for more information). The client has received information about two ways of walking around a horse that is standing tied (either very close to the horse's hindquarters with a hand on the horse or giving copious amounts of space when walking around the horse, remembering to say something to the horse when coming back around). The client is familiar with, and enjoys, gently brushing a horse and knows that walking around the horse is part of that interaction. The therapist will use the brushing time for the client to practice other regulation skills. If walking around the back of the horse does not create a slight apprehension in the client, other functions and activities typical in a horse-care setting, such as picking up feet, can be used.

Step 1: Introduction to Walking Around the Horse

The therapist and client are standing side by side next to Prime, approximately by the shoulder.

Transcript Analysis of Case Example

The following transcript analysis is about a composite client:

Table 8.1 Case Example Transcript

Transcript	Analysis
Therapist: We talked earlier about walking around Prime *(horse)* to brush on the other side. How does that sound?	The therapist reminds the client about what was previously discussed and checks in.
Client: It could be dangerous, I mean, I know that horses kick, I heard about someone who was really injured by that.	The client is communicating some anxiety based on past experience.
Therapist: Kicking is part of the horse's defense repertoire. If a horse startles or feels threatened, they usually try to flee first, and if they can't, they might use their legs to protect themselves. In a setting like this, unless the horse gets startled somehow, there really wouldn't be a need for them to defend themselves in that way.	It is important not to undermine the client's anxiety but not to expand on it either. By providing a functional reason for the horse's behavior, the client can start sensing similarities between themselves and the horse *(comparative health perspective)*.
Therapist: We can use information from our surroundings to evaluate in the moment if there is immediate danger and need for defense, just like Prime would do.	The therapist is introducing a mechanism behind what the client will be doing when walking around the horse.
Client: Okay *(tense body and glazed stare)*.	The client is approaching the edge of the current window of tolerance (e.g., Ogden, Minton & Pain, 2006).
Therapist: Let's pause for a second.	The therapist slows the pace of their speech and intentionally relaxes their body to help the client regulate.

Table 8.1 Case Example Transcript (Cont.)

Transcript	Analysis
Therapist: I'm here to help apply the brakes, if you appreciate my traffic analogy …	The therapist offers reassurance that they will be attuned to the client and provides a gentle reminder of the focus of the client's current trauma work. The second part of the sentence is offered with a light, humorous tone.
Client: Laughs a little *(seeks eye contact).*	The client is orienting to the present and seeks social engagement.
Therapist: Why don't you touch Prime a bit here *(also gently strokes Prime).*	The therapist encourages further regulation by orienting to sensory input.
Therapist: What's your number?	The therapist is asking the client how they rate themselves on a scale from 1 to 10, also commonly referred to as the subjective units of distress (SUDs) scale, a tool that the client is familiar with.
Client: I think about a 6 now.	The client is rating themselves in a middle range on the SUDs scale and has checked in with their body.
Therapist: Okay. So, we talked about two ways to walk around a horse, and you remember the demonstration around the chair?	The therapist is refocusing the client on the task ahead and assesses whether the client has access to information shared earlier in the session.
Client: Yes *(nods).*	Hearing this answer, the therapist is assessing the client's body language, not just their words.
Therapist: We have the two options we talked about, with one being more preferred, and you are free to choose which one you want to do today.	The therapist offers choice to the client and intentionally uses "and" instead of "but" when presenting these choices.
Client: Walking close so that Prime feels better.	The client takes the experience of the other (in this case Prime) into consideration.

Step 2: Starting the Process

The therapist positions themselves slightly in front of the client with their near hand on the horse's side and turns slightly to speak with client. The therapist is positioned in the direction of travel and not behind the client (which might feel threatening) and so creates an opportunity for some autonomy by being present but not directly facing the client.

Transcript Analysis of Case Example Continued

Table 8.2 Case Example Transcript Continued

Transcript	Analysis
Therapist: So, I'll walk with you like this *(positions themselves)*. We're going to be checking in and letting some information come from our body and memory, and some information from the outside. It's helpful to know what signals our body is sending, but sometimes we are operating on old information. So, we'll keep looking at what is actually happening right now.	The therapist emphasizes the mechanism of the activity. The therapist reminds the client to pay attention to their body *and* to information that is accessible in the current situation. The therapist is gently reminding the client to allow information from past experiences to be felt, and that the old information may also need to be re-evaluated.
Therapist: What's your number now?	The therapist is reminding the client to check in with their body.
Client: Still about a 6.	The client has not escalated further and it is likely that they are able to process what the therapist is saying to them.
Therapist: Let your breath out and take a deep one. Now, let's take a few steps.	It is important that the therapist is monitoring their own body in this process and that they model breathing and their own regulation.
Therapist: Let's check in with our surroundings so that we can determine if we should continue. What do you notice?	The therapist engages the client in a *joint venture* and is fully taking part in the experience themselves. The therapist asks for input from the client.
Client: Prime is standing still. I can see his head and eyes. He just moved his tail, maybe a fly.	The client is orienting to factual aspects of the environment as opposed to abstract or past experiences.
Therapist: What can you say about Prime's body state?	The therapist encourages the client to also orient relationally using their body sense.
Client: He doesn't seem to be tense at all.	The therapist chooses not to ask the client to elaborate at this time.
Therapist: What about your body?	The therapist reminds the client to recognize internal information.
Client: I actually don't feel as tense as I thought I would.	The client is noticing a difference between their preconceived notions about the experience and what is actually happening.
Therapist: Would it be advisable to proceed?	The therapist asks the client to determine whether the two should move or not at this point. Since the client views the therapist as knowing more about horses than they do, this does not represent a reversal of responsibility but instead a deepening of the joint venture that is undertaken.
Client: Yes.	The client chooses to go forward.

Step 3: Being By and Behind the Horse's Hindquarters

This is the position that potentially carries the most risk from the client's perspective and it is helpful for them to first watch the therapist's experience.

Transcript Analysis of Case Example Continued

Table 8.3 Case Example Transcript Continued

Transcript	Analysis
Therapist: Let's have a look at what is happening now that I am right behind the horse. If need be, I could take a step to the side *(demonstrates taking a step to the side of the hind leg)* and then go back again.	The therapist physically demonstrates regulation by taking a step back and then stepping forward again.
Therapist: Right, now I am noticing that Prime has both his ears forward and is looking at something out across the pasture. He hasn't raised his head much and his body seems pretty relaxed. So, I'm going to take a deep breath (why don't you do it with me?) and I'm thinking about continuing walking around. *(Breath)* I am noticing a little tension; maybe I could even be picking it up from you. How are you doing?	The therapist models what the client has been practicing: orienting to the current situation and to their own body state. Even a slight change in the environment might not always warrant a change of plan. This can be hard for some clients who are constantly hypervigilant and who are trying to pick up on the most subtle of cues to prevent a previously harmful situation. The therapist also uses the counseling/helping skill of immediacy by addressing the experience between them and the client. The therapist follows the statement with an open question.
Client: Wow, I can't believe you are standing right there *(laughs a little)*.	The client could be escalating, or a feeling of curiousness and fasciation might divert the escalation. Therapist is assessing the client's body state and decides to proceed.
Therapist: If you remember, it's better to be close to the hind legs like this than midway out, in case Prime *would* startle. But unless there is a plastic bag that appears mid-air right now … You know, accidents could happen, but I am using information from right now to make the best choice possible.	The therapist is touching on another relevant word for the client, accident, and models how they operate in the face of the uncertainty that does exist in the world.

Step 4: On the Other Side of the Horse

The client and therapist have slowly walked to the other side of the horse, ending up by the shoulder.

Transcript Analysis of Case Example Continued

Table 8.4 Case Example Transcript Continued

Transcript	Analysis
Therapist: We're on the other side!	The therapist orients client to physical setting but also uses the phrase to mark the end of the specific experience.
Client: I could feel my heart beating but the whooshing sound in my ears didn't start like it has.	The client offers reflection and notices that they are having a new experience.
Therapist: What do you think was different?	The therapist is facilitating further reflection and is curious about the client's thoughts.
Client: I knew it could be dangerous to me to do this. Like you said, accidents can happen. But I could also see what was in front of me, I think it made me less tense to think that way. And, like, slow it down. Prime was really calm. He's a solid guy, I mean, horse.	The client is able to reflect on their experience with the horse.
Therapist: That's a great reflection. Does it sound like something you're working on?	The therapist expresses genuine appreciation of the client's self-reflection. The therapist connects the experience with Prime to what the client and therapist have identified as goals for treatment.
Client: Yeah ... *(smiles).*	The client recognizes what the therapist is asking.
Therapist: Believe it or not, but doing these kinds of things here helps your body "get it," and for you to practice how to talk to and guide yourself when things start feeling tense, in traffic or otherwise. You don't want to be scaring your body by putting it down or ignoring it.	The therapist has previously established the body as "a part" within the client that also has a "voice" and "feelings" and uses the analogy.
Client: Yeah, I've tried to just ignore it and then it's like I can't do anything.	The client recognizes what does not work for them.
Therapist: That makes sense to me.	The therapist affirms what the client expressed about previously failed strategies.
Therapist: Now that we're on this side, why don't you continue brushing Prime for a while, and I want you to pay attention to any of that "sliding out" of anxiety that we talked about, while feeling Prime's coat and mane. Be sure to check in with how he is doing, too! Then after a while, we'll go around again, but this time I'll be next to you, on the outside. Time to get back in the mind gym!	The therapist is orienting the client to what it feels like when anxiety gradually decreases and reminds the client to connect a psychoeducational topic to their immediate experience. The therapist has established an analogy of a gym and building muscles in the mind with the client since the client likes lifting weights.

Multicultural Considerations and Ethical Considerations for this Intervention

What makes this technique different from those typically employed in a more traditional office-based trauma treatment session is the physical positioning of the therapist in relation to the client, in addition to elements of movement and touch. Although the therapist during this technique does not touch the client (any use of touch here is mediated through the horse), other techniques, especially with mounted work, can include some functional touch by the therapist. The equine setting allows for a broader range of options for how the therapist and client position themselves, as a stationary position directly facing another might not always be the best option. However, physical positioning holds different meanings for different individuals and the therapist needs to carefully explore the impact of their position on the therapeutic relationship in tandem with asking the client about their experiences and preferences. When asking clients about their preferences it is important to also assess the client's ability to self-advocate within the therapeutic relationship and to mitigate the systemic and perceived differences in power that this relationship might constitute. It is also the therapist's responsibility to exercise cultural humility (Tervalon & Murray-Garcia, 1998) in seeking to understand themselves and their client, as individuals and as part of larger social systems.

In this technique, the horse is standing tied, and while this is a typical feature of human–horse interactions, careful attention should be paid to the nature of these interactions. The therapist needs to be sensitive to features of human–horse interactions that perpetuate the power differences between humans and horses in a way that might introduce a sense of exploitation into the therapeutic environment. Through experiencing the relationship between the therapist and the horse, the client can assess how the therapist treats and values others, which likely contributes to how safe the client will feel in the context of treatment.

References

American Counseling Association (2014). ACA code of ethics, section C.2.b: New specialty areas of practice. Alexandria, VA: Author.

American Counseling Association (2016). Animal assisted therapy in counseling competencies. Available online at: www.counseling.org/knowledge-center/competencies.

American Psychiatric Association (2013). *Diagnostic and statistical manual of mental disorders* (5th ed.). Washington, DC: Author.

American Psychological Association (2017). Clinical practice guideline for the treatment of PTSD. Retrieved from: www.apa.org/about/offices/directorates/guidelines/ptsd.pdf.

Briere, J., & Scott, C. (2006). *Principles of trauma therapy: A guide to symptoms, evaluation, and treatment.* Thousand Oaks, CA: SAGE.

Certification Board for Equine Interaction Professionals (2017). Certification explained. Retrieved from: www.cbeip.org.

Ekholm Fry, N. (in press). Horses in the treatment of trauma. In P. Tedeschi and M. Jenkins (Eds.), *Transforming trauma: Resilience and healing through human–animal connection*. West Lafayette, IN: Purdue University Press.

Farm Animal Welfare Council (n. d.). Five freedoms. Archived 2012-10-07 at: http://webarchive.nationalarchives.gov.uk/20121010012427/www.fawc.org.uk/freedoms.htm.

Gandubert C., Scali, J., Ancelin M.-L., Carriere, I., Dupuy, A.-M., Bagnolini, G., Ritchie, K, Sebanne, M., Martrille, L., Baccino, E., Hermes, A., Attal J., & Chaudieu I. (2016). Biological and psychological predictors of posttraumatic stress disorder onset and chronicity: A one-year prospective study. *Neurobiology of stress*, 3, 61–67.

Gehrke, E. K., Baldwin, A., & Schiltz, P. M. (2011). Heart rate variability in horses engaged in equine-assisted activities. *Journal of Equine Veterinary Science*, 31(2), 78–84.

Hama, H., Yogo, M., & Matsuyama, Y. (1996). Effects of stroking horses on both humans and horses heart rate responses. *Japanese Psychological Research*, 38(2), 66–73.

Herman, J. (1992). *Trauma and recovery*. New York: Basic Books.

Heron-Delaney, M., Kenardy, J., Charlton, E., & Matsuoka, Y. (2013). A systematic review of predictors of posttraumatic stress disorder (PTSD) for adult road traffic crash survivors. *Injury*, 44(11), 1413–1422.

Keeling, L., Jonare, L., & Lanneborn, L. (2009). Investigating horse–human interactions: The effect of a nervous human. *Veterinary Journal*, 181(1), 70–71. doi:10.1016/j.tvjl.2009.03.013.

Kozlowska, K., Walker, P., McLean, L., & Carrive, P. (2015). Fear and the defense cascade: Clinical implications and management. *Harvard Review of Psychiatry*, 23(4): 263–287.

Lanius R. A., Hopper J. W., & Menon R. S. (2003). Individual differences in a husband and wife who developed PTSD after a motor vehicle accident: A functional MRI case study. *American Journal of Psychiatry*, 160(2), 667–669.

Lanius R. A., & Hopper J. W. (2004). Letter to the editor: Drs Lanius and Hopper reply. *American Journal of Psychiatry*, 161(3), 584–585.

McGreevy, P., (2012). *Equine behavior: A guide for veterinarians and equine scientists* (2nd ed.). Edinburgh: Elsevier.

Merkies, K., Sievers, A., Zakrajsek, E., MacGregor, H, Bergeron, R., & Köning von Borstel, U. (2014). Preliminary results suggest an influence of psychological and physiological stress in humans on horse heart rate and behavior. *Journal of Veterinary Behavior*, 9, 242–247.

Merkies, K. (2016). Can horses distinguish between neurotypical and mentally traumatized humans? Final report, Horses and Humans Research Foundation. Retrieved from: www.horsesandhumans.org/HHRF_dec16_report_K_Merkies.pdf.

Najavits, L. M. (2015). The problem of dropout from "gold standard" PTSD therapies. *F1000 Prime Report*, 7, 43. doi:10.12703/P7-43.

Ogden, P., Minton, K., & Pain, C. (2006). *Trauma and the body: A sensorimotor approach to psychotherapy*. New York: W.W. Norton & Co.

Rui, P., Kang, K., & Albert, M. (2013). National hospital ambulatory medical care survey: Emergency department summary, table 16. Retrieved from: www.cdc.gov/nchs/data/ahcd/nhamcs_emergency/2013_ed_web_tables.pdf.

Sayer, N. A., Friedemann-Sanchez, G., Spoont, M., Murdoch, M., Parker, L. E., Chiros, C., & Rosenheck R. (2009). A qualitative study of determinants of PTSD treatment initiation in veterans. *Psychiatry: Interpersonal and Biological Processes*, 72 (3), 238–255.

Shapiro, F. (2001). *Eye movement desensitization and reprocessing: Basic principles, protocols, and procedures* (2nd ed.). New York: Guilford Press.

Siegel, D. (2012). *The developing mind: How relationships and the brain interact to shape who we are* (2nd ed.). New York: W.W. Norton & Company.

Tervalon, M., & Murray-Garcia, J. (1998). Cultural humility versus cultural competence: A critical distinction in defining physician training outcomes in multicultural education. *Journal of Health Care for the Poor and Undeserved*, 9, 117–125.

van der Kolk, B. (2014). *The body keeps the score: Brain, mind, and body in the healing of trauma*. New York: Viking.

9 Families and Trauma

Rebecca F. Bailey and Elizabeth Bailey

Introduction

Description of Problem

Families disconnected by time, distance, trauma, or other stressful change such as divorce, moving, or death face the challenge of recovery and of reconnecting to one another. The effects of trauma and adverse stressful events are numerous. "Childhood trauma may be accompanied by as yet unknown biological changes that are stimulated by the external events" (Terr, 2003, p. 321). The research suggests that the risk for emotional problems increases in response to the experience of stressful life events (Kraaij et al., 2003; Oliva Jimenez, & Parra, 2007). The primary point is that the family is in crisis, the primary relationships have been disrupted, and the family needs treatment.

A child affected by trauma has, most likely, lost a sense of safety. The limbic system has been activated to manage the distress or threat: "importantly, the limbic system may cause us to over-react to perceived threats that we only perceive on an unconscious level" (Hosier, 2016). Some children will respond to a threat with a full shutdown, becoming paralyzed in their ability to move forward (Kinniburgh et al., 2005). This primitive and appropriate "child-like" response to fear can promote a similar response in other family members. For example, a parent who sees a child shut down can become so concerned they too close themselves off to the world. Each family member may have a different and unique response to fear, and each response may contribute to a home environment that feels "unsafe," "unsupportive," or "inauthentic" to the entire family. This reaction may cause family members to doubt themselves, and to question what is safe and what is not. Families may be susceptible to perceived threats (real or unreal), and contrived responses or inaccurate information, partly due to an amplified emotional state. Authenticity is imperative to counteract some of the effects of trauma and create a "safe" environment. The child and his/her family may calm and be less reactive in the containment of a trusting and secure environment.

The Transitioning Families Therapeutic Reunification Model (TFTRM)

How can the disconnected family be supported? Families need a trusting and safe environment, and experienced professionals to help them learn to manage their anxieties, fears, and feelings of detachment from one another. The purpose of the Transitioning Families Therapeutic Reunification model (TFTRM) is to treat and process the trauma or major stressor as a family, to provide a pathway to recovery, to reduce and cope with responses to the stressor, and to help the family to connect in a therapeutic context. The treatment model supports the family in their work to heal from within, allowing and acknowledging the individual, and the sometimes-conflicting needs of all involved parties. In utilizing a trauma informed family therapy model "family members should be able to gain a deeper understanding of the impact of the trauma on the individual and on the family dynamic, better understand each family member's individual healing process, and feel empowered to provide support and advocacy" (Connecticut Department of Children and Families, 2016).

The TFTRM approach is based on intervention guidelines for responding to child abduction developed by the Department of Justice (Hatcher et al., 1992). The founding clinicians have expertise with family systems therapy, psychodynamic therapy and advanced training in animal assisted therapy (Transitioning Families, 2017). The Transitioning Families website goes on to describe itself as having an "onsite intensive structure; the combination of intellectual, emotional, and physical participation by the family members; and the integration of equine, recreational, and culinary intervention with traditional talk therapy" (2017). The TFTRM is designed to be applicable to trauma and other stressors; "The overarching goal of the TFTRM is to assist families in transitioning from crisis, challenge or conflict to connection and growth" (Judge et al., 2016, p. 235). The program is multifaceted and is usually provided over three to five days by a collaborative treatment team. The treatment plan is customized to fit the needs of the individual family, as assessed by the treatment team. Acceptance into the program is made on a case-by-case basis.

Theoretical Approaches behind the Transitioning Families Approach

Family Therapy

Family therapy "first emerged in the mid-1950s" (Goldenberg & Goldenberg, 2013, p. xxiii). "The one central principle agreed upon by family therapy practitioners, regardless of their particular approach, is that the client is connected to living systems. Attempts at change are best facilitated by working with and considering the family or set of relationships as a whole" (Corey, 2013, p. 397). In a family in crisis or suffering a traumatic event "actions by any individual family member will influence all the others in the family, and their reactions will have a reciprocal effect on the individual" (p. 397). Traditional therapeutic models focus primarily on the individual, leaving the rest of the family out of the recovery process. In 2009, Charles Figley (as cited by James and McKinnon, 2012, pp. 189–209) gave two reasons why it was "better to keep the entire family together" (p. 190) in addressing and processing trauma:

> family members may be vicariously traumatized by one of their member's traumatic experiences … and … the family has the potential to be an important source of support and validation for a traumatized member and may therefore provide the "antidote" for the trauma …The family is the context in which most traumatized people are relieved of their negative traumatic effects through meaning-making.
>
> (Figley, 2009, pp. 179–180)

Reunification Therapy

The term "reunification therapy" has been used within the child welfare context when the intention was made to reunite biological parent(s) and their child(ren) by child welfare workers. These parents often may have committed child abuse or suffered from severe addiction problems, and the child(ren) may have been placed in protective custody or foster care (Sauber, 2013) and subsequently required reunification therapy upon being returned to their family. The term has also been used to refer to the work of mental health professionals in the appropriate reunification of recovered abducted children with families or parent (Hatcher et al., 1992). Reunification therapy has been used to describe therapy used when a member of the military returns to his/her family after active duty (Sayers, 2010) and has been utilized to describe to the therapeutic modality that addresses parent–child issues in families of high-conflict divorce (Polak & Moran, 2017).

In treating families and trauma, the goal of reunification therapy is to reconnect the child(ren) to the parents, to one another, and to improve family function. There are few detailed evidence-based treatment protocols or best-practice guidelines for this type of treatment for families and trauma within the literature. Polak & Moran suggest that the treatment team should be specialized and have competence in family therapy as well as cognitive behavioral therapy (Polak & Moran, 2017).

Psychodynamic Therapy

The TRTFM does not take a strictly psychodynamic approach, but it does utilize psychodynamic techniques and principles (e.g., Shedler, 2010). These basic principles include the use of transference and countertransference to understand family functioning and to select interventions. In addition, projection can be used to name aspects of the family's history and current sources of impasse. Although the TFTRM may explore the family's past through techniques and exercises, the focus remains on present and future family functioning.

In equine-assisted therapy, horses provide opportunities for projection and transference from a new perspective, and the family's various reactions can be considered within the framework of psychodynamic therapy. Some schools of equine work suggest that the work "provides a portal for the resolution of unfinished business by bringing forth – and addressing reactions in the here and now of therapy" (Klontz et al., 2007, p. 259)

Psychoeducation

Psychoeducation has been shown to help families resolve a range of difficulties (Lebow & Gurman, 1995) including children's reactions to trauma, understanding the negative effects of conflict and trauma on child development, and teaching parents how to understand behaviors and adaptations related to the children's distress around the experience of trauma. Incorporating equine work can encourage and promote open dialogue around difficult conversations. Because it is information and educationally based, psychoeducation is most often neutral in presentation, which may help the family to take in the information with a less intense emotional response. For example, at the core of many issues facing individuals and families is unprocessed grief and helping children access emotions related to loss can be, at its best, challenging. Psychoeducation provided to families regarding grief, loss, and resilience may help the family to understand where they are in the process of recovery, and may provide insight and perspective into what's happening now so that the family might process and integrate their feelings in a healthy manner.

Experiential and Play Therapy

In experiential therapy, direct experience is considered the primary agent of change (Mahrer, 1983). A wide range of experiential modalities including equine- and animal-assisted therapy, art and music therapy, cooking, and recreational activities may be embraced. Experiential techniques may be helpful with groups that are difficult to engage and integrate into traditional therapy, and can help a resistant individual to access previously unrecognized or unprocessed emotions. Experiential therapies have their origins in client-centered existential approaches. These approaches value internal processing and promote the notion that individuals can benefit from empathy-based therapeutic interactions. Equine therapy in a peaceful environment can provide an opportunity for the development of empathic relationships within the family, and between the family and therapists, human and equine. This empathic or "attuned" experience can promote "safe" processing of previously unprocessed or unrecognized emotions.

Play may increase engagement (Gil & Sobol, 2005) and motivation among both parents and children (Thompson et al., 2011). Gil and Sobol (2005) suggest that play may help with families that are not verbally facile, may encourage family members to be less analytical and intellectual, and inspire new relational patterns. Winnicott suggests that a playful environment provides an environment in which a problem can be explored and a solution found (Winnicott, 1965). Research has shown how powerful play is for helping traumatized children (Gaskill & Perry, 2014), but its importance in connecting and healing families may be somewhat overlooked. Suggested reasons to incorporate play into therapeutic process with families: "overcoming challenges of a family that is not verbally oriented, helping family members to be less analytical and intellectual, fostering disclosure when shame, discomfort and distrust dominate family interactions and the promoting of new relational patterns" (Gil & Sobol, 2005, Chapter 4). At Transitioning Families, play is not only a way to connect but also a powerful antidote to sadness. Families that learn to play, laugh, and problem-solve often appear at ease and more able to communicate freely after the family has played a game together. The approach taken at Transitioning Families always includes the possibility of humor and playfulness.

Equine-Assisted Therapy and Families with Trauma-Related Issues

Equine-assisted psychotherapies are those that integrate equine activities within a treatment program's broader framework (Klontz et al., 2007), mostly through ground work with less emphasis on riding. Horses are extensions of the intensive reunification team and, as such, are agents of therapeutic change because they draw out a range of emotions and responses in families that may be used as a stimulus for insight and directness, leading to change.

Families who have experienced trauma or major stressful events tend to be hyper-alert; ready in an instant to move into fight or flight mode to respond to perceived threats (Johnston et al., 2009). Observing and understanding equine behavior can teach families to understand the difference between a real perceived threat and an irritation, or other interaction that is not a threat, but a form of communication. The first observation might be that horses are big; they could cause harm but do not (Nurenberg et al., 2015). Secondly, the family may notice that as prey animals (i.e., they are preyed upon by others), horses are finely attuned to their surroundings so that they can react accordingly. Observing horses for a short time can reveal how sensitive they are to their environment; they are quick to move out of harm's way, but just as quick to return to calm grazing when the perceived danger is past. This is what makes them such excellent teachers, almost mirrors, quick to sense and reflect influences coming from their environment, including human behavior. It is easy to understand how well suited they are to address trauma/family issues: "the subtle art of communication, awareness about interpersonal boundaries, the effects of one's posture, demeanor and effect on others, and principles of emotional contagion" (Judge & Deutsch, 2016, p. 99). Understanding that there are new ways to evaluate the perceived threat can calm the family and help them to reinterpret and reframe their environment.

It is not unusual for children and families who have suffered traumatic experiences to have great difficulty articulating and identifying their emotions around the event or events. In addition, many families in treatment may be tired of a heavy emphasis on analysis and "talk." Promoting understanding through verbal exchange only can increase resistance and "promote over-intellectualization" (Judge & Deutsch, 2016, p. 99). Horses respond non-verbally and immediately without judgment or blame, offering new learning and improved insight within families.

Equine-assisted therapy can help with entrenched patterns such as alliances, sub-systems, and other disruptions, which might maintain old systems, by creating "here and now" experiences that the family can observe, with the assistance of the team (EAGALA, 2009, 2010). This type of therapy provides opportunities to learn and practice problem-solving. Experiences such as learning self-regulation when emotionally flooded, understanding differing perceptions and choices in approaching a task, ways to collaborate and use teamwork to complete as task are some areas that can be strengthened with the help of horses (EAGALA, 2009, 2010). Modalities focused on somatic experience through equine ground work may help reduce symptoms of post-traumatic stress (Cloitre et al., 2011). Equine therapy in a peaceful environment can provide an opportunity for the development of empathic relationships. This empathic or "attuned" experience can promote "safe" processing of previously unprocessed or unrecognized emotions.

The Transitioning Families (TF) model and Equine-Assisted Therapy

The TFTRM model focuses on the well-being of the animals by incorporating principles of the Equine-Assisted Growth and Learning Association (EAGALA), as well as guidelines of animal-assisted therapy as established by the International Association of Human–Animal Interaction Organizations in the Prague Declaration of 1998, which state that safeguards should be in place to prevent adverse effects on animals involved in animal-assisted programs, and that animals must be properly cared for. (IAHAIO, 1998). This principled treatment is, of course, the premise behind all ethically run animal-assisted programs.

At Transitioning Families, the equine learning approach identifies and acknowledges the horses as having separate identities and characteristics. In all exercises participants are reminded to display the least amount of stress possible when working them. The very definition of stress may be a topic of conversation prior to the session. The client is encouraged to develop attunement skills by focusing on the needs and responses of the horse or horses in front of them, although there is room for the client's projection should it arise. In some cases, a family or client may be coached to interpret more accurately a response of an animal. Families often discover that they cannot argue with a horse, and may feel that feedback from a horse is less judgmental or shaming than other therapeutic techniques (EAGALA, 2009, 2010), helping them to let go of their defenses and welcome this new learning experience. The role of the horse and the team is to serve as educators, therapists, coaches, and to provide immediate feedback; something they do so well. Horses are seen as colleagues and with their help learning is usually remarkably efficient, given the normal short nature of intensive treatment.

Transitioning Families' practitioners are well versed in a variety of equine-assisted approaches (e.g., Linda Kahonov's work related to boundary setting and her work in herd dynamics is regularly included in TFTRM exercises). They may incorporate exercises from other equine-assisted orientations, always returning to the premise that horses are active team members whose moods and behaviors will contribute to the fabric of the session. Exercises have origins in evidence-based psychological interventions and have evolved from clear theoretical underpinnings (as described above).

One of the important differences in equine-assisted sessions at Transitioning Families and other equine-assisted programs is that Transitioning Families sessions are not dissimilar to standard talk therapy. In fact, what has its beginnings in the arena will often be followed by further discussion in the office. The mental health professional is always trained, and licensed as a therapist, with additional training in equine-assisted therapy. This practitioner functions as a therapist and begins the session with a treatment plan in mind based on goals established by the client(s). Much as in talk therapy, that "plan" is always flexible so that no session is agenda driven. The therapists (including horses and other team members) are in attendance as therapeutic tools for use toward the achievement of the goal. At Transitioning Families, the mental health (MH) professional takes an active role in providing clarification and feedback *during* sessions and may provide psychoeducation *during* sessions as well as discussion and processing *after* the session. The MH professional may step in to refocus direction similar to what might happen during a talk therapy session. Like other experiential therapies, there is usually less talking and more doing, but unlike some other programs the MH professional is actively involved, much as he or she would be in other therapeutic practices.

It is widely accepted that therapeutic alliance is the most predictive of positive outcome across a range of psychotherapies (Norcross & Wampold, 2011) and it is incumbent upon the treating practitioner to develop this alliance. Another reason to utilize equine or other animal assisted therapy is that it can be employed in the treatment of populations less willing to engage in traditional office-based treatment, because they help establish this alliance relatively quickly (Transitioning Families, 2013). As always, cultivation of this therapeutic alliance is essential, both between clients, therapists, and other team members.

Ethical Considerations

Ethical principles underlie mental health practice in forensic and other cases (Greenberg & Gould, 2001; Sullivan & Kelly, 2001). Mental health professionals may do more harm than good if they do not adhere to these ethics.

> These principles include establishing competence (including knowledge of relevant research, legal issues and court rules); explaining service models and role boundaries to clients; obtaining informed consent, explaining

the limits of confidentiality, respecting the parties' rights to information and due process; and limiting reports and opinions to one's role and available data. These issues transcend specific service models and can provide a useful frame of reference for assessing the quality of forensic mental health services

(Greenberg et al., 2004, p. 26)

The TFTRM explicitly reports the multiple theories it draws on for the intervention and highlights the fact that the interventions are not "cookie cutter" or "one size fits all." Rather, family member participation and activities are customized to the individual family. This includes any special needs including medical issues, multicultural matters, and other considerations. As in any type of intervention the well-being of all participants must be considered. Individual differences in temperament, including the horses, should be accounted for when choosing an exercise. It is also imperative that individual responses on any given day be taken into consideration. Additionally, family members maybe at different stages of emotional readiness to process the events that have led to treatment. An individual's ability to participate actively should be considered and acknowledged. The overarching goal of the TFTRM is to "assist families in transitioning from crisis, challenge, or conflict to connection and growth" (Judge et al., 2016).

The question of accessibility and affordability of working with equine partners in treatment must be explored. Treatment must be inclusive to be considered viable and effective. The TFTRM has application as a team-based model only, and does not apply to a solo provider in managing treatment; however, organizations such as EAGALA (www.eagala.org), PATH (www.pathintl. org), and Eponaquest (eponaquest.com) provide information regarding available equine-assisted therapy programs. Such programs could be available for referral by the single practitioner on a case-by-case basis.

Most importantly, the proper care and handling of the horses must be examined and re-examined when utilizing the Transitioning Families model. It is the responsibility of all the human staff to ensure the safety and well-being of each horse and human. The horse professional is expected to know the horses and to be aware that there is an impact when using certain horses with certain populations (e.g., one of the Transitioning Families' mares became colicky three times when she was incorporated into a session with a highly anxious client; this mare is no longer utilized when anxiety is a presenting problem). At all times, the participants are encouraged to be aware of the needs of the horses. The horse professional's role is to remind each participant that although a sand arena may appear to be a large sand tray it is not one. (For those unfamiliar with sand tray therapy, it is a form of expressive therapy using a large sand box and figurines that can be manipulated.) The sand tray is, in its own right, an excellent therapeutic intervention; however, in the Transitioning Families model, the horse brings its individuality and active presence into the session.

Other ethical considerations at Transitioning Families are standard to other professional therapeutic settings, and include: The professional must put the needs of the client first; and must remain aware of his or her own needs, personal problems or sources of countertransference. The practitioner must abide by the ethics of his or her professional organization. "Professionals are expected to exercise prudent judgment when it comes to interpreting and applying ethical principles to specific situations" (Corey, 2013, p. 38). The client has the right to informed consent—to be informed about this therapy and "to make autonomous decisions pertaining to it" (Corey, 2013, p. 40).

The client has the right to privacy—confidentiality is an abiding ethic in every caregiving profession. HIPAA Laws exist to protect the client from having information shared without their explicit knowledge or permission and practitioners have the ethical duty to define the degree of confidentiality that can be promised. This establishes the basic trust between client and provider; though there are laws that mandate breaking this confidentiality in certain circumstances such as abuse of a child, elder, or disabled adult. Many of the clients and families that come to TF would be uncomfortable in a large facility. These families do best in a small private facility with little chance of interruption. The safety and security of the sight cannot be underestimated. Initially, a family or client post-trauma may not be comfortable expressing their need for a very private site, but this must be considered in developing a treatment plan for each family.

Consideration must be made for the safety for humans and horses at all times; respect maintained for the horses as therapists, and protection supervised by the horse professional. Horses may become stressed or otherwise affected by an emotional state of a client, and vice versa. The mental health and horse professional must remain attuned to the well-being of both, and be prepared to intervene if necessary.

Guidelines in Consideration of Multicultural Issues and Ethics

The professional must consider the cultural context of the client including clarification of cultural assumptions and differences. Some clients may not feel able to work with horses due to influences from their culture. Though not always considered to be as multicultural, special needs and health issues must always be considered and accommodated.

Case Example

The family participating in the following exercise was faced with the challenge of reconnecting after an extended period of time. The central victim (a young woman), had been abducted and held captive for ten years in a foreign country. The perpetrator (the victim's father) was still at large. The family (without the father) was coming to a six-day intensive treatment at Transitioning Families to re-connect. The young woman had never met her twin sisters prior to this time, as they had been born after she was abducted. The father had told his daughter (the victim) that her mother had remarried and "moved on" and that her mother was pregnant with another man's children. He convinced his daughter that she needed to go with him because she would be neglected by the new man and her mother. In reality, he took his daughter immediately after he had beaten her mother in the face with a tennis racket, as part of a pattern of violent abuse.

In fact, the victim's mother spent years looking for her daughter and had not remarried. Pictures of the twins posted on the mother's Facebook convinced the daughter that her father's version of the story was correct, but repeated and more accurate postings on the same site were compelling. It took the 17-year-old two years to finally act and reach out to her mother via social media. Once they connected she was rapidly recovered and they were reunited.

The reunion did not go smoothly. One of the sisters was frustrated by the disruption of her life and was jealous of her "new" sibling. The other twin appeared indifferent. The central victim was having difficulty acknowledging and accepting the grief of missing her father, despite his actions. In addition, she had been taught to fear her mother by her father and was clearly uncomfortable in her mother's presence. The mother, on the other hand, was struggling with her own feelings of rejection by her daughter and with the fear that she might disappear again.

The family came to Transitioning Families for reunification treatment, and in later sessions participated in specific treatment for symptoms of anxiety. Incorporating individualized interventions into family based treatment is an important component of TFTRM equine work.

The Exercise Used for This Family: Loss and Attunement

The family (described above) was attending a Transitioning Families Intensive Reunification Workshop. They had been staying in a "safe house" locally for the previous few days. The family spent the first two sessions of equine-assisted therapy getting to know five different horses; the first session was spent observing the herd in the paddock, followed by a session a focused on mindful grooming. The first two sessions were conducted on the same day as the following exercise, with a family lunch in between. The focus of this third session was connection and attunement.

Materials Needed

This exercise involved:

- two mental health professionals and one horse professional;
- dry erase board and markers;
- materials to be used for creating obstacles (e.g., foam "noodles," fence poles, blanket, jump standards).

With the assistance of the facilitators, the family made a list of "needs" that the family believe will help move them forward toward reconnection. The family was invited to go into the arena and build obstacles using the available materials, each obstacle representing a need from the board. (The facilitators do not participate in the building process other than to observe.) The family then told the facilitators what need each obstacle represents. The family selected the horse they wanted to work with for this exercise. (Mental health facilitators are encouraged to support and facilitate conversation related to the process of selection.) The family members and facilitators stand outside of the arena. In this case, the family selected the mother, as primary caregiver and head of the family, to bring the horse with her through, over, or around the various obstacles. The horse is led in to the arena and is turned loose by a facilitator, who then leaves the arena. The mother enters the arena. This part of the exercise begins.

Description

1. The mother approached the horse, who nuzzled her and remained still.
2. The mother attempted to move the horse toward first obstacle.
3. The horse remained friendly but disinterested in following.
4. The mother tried speaking softly, clucking, tapping her own thigh, clapping hands but at all times was noted to be turning away to "get" the horse to follow. Eventually she leaned on the fence in front of the horse, spoke in hushed tones, and reached up to scratch (pat) the horse on the forehead. She asked the facilitators: "I don't know what to do now." The MH facilitator responded by asking what she was trying to do. She responded "I want him to follow me," after which she asked the horse, "I want you to follow me" and then beckoned it to come. The horse did so and walked just behind her for a few steps. The mother strode confidently toward the first object which had been named "trust."
5. As the mother walked toward the first object, the horse lay down behind her; however, she did not notice and kept walking forward. The MH facilitator asked the mother to stop and then asked, "What's happening right now?" The mother noticed that the horse was on the ground behind her. Mother laughed a little and the MH facilitator again asked, "What are you trying to do right now?" The mother stated: "to get to trust, but not all by myself!"
6. At the second obstacle, the horse veered off to the right. The mother stated: "Well, I guess that's close enough!" The MH professional responded by redirecting the client back to the exercise and asked: "What are you trying to do right now?" The mother stated that she was working to get to trust: "I don't think close enough is good enough!"
7. The exercise continued with occasional prompts, redirection, and encouragement from the MH professional.

Discussion

In the Transitioning Families Model of Equine Therapy, every moment provides an opportunity. Success is in the process rather than the achievement of tasks. The horse facilitator observes the behavior of the horse and may intervene if the session becomes too difficult for the horse. The MH facilitator will intervene or comment as described above, much as does a therapist in standard talk therapy. The exercise is ended by time limitations, if any of the participants becomes unable to continue for emotional or physical reasons, or if the facilitators decide it is necessary or beneficial to end it. It is not necessary to complete every task within an exercise—the benefit comes through the process.

The session ends with a discussion. This might begin with a recap, first by the client, of what happened, and then the inclusion of observations by other family members and the facilitators followed by discussion. Criticism is avoided. The point is to engender insight, revelation, better communication, and understanding in the service of re-connection and of the goals set by the family. Given that the session might take some time, the other family members might be scheduled for an additional session later that day, or another. The family may engage in a different exercise specific to individual needs, so that they might experience and benefit from work with equine therapy.

References

American Veterinary Medical Association (AVMA). (1998). The IAHAIO Prague Declaration. Retrieved July 17, 2017, from: www.avma.org/KB/Policies/Pages/The-IAHAIO- Prague-Declaration.aspx.

Cloitre, M., Courtois, C., Charuvastra, A., Carapezza, R., Stolbach, B., & Green, B. (2011, December). Treatment of Complex PTSD: Results of the ISTSS Expert Clinician Survey on Best Practices. *Journal of Traumatic Stress*, 24(6), 615–627.

Connecticut Department of Children and Families. (2016, October). Functional Family Therapy (FFT)/A trauma informed treatment. Retrieved January 9, 2017, from www.ct.gov: www.ct.gov/dcf/lib/dcf/trauma-informed_care/pdf/fft_phases_and_trauma1_pager__2_.pdf.

Corey, G. (2013). *Theory and Practice of Counseling and Psychotherapy* (9th ed.). Belmont, CA: Brooks/Cole.

EAGALA (2009–2010). How it Works. Retrieved March 28, 2017, from: http://home.eagala.org/works.

Figley, C. (2009). Stemming the Tide of Trauma Systemically: The Role of Family Therapy. *The Australian and New Zealand Journal of Family Therapy*, 30(3), 173–183.

Gaskill, R. L., & Perry, B. D. (2014). The Neurobiological Power of Play Using the Neurosequential Model of Therapeutics to Guide Play in the Healing Process. Retrieved December 5, 2016, from: https://childtrauma.org/wp-content/uploads/2014/12/Malchiodi_Perry_Gaskill.pdf.

Gil, E., & Sobol, B. (2005). Engaging families in therapeutic play. In C. E. Bailey (Ed.), *Children in Therapy: Using the Family as a Resource*. New York: W.W. Norton & Co.

Goldenberg, H., & Goldenberg, I. (2013). *Family Therapy: An Overview.* Belmont, CA: Brooks/Cole.

Greenberg, L. R., Martindale, D. A., Gould, J. W., & Gould-Saltman, D. J. (2004). Ethical Issues in Child Custody and Dependency Cases: Enduring Principles and Emerging Challenges. *Journal of Child Custody,* 1(1), 7–30.

Greenberg, L., & Gould, J. (2001). The Treating Expert: A Hybrid Role with Firm Boundaries. *Professional Psychology: Research and Practice,* 32(5), 469–478.

Hatcher, C., Behrman-Lippert, J., Barton, C., & Brooks, L. (1992). *Reunification of Missing Children Project.* Final, US Department of Justice, Office of Juvenile Justice and Delinquency Prevention, Washington, DC.

Hosier, D. (2016, July 14). Effect of Childhood Trauma on the Limbic System. Retrieved January 8, 2017, from: http://childhoodtraumarecovery.com/2016/07/14/effect-of-childhood-trauma-on-the-limbic-system/.

IAHAIO (1998). The Prague Declaration. Retrieved June 20, 2017, from: www.avma.org/KB/Policies/Pages/The-IAHAIO-Prague-Declaration.aspx.

James, K., & McKinnon, L. (2012, September). Integrating a Trauma Lens into a Family Therapy Framework: Ten Principles for Family Therapists. *Australian and New Zealand Journal of Family Therapy,* 33(3), 189–209.

Johnston, J. R., Roseby, V., & Kuehnle, K. (2009). *In the Name of the Child: A Developmental Approach to Understanding and Helping Children of Conflicted and Violent Divorce.* New York: Springer Publishing.

Judge, A. M., & Deutsch, R. M. (2016). *Overcoming Parent–Child Contact Problems.* New York: Oxford University Press.

Judge, A., Bailey, R., Behrman-Lippert, J., Bailey, E., Psaila, C., & Dickel, J. (2016, April). The Therapeutic Reunification Model in Nonfamilial Abductions. *Family Court Review: An Interdisciplinary Journal,* 54(2), 232–249.

Kinniburgh, K. J., Blaustein, M., & Spinazzola, J. (2005, May). Attachment, Self-Regulation, and Competency: A Comprehensive Intervention Framework for Children with Complex Trauma. *Psychiatric Annals,* 35(5), 424–430.

Klontz, B., Bivens, A., Leinart, D., & Klontz, T. (2007). The Effectiveness of Equine-Assisted Experiential Therapy: Results of an Open Clinical Trial. *Sociey and Animals,* 15, 257–267.

Kraaij, V., Garnefski, N., Wilde, E. J., Dijkstra, A., Gebhardt, W., Maes, S., & Doest, L. T. (2003, June). Negative Life Events and Depressive Symptoms in Late Adolescence: Bonding and Cognitive Coping as Vulnerability Factors? *Journal of Youth and Adolescence,* 32(3), 185–193.

Lebow, J., & Gurman, A. (1995). Research Assessing Couple and Family Therapy. *Annual of Psychology,* 46, 27–57.

Mahrer, A. (1983). *Experiential Psychotherapy: Basic Practices.* Ottawa, ON: Ottawa University Press.

Norcross, J., & Wampold, B. (2011, February 1). What Works for Whom: Tailoring Psychotherapy to the Person. *Journal of Clinical Psychology,* 67(2), 127–132.

Nurenberg, J., Scleifer, S., & Shaffer, T. (2015). Animal-Assisted Therapy with Chronic Psychiatric Inpatients: Equine-Assisted Psychotherapy and Aggressive Behavior. *Psychiatric Services,* 66(1), 80–86.

Oliva, A., Jimenez, J. M., & Parra, A. (2007, March). Protective Effect of Supportive Family Relationships and the Influence of Stressful Life Events on Adolescent Adjustment. *Anxiety, Stress and Coping,* 22(2), 137–152.

Polak, S., & Moran, J. (2017). The Current Status of Outpatient Approaches to Parent–Child Contact Problems. In A. J. Deutsch (Ed.), *Overcoming Parent–Child Contact Problems: Family-Based Interventions for Resistance, Rejection and Alienation*. New York: Oxford University Press.

Sauber, S. (2013). Reunification Planning and Therapy. In D. Lorandos, W. W. Bernet, & S. Sauber (Eds.), *Parental Alienation: The Handbook for Mental Health and Legal Professionals* (pp. 190–231). Springfield, IL: Charles C Thomas.

Sayers, S. L. (2010, March). Family Reintegration Difficulties and Couples Therapy for Military Veterans and Their Spouses. *Cognitive and Behavioral Practice*, 18, 108–119.

Shedler, J. (2010, February–March). The Efficacy of Psychodynamic Psychotherarapy. *American Psychologist*, 65(2), 98–109.

Sullivan, M., & Kelly, J. (2001). Legal and Psychological Management of Cases with an Alienated Child. *Family Court Journal*, 39(3), 299–315.

Terr, L. C. (2003, Summer). Childhood Traumas: An Outline and Overview. *FOCUS The Journal of Lifelong Learning in Psychiatry*, 1(3), 322–324.

Thompson, S. J., Bender, K., Cardoso, J. B., & Flynn, P. M. (2011, October). Experiential Activities in Family Therapy: Perceptions of Caregivers and Youth. *Journal of Child and Family Studies*, 20, 560–568.

Transitioning Families (2011–2017). Reunification Brief and Extended. Retrieved March 15, 2017, from: http://transitioningfamilies.com/Program/reunification-brief-and-extended/.

Winnicott, D. (1965). *The Maturational Processes and the Facilitating Environment*. London: Hogarth Press.

10 Natural Lifemanship's Trauma-Focused Equine-Assisted Psychotherapy (EAP)

Equine-Connected Eye-Movement Desensitization and Reprocessing (EC-EMDR)

Bettina Shultz-Jobe, Kathleen Choe, and Tim Jobe

Introduction

Description of the Problem

The prevalence of trauma in today's world cannot be overstated. Whether on a personal level or a collective one, most people have experienced one or more crises in their lifetime. Incidents such as sexual assault, abuse of any kind, unexpected loss, serious injury or illness, or on a more global level, terrorism and natural disasters, may be acute, singular events, or chronic, longer-lasting episodes. For our purposes, we will define trauma as any situation in which survival is the overriding concern, and therefore the brain must make changes to accommodate that need for survival (Jobe et al., 2016).

According to the U.S. Department of Veterans Affairs' National Center for Post Traumatic Stress Disorder (PTSD), 10% of women and 4% of men will develop PTSD following a shocking or life-threatening event (National Center for PTSD, 2016). PTSD is characterized by intrusive thoughts or memories, nightmares, flashbacks, psychological and physical reactivity to triggers, avoiding thoughts, feelings, people, and/or situations connected to the traumatic event, increased arousal symptoms including hyper-vigilance, insomnia, and irritability, and negative alterations in mood or cognition including issues with memory, flat or detached affect, negative thoughts or beliefs about self, and reduced interest in pre-trauma activities. Dissociative symptoms like depersonalization and derealization may also occur (American Psychiatric Association, [APA, 2013]). All of these symptoms combine to interfere with a person's ability to function in activities of daily living including those related to the work environment and inter-personal relationships.

Theoretical Approach

Equine-connected eye-movement desensitization and reprocessing (EC-EMDR), a specialization within the broader Natural Lifemanship treatment model of trauma-focused equine-assisted psychotherapy (TF-EAP), can effectively address both the psychological and physiological effects of PTSD.

In 1987, Dr. Francine Shapiro discovered that eye movements appear to reduce the intensity of disturbing thoughts under certain conditions. She continued to study this phenomenon, and in 1989 published an article documenting the successful treatment of trauma victims using EMDR in the *Journal of Traumatic Stress* (Shapiro, 1989). Since then, therapists and researchers all over the world have developed a set of standardized protocols used to treat everything from PTSD and other psychological disorders to migraines and chronic pain. EMDR can be thought of as a physiologically based therapy that helps a person see disturbing material in a new and less distressing way (Eye Movement Desensitization and Reprocessing International Association [EMDRIA], 2017).

EC-EMDR combines the tenets of traditional EMDR with TF-EAP by adding the grounding, regulating, and integrating component of the relationship between the client and the horse to the standard protocol. Research by leaders in the field of neuroscience such as Dr. Bruce Perry increasingly confirms that healthy relationships constitute the essential vehicle for change for those affected by trauma (Perry, 2013). While mounted, an equine partner literally carries the client and the burden of his or her pain while providing dual attention stimulus *and* relational connection, which adds support and safety to the processing of disturbing material. The movement of the horse provides passive, or bottom-up regulation from the lower regions of the brain where implicit memory is stored to the upper regions of the brain where explicit memory is held, promoting the integration of neural networks compromised by trauma (Shultz-Jobe et al., 2017).

Not only does the relational connection between the client and horse add a component of emotional safety to processing potentially disturbing material, but the quality of the dual attention stimulus (DAS) is greatly enhanced by the rich multi-sensory input involving the client's whole body. On horseback, the client's rhythmic and repetitive sensory experience includes feeling the horse's fur and movement, hearing hoof beats on the ground, watching the horse's ears flick back and forth and his head bob up and down, as well as other sensory input provided by the environment such as the breeze, sunshine, birds singing, and so on. The continuous bilateral, patterned, rhythmic movement of the horse provides DAS in much longer sets than are typically used in the office to allow for grounding and ongoing processing without abreaction. The client is both physically and emotionally connected to the horse throughout the processing.

Rationale for EAP

At the core of trauma is a disconnect between one's internal state and the surrounding environment. A traumatized individual is literally "frozen" in an emotional state of alarm or terror despite the fact that the trauma is no longer occurring and the immediate environment may be relatively safe. Horses have a unique ability to address the somatic experience or "body script" (Levine & Frederick, 1997) of a trauma client. As prey animals, in their natural habitat horses are actively concerned with safety and survival much of the time. Like victims of trauma, the lower regions of horses' brains are engaged, attending to environmental cues to determine whether they need to fight or flee, or can be at rest. When an individual's insides do not match their outsides, i.e., there is inner turmoil in the form of emotional dysregulation but a relatively calm external presentation, horses are alarmed by this incongruence. Horses will respond to the internal emotional state of the person rather than the physical exterior. They read body energy, a skill that allows them to distinguish between a lion stalking and a sheep grazing near the herd. The lion may be crouching low to the ground and moving slowly so as to appear less like a threat, but has a high, predatory internal energy, poised to chase and spring. A sheep, on the other hand, will similarly be low to the ground and moving slowly, but has low, calm body energy. The horse can distinguish between the similar external presentation of a predator and fellow prey animal through this awareness of internal states. Horses are not necessarily alarmed by a person who is anxious or upset unless that emotional state is unconsciously or consciously being suppressed—this feels unsafe and possibly threatening to the horse's survival. The horse's keen attunement to nonverbal signals is helpful in identifying any emotional disconnect in the trauma victim (Jobe et al., 2016).

Ethical Issues in Animal-Assisted Therapy Programs

Horses are sentient beings, i.e., they possess the ability to feel, perceive, and exhibit consciousness (Proctor, 2012). In EC-EMDR we view the horse as a therapy partner rather than as a robotic rocking chair or other object that provides DAS (like mechanized tappers or bilateral headphones). The horse's welfare is continually considered; and the principles of healthy relationship, including the principle "If it's not good for both, it is eventually not good for either" (Jobe et al., 2016), are applied to every interaction between the horse and human. When doing mounted work, we must consider the ability of the horse to dissociate from pain, a valuable skill for a prey animal when any physical impairment threatens the ability to escape from predators. When the horse is allowed to make choices in a relationship and develops connections from the lower regions of the brain to the neocortex, lameness or other injuries may suddenly become apparent as the horse no longer dissociates from them. Caring well for the needs of the horse is essential to effective EC-EMDR. Many trauma victims have been objectified or have had their pain ignored or dismissed. Attending to the horse's well-being affirms their value as a relationship partner in the therapy and models a similar valuing of and for the client. We believe that healing at the expense of another is not true healing. As such, we understand that animal welfare issues are also clinical issues.

Description of Technique

Goals and Objectives of the Connected Calm Space Technique

The goal of the Connected Calm Space technique in EC-EMDR is to help clients connect to their body in a regulated manner without dissociating or abreacting. Such resourcing helps clients manage what is happening inside of their body regardless of the environment so that they can learn to "control the chaos inside regardless of what is going on outside" (Jobe et al., 2016). When triggered, clients exercise the ability they have developed to access a calm internal space to ground and regulate. Developing this resource is typically part of phase 2, the preparation phase of EMDR, but can stand alone and be taught as a grounding skill by a non-EMDR trained therapist as part of rhythmic riding (Williams & Choe, 2017).

Materials Needed

Helmet, bareback pad, halter, lead rope.

Step-by-Step Description

Note: Prior to implementing the Connected Calm Space protocol, the client has done relationship logic work on the ground to build relational connection with the horse and rhythmic riding to promote emotional regulation and cross-brain integration (see Chapter 4 in this book on reactive attachment disorder).

The horse is at liberty, untacked, at the beginning of the session. Depending on how much relationship work the client has done with this particular horse, the client or equine professional (EP) requests connection with the horse prior to putting on the halter and bareback pad and leading the horse to the round pen or arena where the session will take place. The EP always asks for connection and the client is encouraged to do so also. It is through attunement and connection that the client and therapy team know when the horse gives nonverbal consent to participate in the EC-EMDR session in a connected manner.

Clients are asked how they would like to get on their horse's back. Depending upon the policy of the facility, typically a mounting block, or a "leg up" are options for mounting. Before mounting, clients are prompted to take three deep, cleansing breaths with the therapy team.

After mounting the horse, the client is asked to take three more deep, cleansing breaths, with the therapy team participating. Note is taken of whether the horse appears to be releasing any tension which may be an indicator of the horse's or client's level of anxiety or discomfort. The therapist asks if the client is ready to begin walking. The client may give verbal and/or nonverbal consent when ready. For example, the client may say, "Yes, I am ready," while gently squeezing with the legs. The EP begins to lead the horse with the therapist walking beside (the therapist offers to put an arm across the client's leg if touch is appropriate and necessary for stabilization). The client is asked to notice the movement of the horse and allow the horse to move the client's body to promote a sense of external connection through physical touch and rhythm. The therapist begins to direct the client's attention to a more internalized sense of connection through a series of questions designed to access a "felt sense" of attachment (Winhall, 2014).

The EP attunes to the horse's experience; if the horse seems to dissociate or disconnect from the client and seek connection elsewhere, such as whinnying to horses outside of the round pen, nudging the therapist or EP, or displaying submissive or aggressive behaviors, the EP brings this to the attention of the therapist who gently re-directs the client to re-establish the connection. The EP may have to maintain some connection with the horse if the client is too dysregulated or dissociative to offer connection to the horse. The EP is responsible for the horse's welfare and emotional as well as physical safety, and must have knowledge of behaviors in horses that signal distress or connection seeking.

The therapist checks in with the client's emotional state to determine how comfortable the client is feeling on the back of the horse. To help the client stabilize, the therapist may suggest some mindfulness and grounding activities such as listening to the horse's hoof beats, watching the horse's head bobbing up and down or the ears flicking back and forth, feeling the horse's fur with her hands, or asking the client to choose a sensory input to notice and ground with (the feel of the breeze on the client's skin, for example). If the client is reporting a great deal of tension or appears stiff and frozen on the horse's back, the therapist may initiate a body scan. The therapist asks the client to notice where the client's body is physically connecting with the horse's body, and what kind of movement is occurring in the client's body as a result. Often the client will observe a back and forth as well as side-to-side type of movement. When the horse walks, he creates six distinct movements simultaneously. The therapist may ask the client to notice further body movements such as the ways in which the horse is moving hips or legs or torso. Starting with the hips, the therapist will direct the client to allow the body to move freely with the horse, noticing any places where tension or stiffness block this natural swing. The therapist must be aware of the language used in bringing awareness to various parts of the body, such as the pelvic area, that may be triggering especially for victims of sexual trauma.

When the client is able to allow the horse to move his or her body freely and feels some sense of connection with the horse, the therapist asks the client to picture a space, whether real or imaginary, that feels relaxed and calm. Unless the client is deeply dissociative, the client may wish to close both eyes during this process. The therapist asks the client to describe this space using the five senses in terms of what can be seen, heard, smelled, touched, or tasted? The therapist asks the client what positive emotions are experienced when picturing this space. The therapist then asks where those positive emotions are being felt in the body.

The EP has been paying attention to the horse's need for connection and notes if the client has lost some or all of the connection with the horse while describing her Connected Calm Space. If so, the EP brings this to the attention of the therapist, who gently re-directs the client's attention to the horse and helps the client re-establish the lost connection, moving from an external to an internal sense of connected attachment. This dual connection, the ability of the client to connect to the internal experience and concurrently with the therapy partner who is rocking and carrying her, is imperative when brain integration is the goal and is, therefore, central to the process of EC-EMDR.

After connection between the client and horse is re-established, the therapist continues to help the client develop the resource of the Connected Calm Space in a manner that maintains the DAS (awareness of the horse as well as awareness of the image). The client is continually re-directed to notice the relational connection with the horse and to re-connect if this is lost. The rhythmic movement of the horse along with the relational affiliation between the horse and the client enhances the power of the Connected Calm Space as a resource for grounding and emotional regulation.

Cross-brain connections are compromised with trauma. Developing the Connected Calm Space resource on the back of the horse promotes re-wiring of the neural pathways from the brainstem up through the diencephalon (producing the movement of the client's body with the horse's body) to the limbic system (where emotional affiliation and relational engagement is occurring) up to the neocortex (where the cognitive and verbal descriptions of the resource are happening). When the client is able to experience the positive, grounding sensations provided by imagining the Connected Calm Space while simultaneously maintaining a connection with the horse, the resource has been fully implemented.

The client is asked to initiate asking the horse to stop moving by thinking, "I would like you to slow down and stop now," and sitting back deeply into the horse while releasing a deep breath. If the client and horse are truly connected the horse will attune to this shift in energy and come to a stop. If the connection is not strong or has been lost and there is time in the session to repair it, the therapist will direct the client back to re-connecting with the horse. If time has run out in the session or the client is too dysregulated to re-connect, the EP may have to help bring the horse to a stop.

The client is asked to take three deep, cleansing breaths with the therapy team participating. The client might like to end the session by sitting backwards on the horse and resting her head and chest on the horse's rump for several minutes. This promotes emotional containment and ends the session in a regulated and connected manner by compressing the client's vagus nerve (which stimulates the parasympathetic nervous system), promoting relaxation as well as connection with the horse (Broersma, 2014). The client returns to a forward-facing position before dismounting. The client is asked to lean forward and "give the horse's neck a hug" before bringing the right leg over the horse's back and sliding off with support from the EP and/or therapist if needed. Saying thank you and goodbye to the horse on the ground reaffirms the client's connection to the horse as the session comes to a close.

Guidelines in Consideration of Multicultural Issues and Ethics

Cultures vary across a range of variables, which must be taken into consideration when working with humans and horses. These variables may include views on what constitutes strength and weakness for each gender (i.e., a culture that values *machismo* may view fear or sadness as a weakness undesirable for men to feel or display), values around touch and physical boundaries, personal space and showing vulnerability. Likewise, some cultures or socioeconomic groups within cultures view animals as sources of labor or income and may be confused by the idea of partnership or building relationship with a horse. The therapist and EP must be aware of their own personal biases and beliefs about ethnicity and race that may influence how they interact with clients from backgrounds different from their own. Listening to understand and avoiding stereotyping or making assumptions is vital to building bridges between cultures. Ethically, understanding the behaviors horses display when distressed or dysregulated and attending to the physical, emotional, and psychological needs of the horse are essential both for the horse's welfare as well as for modeling the importance of partnership and relationship for the client.

Case Example and Sample Case Transcript Brief Description of Client and Case History

Rachel (pseudonym) is a single female veteran in her fifties who is currently on disability benefit and unable to work due to the severity of her PTSD. She joined the military to escape from her abusive uncle, who lived with the family and began to sexually abuse her from the age of three. She became pregnant by him in adolescence and had an abortion. She was gang raped during deployment and began to exhibit symptoms of PTSD shortly after being discharged from the service. Her symptoms included flashbacks, nightmares, insomnia, withdrawal, and isolation from others, depressive episodes, anxiety, hypervigilance and periods of dissociation. Rachel struggled with activities of daily living, and was particularly prone to flashbacks in stores where someone might come into an aisle where she was shopping and startle her. She used alcohol to medicate her anxiety, resulting in further unwanted sexual encounters while inebriated. A keen animal lover, her only sense of safe connection was with her dogs, so she was very open to the idea of equine therapy.

Transcript Analysis of Case Example

The following transcript analysis is about a pseudonym client:

Table 10.1 Case Example Transcript

Transcript	Analysis
Counselor: Before we begin our mounted work, take a few moments to ask for some connection on the ground.	Client has spent several sessions building a connected, attuned relationship with her horse, Moseby, on the ground prior to beginning mounted work. This connection is a vital part of the safety and support system for the client as she prepares to set up a resource called Connected Calm Space prior to beginning trauma processing using EC-EMDR.
Counselor: How would you like to get on your horse, Moseby?	Depending on the facility, the client typically has some options for mounting such as using a mounting block or receiving a "leg up" from the therapist or equine professional. Having choices is empowering for the client and her ability to make a decision shows that she has some access to her neocortex.
Counselor: Before mounting Moseby, let's take three deep, cleansing breaths, together.	Deep, conscious breathing establishes a connection between the client's neocortex and brainstem while activating her parasympathetic nervous system, thus lowering her body energy and promoting an increased sense of calm relaxation. Breathing together facilitates connection and co-regulation between all members of the team—the client, the therapist and EP, and the horse. The breathing exercises are important both before the client mounts and once mounted, as these intervals often are associated with a sudden increase in the client's stress response. A dysregulated client mounting the horse can be distressing to the horse and makes a connection between client and horse more difficult.
Counselor: Now that you are mounted, let's take three more deep breaths, together. When you are ready, I would like you to ask Moseby to move forward using the least amount of pressure. This begins with the thought that you would like to go, which brings your body energy up. If Moseby doesn't take a step forward, give him a gentle squeeze with your legs. Are you ready to move forward?	Asking the client to initiate Moseby's movement allows her to take ownership of her emotional and physical safety while also creating and maintaining a dual connection between the client and her horse. Moseby's movement will provide passive regulation for the client's brainstem, and her use of body energy and legs to ask for his movement engages her diencephalon, so that the lower regions of her brain receive sensory input, which helps to organize and integrate her neural networks.

(continued)

Table 10.1 Case Example Transcript (Cont.)

Transcript	Analysis
Client: Yes, I am ready.	The client's ability to answer the question confirms for the therapist that she has some access to her neocortex and is able to process the verbal communication appropriately.
Equine Professional: Moseby has planted his hooves and seems to be ignoring your requests to move forward.	The equine professional is observing that the connection between the client and Moseby is not strong enough for her to initiate his movement forward. The equine professional may have to hold some connection with Moseby on the ground so that he can ask for Moseby to move forward. Moseby's well-being depends upon being offered safe connection, so if the client is unable to offer it, the equine professional takes that role in whole or part as needed. It is important for Moseby to begin moving so that client will benefit from the passive regulation his bilateral, repetitive, rhythmic movement provides for the lower regions of her brain.
Counselor: I am going to have the equine professional help you ask Moseby to start moving forward by sharing the connection until you can take it over.	The equine professional and client are going to share some connection with Moseby until the client is able to maintain a stronger connection with him.
Counselor: Now that you are going forward, notice the way Moseby is moving your body. Where do you feel the physical connection between your body and his?	The client often needs to experience the external, physical points of connection between herself and the horse before being able to move towards a more internal, emotional experience of it.
Client: I can feel Moseby moving underneath my seat and legs in a rocking motion, back and forth, as well as side to side.	The client's ability to describe her experience of Moseby moving beneath her shows linkages between the sensing and thinking parts of her brain, which promotes cross brain connection and integration.
Counselor: What is it like for you to feel Moseby rocking your body in this way?	The counselor is prompting the client to shift her attention from the physical, external points of connection to a more internal, relational one by asking her to observe and describe her experience.
Client: It is comforting. He feels strong and solid underneath me.	The client is able to identify some positive feelings towards Moseby for his role in the therapy process. This shows that her limbic system and neocortex are engaged and she is capable of forming some level of connection with her horse.

Table 10.1 Case Example Transcript (Cont.)

Transcript	Analysis
Equine Professional: Moseby seems reluctant to keep walking forward. His head is high and his jaw his tight.	The equine professional notices that Moseby is becoming resistant to continuing to move forward and is displaying some tension. When the client was asked to describe her experience of being carried by Moseby, she may have lost her connection with him. It is common that when the client begins to focus more deeply on her internal experience, she loses connection with her horse—simultaneous connection to self and other is a challenge.
Counselor: Notice Moseby's ears flicking back and forth and his head bobbing up and down as he walks. Put your hands on his withers and feel the softness of his fur. Listen to his hoof beats as they strike the ground.	The counselor is helping the client re-connect with Moseby using sensory input by activating her senses of vision, touch, and hearing.
Equine Professional: Moseby is lowering his head and licking and chewing. He seems to be relaxing and moving forward more freely.	Moseby is starting to re-connect with the client and relaxing as she re-focuses on him through her different senses.
Client: He seems so attuned to what I am feeling. I am worried that this is too much for him.	Clients often worry that they will overwhelm their horse with their anxiety and emotional pain. This concern is an important part of being a caring partner in the relationship. They need reassurance that the horse's welfare is being considered in the therapy process.
Counselor: What are some ways Moseby is letting us know how he is feeling about participating in the session?	The counselor encourages the client to use her powers of observation and be attuned to her relationship with Moseby so she can learn to read his signals and strengthen her connection with him.
Client: He can slow down or stop. He tenses his muscles to let us know when he is anxious. I am grateful that he is willing to carry me and my pain even if it is hard for him.	The client demonstrates that she is attuned to Moseby's body language and can read his signals. Feeling gratitude to him is a sign that her limbic system is re-engaged and she can pick up more of the connection.
Counselor: Where do you feel that gratitude in your body?	The counselor seeks to make the feeling more concrete by noticing the body sensations that accompany it.

(continued)

Table 10.1 Case Example Transcript (Cont.)

Transcript	Analysis
Client: I feel a warmth starting in my core and spreading through my whole body.	The client is able to describe the body sensation of her feeling of gratitude which promotes more neuronal connections between the sensing (brainstem and diencephalon), feeling (limbic system), and thinking (neocortex) regions of her brain, which helps her to connect more deeply with Moseby.
Counselor: Does that warmth have a color or a shape?	Through a series of intentional questions, the counselor helps the client begin to increase the power of her resource by expanding and anchoring it in her body.
Client: It is a soft lavender that is diffuse.	The client refines her description of the sensations she is experiencing by adding more details.
Counselor: Allow Moseby to move that lavender warmth into your core and gently allow it to spread to other areas of your body. Is that possible?	The counselor continues to encourage the client to allow her felt experience to grow. Staying connected with the sensations she is experiencing in her body while also staying connected to her horse simultaneously activates functionally distinct areas of the brain in an organized fashion, facilitating pathways for self-regulation and cross-brain integration.
Client: Yes. It feels so good to allow Moseby to move the lavender. My core feels so relaxed and I feel it slowly spreading to my chest. I feel so connected to him right now.	As the client focuses on her body sensations and the positive feelings accompanying them she is experiencing increasing connection with Moseby through linkages and integration between all of the regions of her brain.
Counselor: How would you like to express your gratitude to Moseby as we keep walking?	The counselor seeks to further expand and enhance both the neural integration and connection between the client and Moseby.
Client: I would like to pet his neck.	The client is able to access her neocortex to answer the question and engage her diencephalon to use her hands to pet Moseby's neck.
Equine Professional: Moseby is lowering his head and walking more rhythmically. He seems to be more relaxed since you started expressing your gratitude to him.	The equine professional observes Moseby's relaxation response and reports this to the client so she can see the positive effect of her stronger connection to him as well.
Counselor: While you are petting Moseby's neck and connected to the warm color of lavender in your core and chest, I would like to start setting up the resource we talked about: your calm, connected space. I would like you to picture a real or imaginary space where you feel relaxed and calm.	This is the first step in preparing the calm, connected space resource. This resource can stand alone to help clients regulate their emotions or can be used as part of the set-up for trauma processing by EMDR trained therapists (Williams & Choe, 2017).

Table 10.1 Case Example Transcript (Cont.)

Transcript	Analysis
Client: I am imagining that I am in the mountains.	The client is beginning to set up a resource she can access when she needs to regulate her emotions and come back into the present moment.
Counselor: Use your five senses to describe this space: what do you see, hear, smell, touch, and taste?	Adding sensory details enhances the client's experience of this resource. It also engages the lower sensing regions of the brain that are most affected by trauma.
Client: I can see lots of trees, and a stream, and hear the wind moving through the branches and the water bubbling along. I am sitting on a log near the stream and can feel the rough bark with my fingers. The breeze tastes fresh and brings the smell of the forest with it.	The client continues to add rich sensory details to her calm, connected space to strengthen her experience of it.
Equine Professional: Moseby is nudging me and displaying tension in his jaw.	As the client becomes absorbed in her description, she begins to lose her connection to Moseby. As the horse loses dual connection with his rider, he begins seeking connection with the equine professional instead.
Counselor: Moseby is telling us that he lost some connection with you. Can you feel that?	The counselor checks in with the client to see if she notices the loss of connection. As the client accesses her neocortex to describe her calm, connected space, she loses access to her limbic system. As she connects more deeply to herself, it becomes more difficult to maintain connection with her horse.
Client: Yes, I was thinking about my Calm Space and got distracted!	Client confirms that she notices the loss of connection with Moseby.
Counselor: Oh goodness, of course you did! It definitely takes practice to deeply connect to your experience and stay connected with Moseby as he carries you. I notice that you have stopped stroking Moseby's neck; maybe you can better maintain connection if you put your hands back on his withers and see if you can feel them move while you stroke his fur and watch his head bob up and down. Listen to his hoof beats as they strike the ground. Could you reconnect to that feeling of warmth and color of lavender in your core and chest?	The counselor normalizes the client's experience and helps her re-connect with Moseby by directing her attention to the sensory input of touch, movement, and vision to engage all of the regions of her brain, promoting linkage and integration between the sensing, feeling, and thinking neural networks.

(continued)

Table 10.1 Case Example Transcript (Cont.)

Transcript	Analysis
Client: Yes I can. Really, I hardly ever feel this calm.	Although the client briefly lost some connection with Moseby, she can quickly focus on re-connecting with him due to the regulation and neural integration she has already experienced in the session due to the continuous movement of the horse.
Equine Professional: "Moseby is yawning and stretching his neck. He is regulating himself by releasing tension. That's a good cue for all of us to do the same. Maybe we should all take a deep breath and then release it with a sigh.	The equine professional observes and reports that Moseby is responding to the client's attempts to focus on re-connecting with her horse. The equine professional also encourages the entire team to release tension. This encourages co-regulation for all involved.
Client: I am glad he knows how to do that and that he reminds me to keep breathing. I am so thankful that he is willing to carry and hold me even though I keep losing my connection with him.	The client goes back to expressing her gratitude to Moseby for his participation in her therapy, which illustrates that she has access to her limbic system and neocortex again.
Counselor: While maintaining that connection with Moseby and the connection to the warm lavender in your body, let's go back to your mountain scene. What positive emotions do you experience when you picture this space?	Adding the emotional component to this resource continues to build its power and promotes neural integration by involving the limbic region of the brain.
Client: I feel contentment and peace when I picture myself there. I feel the same way when I think of Moseby. I would like to ride him by the stream.	Clients often invite their horse into their calm, connected space, which strengthens both their dual connection as well as the value of the resource.
Counselor: Notice that Moseby has joined you in your calm, connected space. What is it like having Moseby there with you?	Focusing on the client's relationship with her horse is a vital part of maintaining dual connection, providing valuable support and stability for the development of this resource.
Client: It's wonderful! Moseby has walked into the stream and is drinking some water. I feel so free and happy on his back, like nothing bad could happen to us here.	Inviting Moseby into the calm, connected space strengthened the client's positive emotions as well as her connection with Moseby.

Table 10.1 Case Example Transcript (Cont.)

Transcript	Analysis
Counselor: Notice how happy you feel about having Moseby in your calm, connected space while also noticing him moving beneath you right now in the round pen. Ask him to keep moving forward while you imagine riding him into the stream and hearing him splash in the water.	Asking the client to notice both what is happening in the present moment while also imagining her calm, connected space continues to promote linkage and integration in all the regions of her brain. We will keep building the resource with the horse continuously moving to provide both passive and active regulation. When the horse stops, shows signs of anxiety, or seeks connection with the equine professional or therapist, the client will be re-directed towards her connection with the horse before proceeding to work on her resource.
Counselor: As we come to the end of the session, we are going to stop and have you turn around and sit backwards on Moseby, laying your head on his rump and letting yourself be thankful for his partnership in building this resource for you.	This activity compresses the client's vagus nerve, initiating a relaxation response from the parasympathetic nervous system, and allowing her a final moment of deep connection with Moseby before dismounting and ending her session.

Sample Client Session Note

Table 10.2 Sample Client Session Note

CONFIDENTIAL

Session Note	
Name: *Rachel M.*	*Date:*
Start Time: *9:00 AM* **End Time:** *10:00 AM*	**Diagnosis:** *Post Traumatic Stress Disorder, Chronic (F43.12)*
Service Type: *CPT Code* ☐	
Therapeutic Goals: Re-connect with self through mindfulness and grounding Pursue healthy connection with others Reduce symptoms of insomnia, hypervigilance, anxiety Process traumatic memories	

(continued)

Table 10.2 Sample Client Session Note (Cont.)

Check in with client (degree to which learning in session is transferring to other areas of life): Client reports that she is more aware of when she dissociates and is able to return to the present moment more readily using the mindfulness and grounding techniques practiced in sessions. She has been transferring the relationship principles of connected attachment and detachment that she has been learning and practicing in session to her human relationships and is experiencing less anxiety when grocery shopping alone or at night when she is trying to fall asleep.
Intervention/s used: The resource of calm, connected space was developed today in session in preparation for processing a trauma target. Passive regulation provided by rhythmic, patterned, bilateral movement provided Rachel with the lower brain support needed for her limbic system and neocortex to begin to be engaged.
Client's response to intervention/s: Client was able to practice body awareness, mindfulness, grounding, attachment, and affect tolerance, which are all key elements necessary for processing trauma. She expanded and enhanced her calm, connected space resource by noticing where she felt her gratitude in her body, then giving it a color and a shape and allowing it to grow. Working on connection to herself as well as others engaged both her limbic system as well as her neocortex, facilitating cross-brain connection and integration.
Future Plan: We will continue to strengthen the resource of calm, connected space and process traumatic memories.

Therapist Signature/Credentials and Date

Blank Client Session Note

See Table 10.3 at the end of the chapter.

References

American Psychiatric Association. (2013). *Diagnostic and statistical manual of mental disorders* (5th ed.). Arlington, VA: American Psychiatric Publishing.

Broersma, T. (2014). *Research on Horse/Human Connection.* Retrieved October 22, 2017, from http://ridingbeyond.org/research-horsehuman-connection/.

Eye Movement Desensitization and Reprocessing International Association: Definition of EMDR. Retrieved October 22, 2017, from: http://c.ymcdn.com/sites/www.emdria.org/resource/resmgr/imported/EMDRIA%20Definition%20of%20EMDR.pdf.

Jobe, T., Shultz-Jobe, B., & McFarland, L. (2016). *Fundamentals of Natural Lifemanship: Trauma-Focused Equine Psychotherapy (TF-EAP^{TM}).* Publisher: Author.

Levine, P. & Frederick, A. (1997). *Waking the Tiger: Healing Trauma.* Berkeley, CA: North Atlantic Books.

National Center for PTSD (2016). Retrieved October 22, 2017, from: www.ptsd.va.gov/public/PTSD-overview/basics/how-common-is-ptsd.asp.

Perry, B. (2013). *Bonding and Attachment in Maltreated Children: Consequences of Emotional Neglect in Childhood*. Retrieved October 22, 2017, from https://childtrauma.org/wp-content/uploads/2013/11/Bonding_13.pdf.

Proctor, H. (2012). Animal Sentience: Where Are We and Where Are We Heading? *Animals*, 2(4), 628–639. MCPI AG. Retrieved from: http://dx.doi.org/10.3390/ani2040628.

Shapiro, F. (1989). Efficacy of the Eye Movement Desensitization Procedure in the Treatment of Traumatic Memories. *Journal of Traumatic Stress*, 2, 199–223.

Shultz-Jobe, B., Jobe, T., & Williams, E. (2017). Equine Connected Eye Movement Desensitization and Reprocessing (EC-EMDR). Presented at the 2017 Natural Lifemanship Conference, Brenham, TX.

Williams, E. and Choe, K. (2017). Connected Calm Space: Resourcing for Equine Connected Eye Movement Desensitization and Reprocessing (EC-EMDR). Presented at the 2017 Natural Lifemanship Conference, Brenham, TX.

Winhall, J. (2014). Understanding and treating addiction with the felt sense experience model. In G. Madison (Ed.), *Emerging practices in focusing-oriented psychotherapy: Innovative theory and application* (pp. 178–193). London: Jessica Kingsley Publishers.

Table 10.3 Blank Client Session Note

CONFIDENTIAL

Session Note	
Name:	Date:
Start Time: End Time:	Diagnosis:
Service Type: CPT Code☐	
Therapeutic Goals:	
Check in with client (degree to which learning in session is transferring to other areas of life):	
Intervention/s used:	
Client's response to intervention/s:	
Future Plan:	

_____

Therapist Signature/Credentials and Date

11 Warrior PATHH

Integrated Equine-Assisted Psychotherapy
for Posttraumatic Growth in Combat
Veterans

Rob Pliskin

Introduction

The need for a comprehensive opportunity for combat veterans to heal and grow is prevalent and not going away any time soon. By the end of 2014 there were more than 2.7 million veterans of Iraq and Afghanistan, and today there are even more. Veterans who went to Vietnam number about 2.6 million. Many of these more than 5.3 million Americans endured the trials of combat. Many of them have returned missing limbs, were otherwise painfully wounded, and/or suffer from the hidden wounds of war—traumatic brain injury (TBI), combat stress, and posttraumatic stress disorder (PTSD) (Spelman et al., 2012). It is estimated that 20% of all Iraq and Afghanistan veterans suffer from PTSD. The most recent statistical studies show the suicide rate among all veterans at 20 a day (Veterans Affairs Office of Public and Intergovernmental Affairs, 2016).

At the same time Veterans Administration (VA) services have significantly lagged behind demand. Some veterans have waited as long as 279 days for an appointment for care of any kind (Government Accountability Office [GAO], 2015). Further, there are explicit barriers cited by veterans towards seeking mental health treatment. Examples include shame and embarrassment, viewing mental health problems as a sign of weakness, or believing it is possible to "tough it out" on their own. Co-morbidity of PTSD with disorders like depression lead to avoidant coping mechanisms. Competing family, work, or school obligations can be further barriers (Spelman et al., 2012). I agree with Reisman (2016) that there is a need to broaden the search for effective community approaches as veterans and their families also turn in this direction.

The VA is doing what it can today to adapt and address the issues confounding its effectiveness, but sending a veteran home from a group session or an appointment with prescription drugs and an emergency telephone number may not actually promote a veteran's experience of truly "coming home." It may help them survive, but does it help them really connect, build relationships important to them and their close others, rejoin or build their community, personally grow, and thrive? Shouldn't they as much as any of us have that opportunity and be supported in reaching for it?

Theoretical Approach

Posttraumatic growth (PTG) is a theoretical approach supporting "the experience of positive change that occurs as a result of the struggle with highly challenging life crises." (Tedeschi & Calhoun, 2004). PTG has long been known and experienced in spiritual practice and religion across history and culture (Tedeschi & McNally, 2011). It enters our modern lexicon of trauma recovery in sayings such as "what doesn't kill you will make you stronger." One of its most compelling examples comes from Viktor Frankl, Holocaust survivor and psychologist. In *Man's Search for Meaning* he writes of his World War II captivity at Auschwitz concentration camp about what matters: "to transform a personal tragedy into a triumph, to turn one's predicament into a human achievement. When we are no longer able to change a situation…we are challenged to change ourselves" (Frankl, 1985, p. 35). Theoretical work and research on PTG remained rare until the mid-1990s but has since blossomed with roughly 700 articles in the professional literature (Swanson, 2015; Tedeschi & McNally, 2011; Tedeschi, personal correspondence, September 1, 2017).

According to the Posttraumatic Growth Research Group of the Department of Psychology at the University of North Carolina-Charlotte, PTG can evince for a trauma survivor in five major ways:

1) increased awareness of new opportunities and possibilities ahead;
2) closer relationships with specific people, and relating to the suffering of others;
3) increased experience of personal strength based on coming through trauma;
4) enhanced appreciation for life;
5) deepening spirituality that may include new or changing beliefs.

PTG is both a post-trauma state of being as well as the process that leads to growth in a trauma survivor's post-trauma world. This process can arise within an individual as well as be consciously activated and enhanced through practice (Posttraumatic Growth Research Group, 2014).

Research has shown post-treatment measures of increased PTG is associated with decreased PTSD symptoms, helping trauma survivors experience healing and growth that goes beyond merely surviving their struggles (Swanson, 2015). Tedeschi et al. (2015) present guidelines for clinical treatment of PTSD integrated with PTG principles. They coach the clinician on being an "expert companion" in the client's struggle to adapt to his or her new situation rather than focus on the experience of the trauma itself.

Expert companionship can mean listening for the metaphors of clients due to the difficulty of describing such horrific events in everyday language. Engaging with the client in these metaphors may help trauma survivors to acknowledge what they couldn't find words for previously. Group work with trauma survivors also provides the opportunity for clients to experience PTG among others who are also experiencing it, giving rise to recognition of each participant's personal strength, empathy, and compassion, as well as sharing and contributing to the group experience (Tedeschi et al., 2015). Meichenbaum (2006), in discussing the five elements of PTG, sees relationship building as a key component in moving forward to build social supports.

How Equine-Assisted Psychotherapy (EAP) Helps

The opportunity for clients to make metaphor out of their experience with horses is widely recognized by EAP professionals as a hallmark of the modality. Growth from group work can achieve strong expression in the EAP arena. Horses and other equines are expert companions with "whom" to practice building relationships (EAGALA, 2010).

These findings set the stage for treatment of PTSD and other posttraumatic stress conditions in programs that build PTG through the power of EAP. Research results, while limited and still maturing, show EAP is well-suited to provide healing opportunities for posttraumatic growth. In one study results showed participants reporting significant reduction in symptoms of stress with a corresponding increase in well-being over monthly sessions for a period of eight months. Results included less guilt, resentment, and regret of the past; less fear of the future; and being more independent and self-supportive (Klontz et al., 2007). In another study, measures of increased hope and decreased depression in at-risk youth were statistically significant in a five-week program (Frederick et al., 2015). McCullough et al. (2015) viewed equine-facilitated psychotherapy as an integrated mind–body–emotion–spirit intervention that responds to the complex contextual aspects of posttraumatic stress.

Equine-Assisted Psychotherapy, Posttraumatic Growth, and Combat Veterans at Boulder Crest Retreat

Boulder Crest Retreat serves combat veterans who have encountered the physical and psychological wounds of war. Its vision is "a model of healing that integrates evidence-based therapies, a safe, peaceful space and unparalleled customer service to improve physical, emotional, spiritual and economic well-being for our nation's combat veterans and their families" (Boulder Crest Retreat, 2017).

Warrior PATHH at Boulder Crest is a comprehensive seven-day intensive retreat program that begins an 18-month PTG experience for a cohort of about six individual participants who return to their homes and become a mutually supportive "fire team" going forward for the 18-month duration of the program. While highly therapeutic, it is a non-clinical approach grounded in the science of PTG that engages the cohort in integrated group work, psychoeducation, and experiential practice. It fits for combat veterans who may shy away from seeking traditional treatment but who have survived as war fighters via their personal strengths, their training, and the support of their fellow warriors at the time of trauma (Boulder Crest Retreat, 2017a, 2017b; Resiman, 2016;

Spelman et al., 2012). Here are results from Warrior PATHH's first six months of a longitudinal study:

- 40–60 percent overall reduction in PCL scores
- 50% reduction in depression and anxiety; 40% reduction in stress
- Upwards of 75% improvement in level of psychological, spiritual/existential, and relationship growth, according to the Posttraumatic Growth Inventory (Tedeschi and Calhoun, 1996)
- 100% of participants would recommend PATHH to a fellow Warrior (Boulder Crest Retreat, 2017b).

The Warrior PATHH acronym stands for Progressive and Alternative Training for Healing Heroes. The equine assisted component of Warrior PATHH provides the experience and practice for participants to do just that for themselves and each other.

An underlying assumption of the equine segment of the Warrior PATHH retreat is its integral experiential support for the rest of the PATHH model. In the EAP portion of Warrior PATHH participants are guided to recognize their personal strengths and those of their cohort. They build lines of social connection and support during the EAP component, based on their mutual experience with the horses and practice of the five elements of PTG. This makes PTG more portable in the veteran's wider environment of home, family, work, and society. EAP as a segment of Warrior PATHH fits well with Spelman et al. (2012), who found that multi-dimensional needs of combat veterans and their families suggest an interdisciplinary approach to address the long-term health impacts of combat.

EAP builds personal strength and courage through the need to relate to a 1–2,000-pound animal that can move quickly and may not be predictable. This kind of relationship building takes honesty as well as connection to self, others, and the environment in the here and now. (Eagala, 2017; Meichenbaum, 2006; Tedeschi et al., 2015).

As a final point, Tedeschi et al. (2015) personally note that the benefits of PTG for clients are also shared by the professionals who work with them. In other words, when you do this work with humility and respect, your reward can be your own posttraumatic growth and a more deeply energized daily life. As professionals who look forward to being with their clients and their horses, we know this happens session after session. It is one reason we do this work.

Ethical Issues

Evans and Gray (2012) explores ethical questions in animal-assisted therapy from the standpoint of animal welfare and wellness. In the ecology of a client, this can extend to examining client interactions with animals in their own world. Walker et al. (2015) sees focusing with the client on the ethical issues involved in working with therapy animals as a way to build ethical strengths for the client in his or her world.

Similarly, EAGALA includes standards of equine wellness and welfare along with those of clients within its Code of Ethics (EAGALA, 2017). Sample client issues for Warrior PATHH might be readiness of the client to participate from both a mental health as well as physical health standpoint, and staff readiness to accept the role of an "expert guide" offering expert companionship. The ongoing equine-related concerns such as "knowing your horses" and providing for the health and safety of both equines and humans are woven into ethical practice of the model.

The Technique

The Horse Inspired Growth and Learning (HIGH) model of EAL is the basis for the equine component of Warrior PATHH because of its fundamental orientation to the posttraumatic growth of its participants (Landolphi, personal communication, 2017).

Goals

1. Facilitate posttraumatic growth for participants with horses.
2. Create experiences to transform participants' struggles into recognition of their own and others' personal strength and growth.
3. Hold space and support participants in gaining from group process.
4. Contribute to connecting participants as accountable team members.

Objectives for Participants

1. Practice self, other, and environmental awareness to maintain personal safety, the safety of others, and the safety of the horses.
2. Safely engage in the steps of each equine-assisted experience as an individual and as a group participant.
3. Be open to the disclosure of others and the opportunity for self-disclosing and feedback during all phases of the experience.

Materials Needed

- arena, fenced pasture/paddock, or other suitable enclosure of sufficient size in which a group of six participants, staff, and several horses can move about freely and safely
- oversized round pen or small arena large enough to accommodate the group and staff—the area will be a space in which an able-bodied equine will carry a participant rider wearing a helmet around the rail at a walk while being led by staff and assisted in mounting, dismounting, and side-walking by participants;
- several riding helmets of assorted sizes;
- rope halters, lead ropes of various lengths;

- at least four traffic cones;
- 15–20 pieces of 2 x 10 feet lumber cut about 18 inches long;
- option: two sets of PVC or other lightweight lengths of ground poles or pieces of rope at least 40 feet long;
- option: other materials to lead horses with such as baling twine, yarn, or ribbon;
- option: availability of other assorted props.

Step-by-Step Description

Part I: Meeting (Individual Experiential—45 Minutes)

Assemble participants and staff at the rail or fence outside the arena or pasture. Tell participants they are going to meet the horses. Tell them their task is to take their time to move around the horses and interact with them. While doing this they are to decide which horse is most like them based on an observable behavior. Demonstrate appropriate contact if determined this is necessary. Remind them to be mindful of themselves, each other, and the horses for the safety of all. After sufficient time reassemble the group inside the enclosure and debrief.

Debrief

- Ask a participant which horse they decided was most like them and to name the qualities and behaviors of the horse that the participant sees in herself/ himself.
- Describe the horse in terms of what you and/or the horse's keeper know of the horse's unique past and its "horseanality." Be sure to include its standout positive role in the herd, its strengths, and how it is appreciated.
- Ask the group to further comment on the qualities they recognize in the participant and the horse.
- Move from one participant to the next in the debrief.
- Ask the participants as a group for closing feedback about the experience, what they noticed about the horses, and what they notice about themselves.

Part II: Leading (Buddy Experiential—45 Minutes)

Tell participants to buddy up. Their task is to halter and lead the horse most like them from the staging area beside a nearby cone to and around a distant cone and back, using the rope halter and lead rope any way they want.

- Allow participants time for this experience and support them if necessary.
- After sufficient time gather the group together to debrief.
- Sample debrief questions (note: most questions can be adapted so participants can also talk about their buddy and their experience of their buddy).
- What was the best part of this experience?
- What was the hardest part?

- What worked the best?
- What did you learn about yourself?
- What did you learn about being buddied up?
- How was it at the beginning of the experience? How about at the end?
- What did you learn about getting the horse out there to the cone and back?
- What are you learning about the nature of success?
- How did you behave as a good team member to help make success?

Part III: The Desert (Team Experiential—60 Minutes)

(Adapted from an EAGALA activity called "The Raging River")
Use cones, ropes, or lightweight poles to mark two parallel lines on the ground roughly 40 feet away from each other, each about 40 feet long. Tell participants their task is to get their entire team across the desert between the two lines while at the same time taking an important mission component with them—a horse. The horse is uniquely adapted to survive in the desert, but they must rely on their own unique strengths and guiding principles as individuals and as a team to make it across. They can do this by laying down the lumber cuts and using them to step safely one by one.

First the participants must label three "principles they will stand on going forward" on adhesive-backed material. Each participant names these out loud and then attaches them to one of the lumber pieces. Participants are warned that there are "desert denizens" (or coyotes) that live in the area. Facilitators secretly arrange with several staff to be these denizens. One facilitator always remains trustworthy. Option: Another facilitator will manage to "steal" the horse using some form of misinformation and guile. The cohort is then encouraged by staff to decide which facilitator is most trustworthy and enlist their support. This demonstrates an example of asking for help from a safe person when a situation warrants, which in this case is getting the horse back.

Rules are stated:

- Participants are safe from denizens and can survive the desert as long as they are standing on their principles, the lumber pieces.
- Denizens may not touch participants or steal the lumber pieces as long as participants are in contact with the lumber pieces in any way, or not actually in the desert.

As the experience begins, denizens may impede participants, trick them into surrendering the lumber pieces in their hands, steal unattended lumber pieces on the desert floor, etc. Debriefing follows as in Part II above. Attention can be given to discussing the meaning of the horse.

Part IV: Moving Forward Together (Team Experiential—60 Minutes)

In an arena or large round pen, participants work as a team supported by facilitators and staff to safely help each helmeted team member approach and mount a bareback horse. First, the rider takes time on the ground to connect with the horse either silently or with words. The rider tells the horse his or her safety needs and asks the horse to behave in a way that respects them. Then the rider must tell the horse how he or she will behave to ensure the safety and care of the horse. When mounted, the rider is asked to relax and lay forward to do mindful breathing, then sit up and lay back to breathe, and then sit up and move with the horse as the horse is led by a staff member and walked for about two minutes. Team members and/or staff accompany the horse and rider as side walkers while the horse is moving. The facilitator asks the rider to tell when the left front hoof strikes the ground without looking down; then the right rear hoof.

- The horse is then halted with a verbal "whoa" from the rider.
- The rider is assisted by participants and supported by staff in dismounting safely.
- After each participant has had a turn, the team debriefs.

Multicultural Guidelines

Staff and volunteers need to be comfortable and respectful regarding missing limbs, prosthetics, and scars of participants. Cultural safety issues such as differences in making eye contact, staff diversity, and speaking out in a group are to be recognized and respected. A hand gesture or other "stop sign" can support privacy with no explanation needed. Leave open the opportunity for 1:1 guidance and assistance with a trusted staff member. Provide whatever least restrictive environment is necessary during sessions to support every participant.

It is my belief that horses and other equines live in their own culture. Managing horses at all times for their well-being and involving them safely in session work can benefit the horses, serve as a model for clients, and mitigate the possibility of harm to everyone.

Case Example Compilation

The participants in the cohort I joined are six adult male combat veterans with five legs and 11 arms between them, TBI, PTSD, and a broken back. One received his injuries in Vietnam while the rest were injured in either Iraq or Afghanistan (Landolphi, personal communication, 2017). All that is necessary to understand the relevance of building PTG for combat veterans is to imagine the journey these men have taken from home to the battleground and back. Now imagine them working as an integrated team to safely hoist each other one at a time onto the bare back of a 19-hand Percheron; the rider's experience of being up there safely supported; and the rider's feeling of moving forward in unison *with this horse*, and with a *new view* of his or her world and its *new possibilities* for life.

Transcript Analysis of Case Example Compilation

The following transcript analysis is about a pseudonym client:

Table 11.1 Case Example Transcript

Client(s) Warrior Path August Cohort **Horse(s)** Clayton Gabriel Danny Boy	
Session on site **Goal** Experience Individual PTG and Group Cohesion	
Client A : Missing legs, has prosthetics Client C : PTSD, broken back	Client B : Missing legs, with prosthetics Client D : Missing legs, left arm, no prosthetics

Transcript	Analysis
Meeting the Horses **Client A:** He knew me. I knew him. I spent some time with him. I felt his energy, his way. He felt mine.	Client A is practicing building close positive relationship with the horse.
Facilitator: You felt who Clayton [horse] is. He needs to move others around. He's pretending to be a leader. He is very wise and talented, has the opportunity to see if he can be a leader. But he spooks and runs away.	The facilitator describes Clayton to client A, who picked him as most like himself.
Client A: *(Hesitantly)* It fits. I agree. It is what I do at home.	Client A gains self-knowledge and a new possibility of growth, with increase awareness of self and others.
Moving Forward Together **Facilitator:** OK, Client B makes a connection with Danny Boy [19-hand Percheron]. Tell him your needs. What you want to happen.	The facilitator guides client. B, to become self-aware, and to honestly communicate wants and needs.
Client B: *(Leaning in close to the horse's cheek talking speaking softly and slowly)* Danny Boy, thank you for doing this for me. I've never quite done anything like it. I know I got you and all my team around me. I just want it to be good. For everybody. I am going to stay calm and trust you and practice my breathing so I can just relax and move with it. Maybe you could not move around too much while I am getting on, even though a lot of us are surrounding you. That would be good. And thank you. Ok. Thank you. *(Team helps client B mount Danny Boy)*	Client B practices trust, honesty, and loyalty, teaming up to experience new possibilities while using his own strengths.
Facilitator: OK? Now practice your 4-7-8 [mindfulness] breathing and lay back on Danny Boy when you are ready.	The facilitator is checking in with client B while expertly guiding him to the next step.

(continued)

Table 11.1 Case Example Transcript (Cont.)

Client B: *(Mounted: sighing, breathing out, doing relaxation breathing lays back, relaxing. After a moment, he brings his arms down on the barrel of the horse to reposition himself more comfortably on the back of the horse)*	The client is visibly more comfortable, body and arms more relaxed, and sighs again.
Facilitator: Wow, client B! It didn't feel quite right so you adjusted yourself. You adjusted to make it better. Really awesome.	The facilitator is reflecting back and reinforcing client B's strengths and ability to manage self-care.
Facilitator: *(to client C on Danny Boy, while horse is moving forward at a walk)* How does it feel up there?	The facilitator is checking in with client C while guiding and supporting him.
Client C: Pretty good, pretty good.	Client C's voice in monotone, soft, terse.
Facilitator: Now let go and relax, feel Danny moving and move with him. Breathe.	The facilitator offers expert guidance and support.
Facilitator: *(after seeing client C's posture relax and back and legs start moving with the horse's footfalls)* OK, client C, now you are moving with him! Do you feel it? How is it now?	The facilitator continues expert guidance as client C follows through new experience.
Client C: Yeah, I can feel it. Feels pretty good.	Client C's body is more relaxed. He is starting to smile slightly. He is using his own physical skills while supported by his facilitator and PATHH training to the experience.
Facilitator: See! That's what happens when you move with him. He is a 2,000-pound Percheron draft horse. You can't control him. But you can move *with* him. He is like the universe! You can't control it, so you move with it, you move through stuff with it. Like moving with him!	The facilitator and horse guide client C in exploring his world inside the arena while allowing client C to practice a new way to explore his world outside the arena.
Facilitator: Now look straight ahead, don't look down, and tell me when his left front hoof hits the ground.	The facilitator is challenging client C to reinforce new experiential learning of moving forward.
Client C: *(correctly)* Yeah, now, now, now. **Facilitator:** Yep, great! Now tell me when his right rear hoof hits the ground. **Client C** *is again successful.* **Facilitator:** See, awesome, you got it.	Client C is really practicing moving forward with self and other awareness, instead of resisting it. Continuing and reinforcing the experience as an expert guide for client C. Client C is visibly relaxed with a bigger smile. Facilitator recognizes new ability of client C.

Table 11.1 Case Example Transcript (Cont.)

Client D: *(before being lifted onto the horse)* I'm scared. *(A few seconds later)* I'm afraid. **Facilitator:** Client D, I've seen everything you can do, how you hop down from your chair using your arms, how you balance and move across the floor to swing up into your chair, how strong you are, how much you give. These guys are here for you. Are you ready? *(Client D allows the cohort to lift him up onto the horse's back. He finds his balance and completes the experience with the help of the cohort and the staff. After completing the experience, he moving to each staff member and his cohort with handshakes and hugs.)* **Client D:** I couldn't have done it without you. Without all of you. Thank you.	Client D is being honest and trusting his team with his honesty. The facilitator is mirroring for client D his strength and the connection with his team. Only then does she ask him if he is ready to continue.

Sample Group Session Note

Table 11.2 Sample Group Session Note

EAP GROUP SESSION NOTE FOR : August Warrior PATHH—Clients B, C, D, E, and F
Date: 8-28-17   **Time:** 1–4pm   **Weather:** seasonal, partly cloudy, dry, breeze
Staff: 1 Lead PATHH Guide, 3 PATHH Guides, 3 Volunteers
Outside Staff:
Horses/Equines: Clayton, Gabriel, Danny Boy
EXPERIENCE: HIGH 1) Meet the Horses 2) Lead the Horses 3) The Desert 4) Moving Forward

Clients	Horse(s)
Beginning	
Group is relaxed, outside rail, bantering. Focus attention well when receiving direction. Maintain attention going into "Meet the Horses."	Horses relaxed, grazing, or standing quietly. When group enters, Clayton moves alongside Gabriel and noses him away. Danny Boy later noses Clayton away from Danny Boy's grazing.
Client E refrains from meeting the horses until redirected to do so. Client E complies	

(continued)

Table 11.2 Sample Group Session Note (Cont.)

Middle	
Group is engaged in "Leading Horses." They support each other in haltering and leading as buddies. Then teammates from other teams interact with teams that need support.	Horses are remaining calm and compliant. Most walk with minimal guidance to stay with buddy teams. Buddy teams redirect horses when necessary.
Group is highly engaged for "The Desert." Sharing planning and gamesmanship. Focused, aware of environment and each other, positive, light.	Danny Boy is calm and mostly compliant during "The Desert."
End	
Group remains highly engaged and supportive of each other and the experience. Each member mounts and rides with support of the group and staff. Client F adds focus to get horse to whoa. Client E loses focus while mounted and moving so horse stops moving. Client E reapplies focus and horse begins to move again. Client C adds extra adjustment to ride more comfortably. Client D expresses fear to team and gets support. Client B removes prosthetics while mounted.	Danny Boy remains mostly calm, appropriately responsive, and compliant regarding minor interventions, e.g., stopping and restarting for Client E and halting for Client F's stronger whoa.

Assessment: Much more integrated focus, cohesion, and support amongst group members with individual group members more present in the here and now post-session

Plan: NOTE: REVIEWING MOTORIZED WHEELCHAIR WITH DANNY BOY WAS HIGHLY EFFECTIVE. MAKE SURE TO CONTINUE TO REVIEW WITH HORSES WHAT THEY WILL ENCOUNTER ON AN ONGOING BASIS. Continue to integrate experiences into the week's work as planned.

By: **Date:**

Blank Group Session Note

See Table 11.3 at the end of the chapter.

References

Boulder Crest Retreat (2017a). Warrior PATHH. Retrieved from www.boulder crestretreat.org/warriorpathh/.
Boulder Crest Retreat (2017b). Why We Exist. Retrieved from www.bouldercrestre treat.org/why-we-exist/.

EAGALA (2010). How It Works. Retrieved from http://home.eagala.org/works.

Evans, N., & Gray, C. (2012). The Practice and Ethics of Animal-Assisted Therapy with Children and Young People: Is It Enough that We Don't Eat Our Co-Workers? *British Journal of Social Work*, 42(4), 600–617. doi:10.1093/bjsw/bcr091.

Frankl, Viktor E. (1985). Man's search for meaning. New York: Washington Square Press/Pocket Books.

Frederick, K. E., Hatz, J. I., & Lanning, B. (2015). Not Just Horsing Around: The Impact of Equine-Assisted Learning on Levels of Hope and Depression in At-Risk Adolescents. *Community Mental Health Journal*, 51(7), 809–17. doi:10.1007/s10597-015-9836-x.1–9.

Government Accountability Office (GAO) (2015, October 28). Veterans Affairs Mental Health: Clearer Guidance on Access Policies and Wait-Time Data Needed. Retrieved from www.gao.gov/products/GAO-16–24.

Klontz, B. T., Bivens, A., Leinart, D., & Klontz, T. (2007). The Effectiveness of Equine-Assisted Experiential Therapy: Results of an Open Clinical Trial. *Society and Animals*, 15(3): 257–267. Retrieved from www.animalsandsociety.org/wp-content/uploads/2016/04/klontz.pdf.

Mccullough, L., Risley-Curtiss, C., & Rorke, J. (2015). Equine Facilitated Psychotherapy: A Pilot Study of Effect on Posttraumatic Stress Symptoms in Maltreated Youth. *Journal of Infant, Child, and Adolescent Psychotherapy*, 14(2), 158–173. doi:10.1080/15289168.2015.1021658.

Meichenbaum, D. (2006). Resilience and Posttraumatic Growth: A Constructive Narrative Perspective. In L.G. Calhoun & R. G. Tedeschi (Eds.), Handbook of post-traumatic growth: Research and practice (pp. 355–368). Mahwah, NJ: Lawrence Erlbaum Associates. Retrieved from https://books.google.com/books?hl=en&lr=&id=BHEABAAAQBAJ&oi=fnd&pg=PA355&dq=Meichenbaum,+D.+(2006).+Resilience+and+posttraumatic+growth:+A+constructive+narrative+perspective.&ots=o4vJBa6Blt&sig=8ODaie9teCrYY5nxnmxEpPvqViM#v=onepage&q&f=false.

Posttraumatic Growth Research Group (2014). What is PTG? Retrieved from https://ptgi.uncc.edu/what-is-ptg/.

Reisman, M. (2016). PTSD Treatment for Veterans: What's Working, What's New, and What's Next. *Pharmacy and Therapeutics*, 41(10), 623–634. Retrieved from www.ncbi.nlm.nih.gov/pmc/articles/PMC5047000/.

Spelman, J. F., Hunt, S. C., Seal, K. H., & Burgo-Black, A. L. (2012). Post Deployment Care for Returning Combat Veterans. *Journal of General Internal Medicine*, 27(9), 1200–1209. doi.org/10.1007/s11606-012-2061-1.

Swanson, A. C. (2015). Posttraumatic growth among Latina victims of interpersonal violence in psychological treatment. Open Access Dissertations. 1493. University of Miami, Miami. Retrieved from http://scholarlyrepository.miami.edu/cgi/viewcontent.cgi?article=2500&context=oa_dissertations.

Tedeschi, R. G., & Calhoun, L. G. (2004). Posttraumatic Growth: Conceptual Foundations and Empirical Evidence. *Psychological Inquiry*, 15(1), 1–18. Retrieved from http://sites.uncc.edu/ptgi/wp-content/uploads/sites/9/2013/01/PTG-Conceptual-Foundtns.pdf.

Tedeschi, R. G., & McNally, R. J. (2011). Can We Facilitate Posttraumatic Growth in Combat Veterans? *American Psychologist*, 66(1), 19–24. Retrieved from http://sites.uncc.edu/ptgi/wp-content/uploads/sites/9/2015/01/Can-we-facilitate-posttraumatic-growth-in-combat-veterans.pdf.

Tedeschi, R. G., Calhoun, L. G., & Groleau, J. M. (2015). Clinical Applications of Posttraumatic Growth. In S. Joseph (Ed.), Positive psychology in practice: Promoting human flourishing in work, health, education and everyday life. (pp. 503–518). Hoboken, NJ: Wiley. Retrieved from https://ptgi.uncc.edu/wp-content/uploads/sites/9/2015/01/Tedeschi-et-al-Joseph-Ch-30-Clinical-applications-of-PTG.pdf.

Tedeschi, R. G., & Calhoun, L. G. (1996). The Posttraumatic Growth Inventory: Measuring the Positive Legacy of Trauma. *Journal of Traumatic Stress*, 9(3), 455–471. doi:10.1007/BF02103658.

Veterans Affairs Office of Public and Intergovernmental Affairs (2016, July 7). VA Conducts Nation's Largest Analysis of Veteran Suicide. Retrieved from www.va.gov/opa/pressrel/pressrelease.cfm?id=2801.

Walker, P., Aimers, J., & Perry, C. (2015). Animals and social work: An emerging field of practice for Aotearoa New Zealand. *Aotearoa New Zealand Social Work*, 27(1), 24–35.

Table 11.3 Blank Client Session Note

EAP GROUP SESSION NOTE FOR :
Date: **Time:**   **Weather:**
Staff:
Outside Staff:
Horses/Equines:
EXPERIENCE:

Clients	*Horse(s)*
Beginning	
Middle	
End	

Assessment:

Plan:

By: *Date:*

12 Treating Combat-Related Posttraumatic Stress Disorder through Psychodynamic Equine-Assisted Traumatherapy

Ilka Parent

Combat Posttraumatic Stress Disorder

Posttraumatic stress disorder (PTSD) is associated with serious consequences that may lead to poor quality of life and many comorbid occurrences (APA, 2013; Atwoli et al., 2015). In the United States, approximately 7 to 8% of the population will have PTSD at some point in their lifetime (U.S. Department of Veterans Affairs, 2016). However, the rate of PTSD in combat military veterans is even higher, ranging from 11 to 20% (U.S. Department of Veterans Affairs, 2016). Since 2001, 2.7 million United States service members have deployed to the war zones of Iraq and Afghanistan, where 90% of troops were confronted with direct combat and other potentially traumatic events. As a result, it is estimated that over 300,000 Veterans will suffer from PTSD. In addition, 23% of women veterans receiving Veterans Administration health care experienced sexual assault while in the military (U.S. Department of Veterans Affairs, 2016). Therefore, risk of PTSD is even higher for female veterans.

Common mental health treatments for military veterans primarily include prolonged exposure therapy, eye movement desensitization and reprocessing (EMDR), cognitive processing therapy (CPT), and drug therapy (U.S. Department of Veterans Affairs, 2016). As of late, equine-assisted modalities have been included and are well worth exploring. One example of such an equine intervention treatment method is psychodynamic equine-assisted traumatherapy (PEATT), conceptualized by Ilka Parent (2016). PEATT combines key elements from the equine world with established psychoanalytically-based psychodynamic concepts and proven methods from the psychotraumatology world. Treatment guidelines can either be applied in a time-restricted (inpatient) setting with focus on promoting resilience and reintegration after redeployment, or an open-ended outpatient setting.

Psychodynamic Equine-Assisted Traumatherapy (PEATT)

PEATT (Parent, 2016) is rooted in a neurological understanding of trauma. Traumatic events change and block certain neuro-information and information-storage processes in the brain and body (van der Kolk et al., 2007). Simplistically put, human beings have two types of memory systems regarding information processing: an explicit-declarative memory which contains all that is or is to be thought and spoken, and an implicit-procedural memory which contains unconscious knowledge—without temporal and spatial attribution or attribution to the self. Contents in the latter are not stored linguistically or symbolically, but rather in an emotional-sensory way (van der Kolk et al., 2007). Therefore, the information stored is not accessible to the consciousness, but only noticeable on some minor, unconscious level.

Overwhelming traumatic experiences lead to information being stored in the implicit-procedural memory. In order to be able to integrate such experiences by making them accessible to the conscious mind, verbalization is, to some extent, necessary. Verbalizing and labeling leads to an activation of the cortex, which in turn can facilitate the updating of fragmented bits of memory stored in the implicit-procedural memory into the explicit-declarative memory. Treatment, therefore, strives for an integration of implicitly stored elements in the episodic memory.

However, for a traumatized person, speaking about their traumatic experiences it often overwhelming and can lead to re-traumatization (van der Kolk et al., 2007). To be capable of dealing with the experience, resources such as coping skills and strategies need to first be built, and then utilized.

In light of this neurological perspective of trauma, PEATT (Parent, 2016) builds on the psychoanalytical elements concerning the theory of ego-function development. During the human–horse interaction, self- and object representations and relational regulations may be experienced. Symbols are used in an experiential way. Symbols are similar to metaphors in that they are objects that are used to represent something else. Sometimes clients are asked to create a situation or an event; in a way, they build a stage. Experiencing interactions with horses on a stage that represents the clients' real life facilitates an insight into everyday behaviors that they may not be able to verbalize or be conscious of at that point. Yet utilizing symbols changes the relationship between therapist and client. From a purely psychoanalytical point of view, the "projection area therapist" is broken up. There is room to "act out" (i.e., display un-reflected actions and behaviors that present as resistance to treatment). In equine-assisted psychotherapy this technique is used deliberately to facilitate an ensuing transfer to everyday life.

During regular psychotherapeutic sessions, the therapist–client relationship is observed. In PEATT, the client is invited to interact not so much with the therapist but instead with the horses. The relationship with the horse(s) is not forced, but rather unfolds organically. Consequently, unconscious thoughts, feelings, and wishes are projected onto the horses. The horse, in turn, responds and reacts to nonverbal cues and communication emitted from the person. An interaction ensues. The treatment team, consisting of a licensed trauma therapist and a knowledgeable equine behavior specialist, observes the human–horse interactions and designs activities to pursue emerging topics. Aspects of developmental and attachment traumatization are considered. In accordance with practiced trauma therapeutic procedures, a stage-oriented approach has proven to be most effective (Herman, 1992):

1. At the beginning and forefront of each (trauma) treatment is the establishing of a trusting and reliable working relationship, developing positive bonds and attachments, as well as control and measures that increase self-worth. By adding equines to the interaction, much of the typical projections placed on humans and trust issues are being avoided, as projections are being placed on the horses. These projections onto the horse can then be observed and processed. As trust increases, the human team members can evolve from neutral observers to potential trusted providers.

2. During the stabilization stage, basal key elements of safety, meaningfulness, self-worth and worthiness need to be established and supported. Affect differentiation and affect tolerance are to be built and increased. By engaging in guided interactive experiential activities, unconscious (behavioral) patterns turn visible and can then be processed, explored anew, and changed.

3. The integration of traumatic experiences takes place through a confrontation with the trauma and a respective actualization and update of memory contents from the "here and now" perspective. Key elements of bilateral stimulation (based on evidence-based EMDR) are used in the presence of and fortified by the horses' presence, keeping the person grounded and staying in the here and now.

4. Based on these newly developed and processed experiences and integration of traumatic memories, the aim of the reintegration stage is to develop self-reliability, self-efficacy, and self-control in present life circumstances. Experiential activities with horses offer the opportunity to symbolically work through stages, anticipated situations, and receive feedback about inner mechanisms at play.

Integrative Treatment Plan for Combat Veterans

The treatment of combat-related PTSD in veterans and soldiers differs from the treatment of non-combat trauma for several reasons. First, therapists must understand that soldiers' moral and ethical core values are shaped and influenced by concepts such as patriotism, an inner conviction to "do the right thing," a sense of belonging to the unit, a hierarchical rank structure with firm rules and a self-concept rooted within all of the above. A perceived violation of these values may be disrupting to veterans and soldiers. Second, veterans and soldiers often face massive social prejudice and therefore may present as quite guarded to perceived outsiders. Third, there is often a gap between civilians and members of the Armed Forces because the military system creates their own "culture"—a system with its own language, values, and self-concept.

These unique military values, experiences, and culture are considered and integrated into the PEATT therapeutic framework. The mindset and skillset that helped veterans and soldiers survive and cope with hostile conditions is acknowledged and honored. Not doing so may result in inflexible behavior patterns in civilian life. Integrating the skills they acquired before and during combat requires a re-evaluation of existing priorities and a transfer of those priorities into everyday life. When PEATT therapists help veterans process their values, experiences, and priorities through guided interaction with horses, veterans' coping skills can be enhanced and integrated into everyday life.

Case Example

Seven participants five men and two women, decided to conquer a common obstacle, their PTSD diagnosis. To represent their PTSD diagnosis, they built a five-feet high conglomeration of poles, barrels, crutches, and cloths. In front of the obstacle were several cones, set up in a square. Inside of that square was a combat dress uniform. According to the participants, this was their deployment. There was another, smaller obstacle right in front of the big one: several sticks stuck in the sand were representative of the nightly terrors they all shared. Hoops and tires symbolized the relapses back to the beginning of the obstacle course. All participants agreed that if a person stepped into one of the hoops, they would have to return to the beginning of the obstacle course. Small and big balls were representative of their problems that kept rolling into their life. Colorful cloths stuck in barrels symbolized the lost social connections with family and friends. At the very end, far away from the rest of all objects was a single flag representing their goal, a return to normal life. No other objects were placed next to or beside "normal life" and no other definition or detail could be provided as to what "normal life" looks like.

Participants were invited to overcome, along with one or more horses, the obstacles they had built. Their immediate feedback was, "That is not possible!" Humans and horses stayed far apart from each other. Only after some of the horses approached the big obstacle did the people come together. Horses were seen putting their noses in barrels. Cloths were seen being taken out by horses' teeth. Participants moved closer to the horses. A few tried to move them. Nothing appeared to work. A few times pool noodles could be seen behind horses, at which point horses were seen moving rather quickly away from both participants and pool noodles. Participants unanimously agreed that the animals should overcome the obstacles on their own, without using force. Humans and horses surrounded the obstacles. Nobody visited the area where the single flag named "normal life" had been placed. One horse came too close to the obstacle and a pole fell down. At this point, participants appeared to have the idea to re-construct their obstacle and to make it smaller. Within moments, the obstacle changed so that it now was only about a foot high. One participant regularly stepped into one of the hoops that had been labeled "relapse"—the others sent her back to the beginning of the obstacle course. Continued efforts to move one or more horses across the remaining pole failed. Some horses were seen with colorful cloths around their necks. One participant was seen sitting on the pole of the obstacle, while others were seen behind a horse, attempting to push it from behind. The animal stood with his head high in front of the pole the person was sitting on, until it moved or escaped to the side. Horses were seen following grass in front of their noses, up to the pole of the obstacle where everybody stopped. Participants were seen crossing the obstacle—without horses. Eventually all participants requested a "check-in."

This example clearly shows process-related facilitation. Process-related facilitation focuses on present attitudes, competencies, and strategies. In this instance, the group discussed that they did not need to use force or induce fear to move the horses across the obstacle. They also discussed the use of food (grass) in an attempt to motivate the horses to cooperate and the colorful cloths labeled as "lost social interactions with family and friends" that were then used to move horses. Also the process-related facilitation addressed the clients' idea to break down the obstacle into various smaller elements. These examples gives a raw overview of just some of the many observations with horses that can be addressed and explored further and offer clients the opportunity to project and later reflect their own processes.

Table 12.1 Case Example Transcript

Transcript	Analysis
Traumatherapist: We invite you to build/create your current situation as well as your future situation that you wish to get to. You can use any objects available in this area that represent important aspects of your situations.	Inviting clients to build/create their situations allows for a physical representation of clients' perception in the here and now. The open, non-directive invitation allows for clients to activate internal resources.
Client 1: I do not know how to do this—what do you mean? **Client 2:** Do you want me to use this barrel?	Client is experiencing uncertainty and is attempting to seek help from the provider team.
Traumatherapist: It sounds like you have some ideas—we invite you to explore those and put them into action and let us know when you are done.	Counselor reflects insecurities and re-directs focus to clients' ability to explore internal resources. By inviting to put thoughts into action client is given the opportunity to conceptualize own thoughts. Support is provided by remaining close, yet belief is transpired that each client is self-responsible and able to explore, discover, and put into action internal beliefs.

Table 12.1 Case Example Transcript (Cont.)

Transcript	Analysis
Horses and horse behaviors are observed during set-up. Check-in is conducted once clients let provider team know that they are "done."	
Equine Specialist: How did it go?	By asking an open-ended question, clients are given the opportunity to self-direct and share what stood out foremost in their experience.
Client 1: I set up my current problems. This barrel stands for my family. This loop stands for my relapses. I did not know what to put into my future situation except that I want for things to be better. **Client 2:** I put a flag into the future situation as a symbol that I have overcome all obstacles.	Clients are able to label items, allowing for processing previously unverbalized concepts and storing them in the explicit-declarative memory.
Equine Specialist: What stood out about the horses?	Asking about the horses allows for clients to divert their focus from possible internal struggles to a potential outside perspective and sets the path for future focus on outside actions and reactions by the horses.
Clients: We did not notice anything about the horses, we were busy with setting up the stuff.	Acknowledging that the focus was on internal processes vs. outside circumstances allows for clients to be sensitized to future outside circumstances.
Traumatherapist: When you think about your current situation and your future situation, are there any obstacles along the way? If so, we invite you to set up the obstacles that you think you will encounter when wanting to get to your future.	Asking about possible obstacles along the way and inviting to set them up in a symbolic manner allows for labeling and conceptualization.
(When set-up is done) **Equine Specialist:** We invite you to take one or more horses from your current situation to your future situation. Let us know when you are done.	Describing the various objects that were set up allowed for clients to associate various emotions with them. Taking the horses along the way, who respond to the physiological responses clients experience approaching various emotionally laden objects, magnifies what clients are experiencing. As the horses' reactions and actions are observed, the opportunity is paved to check into previously unknown or non-verbalized emotional reactions clients may experience concerning various obstacles, objects or situations.

(continued)

Table 12.1 Case Example Transcript (Cont.)

Transcript	Analysis
Activity is observed according to Observational Focal Points (OFPs)[1]	
(Check-in) **Equine Specialist:** How did it go?	By asking an open-ended question, clients are given the opportunity to self-direct and share what stood out foremost in their experience.
Clients can share their experience.	
Equine Specialist: Is there anything that stood out about the horses?	Asking about the horses allows for clients to divert their focus from possible internal struggles to a potential outside perspective and sets the path for future focus on outside actions and reactions by the horses. Projection onto the horses is made possible. Listening to the answers provided allows for traumatherapist to hear where clients' focus was, e.g., struggles, perceived failures, used strategies, outside opinions, allowing for insight into clients' self-concept and conflicts. At the same time, it is possible for clients to identify with the horses and draw parallels to their own situation.
Equine Specialist: There was a time when horses were standing, then moving. What changed?	Several horse observations, categorized according to OFPs, are reflected back to clients, allowing for them to reflect on and discuss what happened. Open-ended horse observations without providing specifics allow for clients to interpret events according to own perception, and to share their different experiences, enhancing further reflection in group through varying outside perspectives.
Equine Specialist: There was a time when horses were standing in a corner, and people were standing in a corner—what was that about?	Asking about observed parallels sets the stage for the traumatherapist facilitating a possible transfer from the experience with the horses in the here and now to applicable changed behavior in the clients' regular life.

Table 12.1 Case Example Transcript (Cont.)

Transcript	Analysis
Traumatherapist: What did you do here that you typically do—and what did you do here that you typically do not do? What worked for you?	Speaking about the horses through the horses' perspective has given clients the room to listen to themselves speak about somebody else in a similar situation. Inquiring now about the clients' applied strategies/concepts in the here and now and comparing it to their regular life allows for a conceptualization of what transpired in the here and now and a possible transfer to their life.

Conclusion

By having horses as part of the integral treatment approach, the afflicted person is being given the opportunity to connect with another being in a non-judgmental way, and thus is able to process and re-integrate past experiences from a here-and-now perspective. Research in this area is scarce, particularly as equine inter-action programs are met with a variety of prejudice and treatment applications are not regulated but instead show vast individual differences. However, soldiers and veterans in particular benefit from a treatment approach that is experien-tial in nature, and allows for a trauma processing in a non-judgmental, non-emotion-focused environment that involves all five senses.

Note

1 Observational Focus Points (OFPs; "The Fundamentals of Equine Assisted Trauma Therapy", Ilka Parent, 2016): OFPs provide recommended observational points that assist in adhering to treatment goals while maintaining an agreed upon treatment plan.

References

American Psychiatric Association. (2013). *Diagnostic and statistical manual of mental disorders: DSM-5*. Washington, DC: American Psychiatric Association.

Atwoli, L., Stein, D. J., Koenen, K. C., & McLaughlin, K. A. (2015). *Epidemiology of posttraumatic stress disorder: prevalence, correlates and consequences*. Current Opinion in Psychiatry, July, 28(4): 307–311. DOI:10.1097/YCO.0000000000000167.

Herman, J. L. (1992). Complex PTSD: *A syndrome in survivors of prolonged and repeated trauma*. Traumatic Stress, 5: 377–391.

Parent, I. (2016). *Fundamentals of Equine Assisted Trauma Therapy, with practical examples from working with military service members*. Self-published, Createspace, 1533258899/ 9781533258892.

U.S. Department of Veterans Affairs (2016). *PTSD: National Center for PTSD*. Retrieved from www.ptsd.va.gov/public/PTSD-overview/basics/how-common-is-ptsd.asp.

van der Kolk, B. A., McFarlane, A. C., & Weisaeth, L. (2007). *Traumatic stress: The effects of overwhelming experience on mind, body, and society*. New York: Guilford.

Appendix 1: General Trauma-Informed Therapy Trainings

The chapter authors have recommended the following list of trauma-informed trainings. Although this list is not meant to be comprehensive, it does provide a wide range of trauma-informed trainings to choose from. The trainings listed below are ranked alphabetically. Please note that the trainings listed are provided as a courtesy. Trainings from this page do not represent or imply endorsement.

Ana M. Gomez, MC, LPC

Offers a variety of live classes and online webinars for professionals, including EMDRIA-approved specialty courses on EMDR with children and adolescents, complex trauma, attachment, and dissociative disorders.

http://anagomez.org/live-workshops

Attachment Trauma Center Institute

Provides training in the EMDR Integrative Attachment Trauma Protocol for Children (IATP-C), a combination of EMDR and family therapy for treating abused and neglected children. Live classes and webinars on related topics also available.

http://atcinstitute.com/for-clinicians/trainings/

Attachment and Trauma Treatment Centre for Healing (ATTCH)

Founded by Lori Gill, MA, RP, CTS, the Centre offers the Certified Trauma Integration Professional designation trainings as well as the Certified Trauma Integration Organization certification process.

www.attch.org

Arizona Trauma Institute

Delivers professional training on trauma-informed care and trauma-specific treatment, including the Certified Clinical Trauma Specialist designation for working with individuals or families.

https://aztrauma.org/

Babette Rothschild, MSW

Offers training in trauma treatment from a body-oriented perspective.
www.somatictraumatherapy.com

Bodynamics

Bodynamics was founded by Lisbeth Marcher and her colleagues, and is a somatic approach to working with developmental disruptions encoded in the mind and body and associated character structures and developmental stages.
www.bodynamicusa.com

Brainspotting

Developed by Dr. David Grand, this approach works with identifying and treating eye positions that are related to the energetic or emotional activation of a traumatic or other highly charged unresolved issue in the brain.
https://brainspotting.com

Castellino Prenatal and Birth Therapy Training

Dr. Raymond Castellino offers professional trainings to resolve and re-pattern prenatal and birth trauma imprinting, along with other specialization trainings co-taught with a variety of somatic and attachment professionals.
www.castellinotraining.com

Center for Prenatal and Perinatal Programs

This interdisciplinary group of professionals with specializations in somatics, attachment, touch, trauma, pregnancy, birth, early development, and other related scopes of practice offers training and continuing education for therapists and other professionals.
www.ppncenter.com/

Child Trauma Academy

Offers training in Dr. Bruce Perry's Neurosequential Model of Therapeutics (NMT) and the Neurosequential Model in Education (NME) as frameworks for assessing and treatment planning for children, which are neurodevelopmentally informed and biologically respectful perspectives on human development and functioning.
http://childtrauma.org (NMT/NME) and www.childtraumaacademy.com (online courses)

Circle of Security International

Provides training programs in the COS protocol and principles of supporting secure attachment between children and caregivers in group settings, home visitation, and counseling.

www.circleofsecurityinternational.com

Dave Berger, LCMHC, PT, MA

Dave is a faculty member for the Somatic Experiencing® Trauma Institute who delivers live trainings on Bodywork and Somatic Education (BASE) for working with trauma through touch work, as well as trainings involving relational rupture and repair, and working with concussions and PTSD.

https://daveberger.net/

Diane Poole Heller, PhD, SEP

Dr. Heller is a faculty member for the Somatic Experiencing® Trauma Institute who also delivers live trainings and webinars on the Dynamic Attachment Repatterning Experience (DARe Certification), drawing from SE™, attachment theory, neuroscience, and spiritual perspectives in working with the nervous system in relationships.

https://dianepooleheller.com/

Dyadic Developmental Practice Network

This organization promotes training and consultation in Dyadic Developmental Psychotherapy, an approach developed by Dr. Daniel Hughes, focused on healing developmental trauma and promoting secure attachment.

http://ddpnetwork.org

Ego State Therapy International

This organization provides educational resources and training on Ego State Therapy, an approach developed by Dr. John G. Watkins and Helen Watkins for working with ego states and fragmented parts of the personality in the case of dissociative disorders.

www.egostateinternational.com/

EMDR Solutions

Robin Shapiro, MSW, LICSW, offers EMDRIA-approved specialization trainings, including ego state interventions for working with fragmented parts of the personality and dissociative disorders.

www.emdrsolutions.com

Eye-Movement Desensitization and Reprocessing (EMDR)

The EMDR International Association is the professional body representing EMDR practitioners and researchers worldwide, promoting best practices and offering a list of EMDRIA-approved EMDR training and continuing education options.

www.emdria.org

Gabor Maté, MD

Offers live seminars and online audio podcasts on addictions, trauma, adverse childhood experiences, child development, parenting, ADHD, stress, and mind body health.

https://drgabormate.com

Hellinger Institute

Offers levels 1, 2, and 3 of the Family Constellations training for working with inherited family/intergenerational trauma.

www.hellingerinstitute.com/

Internal Family Systems (The Center for Self-Leadership)

Offers progressive levels of training in Internal Family Systems, an ego state approach developed by Dr. Richard Schwartz to working with parts of the personality with individuals, couples, children, families, and groups.

www.selfleadership.org/

Janina Fisher, PhD

Offers live classes and online seminars on a range of topics related to complex developmental trauma, neurobiology, attachment, shame, and dissociation, incorporating Sensorimotor Psychotherapy, Structural Dissociation, and EMDR.

https://janinafisher.com/

Kathy Steele, MN, CS

Kathy is one of the creators of the Structural Dissociation model of parts work for dissociative disorders, and offers training and consultation in this model and in working with complex trauma and attachment.

www.kathy-steele.com

Laurel Parnell, PhD (The Parnell Institute)

Offers basic and advanced EMDR training, as well as training in Attachment-Focused EMDR and Resource Tapping™.

http://drlaurelparnell.com and http://parnellemdr.com

Mark Wolynn

Offers workshops and trainings on Family Constellations, Inherited Family Trauma, and Bert Hellinger's approach to working with family systems.

www.markwolynn.com

Mindsight Institute

Dr. Daniel Siegel offers live trainings and webinars on interpersonal neurobiology, mindfulness, and developmental neuroscience for therapists, parents, educators, coaches, and other professionals.

www.mindsightinstitute.com/

National Child Traumatic Stress Network (NCTSN)

Offers an online learning center with over 300 free continuing education certificates and over 200 online webinars focused on working with trauma, attachment, trauma-informed care, and trauma treatment in a variety of areas and settings.

https://learn.nctsn.org

National Institute for the Clinical Application of Behavioral Medicine (NICABM)

Offers online continuing education programs featuring leading experts in the area of trauma treatment, mindfulness, mind/body interventions, neuroscience, polyvagal theory, interpersonal neurobiology, Somatic Experiencing®, and Sensorimotor Psychotherapy®, among others.

www.nicabm.com/

National Institute for Trauma and Loss in Children

TLC provides online courses, on-site trainings, and conferences designed to enable schools, crisis teams, child and family counselors, and private practitioners help traumatized children and families. The Institute offers the Certified Trauma Practitioner designation at various levels of specialization as well as case consultation, books, and other resources.

www.starr.org/training/tlc

Neufeld Institute

Dr. Gordon Neufeld and his faculty members offer training in his comprehensive model incorporating developmental neuroscience, attachment theory, and depth psychology.

https://neufeldinstitute.org

NeuroAffective Relational Model (NARM™)

Developed by Dr. Laurence Heller, NARM offers a systemic, somatic, psychodynamic, and resource-oriented approach for working with developmental issues, shock trauma, nervous system regulation, shame, and identity distortions.

www.drlaurenceheller.com/

Organic Intelligence®

Developed by Steven Hoskinson, MA, MAT, Organic Intelligence is a shift away from pathology and trauma to interventions and mapping that supports natural reorganization and healing of the nervous system through increased coherence and the biology's natural rhythms.

https://organicintelligence.org/

PESI®

A continuing education provider offering online webinars and certificate programs in trauma, mental health, and other specialized topics featuring the world's leading authorities and experts.

www.pesi.com

Psychobiological Approach to Couples Therapy® (PACT Institute)

Developed by Dr. Stan Tatkin, the PACT model incorporates attachment theory, developmental neuroscience, and arousal regulation.

https://thepactinstitute.com

Sarah Jenkins, MC, LPC, CPsychol

Offers EMDRIA-approved EMDR training and additional curriculum and training on treating complex developmental trauma and structural dissociation.

www.DragonflyInternationalTherapy.com

Sensorimotor Psychotherapy® Institute

Developed by Dr. Pat Ogden, Sensorimotor Psychotherapy® draws from somatic therapies, neuroscience, attachment theory, and cognitive approaches, as well as from the Hakomi Method. The SPI offers resources and a list of trainings worldwide.

www.sensorimotorpsychotherapy.org/

Somatic Experiencing® Trauma Institute

Developed by Dr. Peter Levine, Somatic Experiencing® is a body-oriented approach to the healing of trauma and other stress disorders, resulting from the multidisciplinary study of stress physiology, psychology, ethology, biology, neuroscience, indigenous healing practices, medical biophysics, and polyvagal theory. SETI offers a list of trainings worldwide.

https://traumahealing.org/

Somatic Practice

Kathy Kain, MA, SEP is a faculty member for the Somatic Experiencing® Trauma Institute who has developed post-advanced trainings on somatic touch, attachment, developmental trauma, and the polyvagal theory. Her offerings include the Touch Skills Training for Trauma Therapists, and the Somatic Resilience and Regulation: Early Trauma Training (on relational rupture and repair and touchwork), co-developed and taught with Stephen Terrell, PsyD, SEP.

www.somaticpractice.net

Stephen Terrell, PsyD, SEP

Offers the Touch Skills Training for Trauma Therapists and the Somatic Resilience and Regulation: Early Trauma Training, in collaboration with Kathy Kain and independently, and Transforming the Experience-Based Brain Training for developmental trauma.

www.austinattach.com

The Theraplay® Institute

Offers training in child and family therapy focused on using play to enhance attachment relationships, self-esteem, trust in others and joyful engagement through play, games, developmentally challenging activities, and nurturing activities that support loving connection and regulation.

www.theraplay.org/

The Trauma Center

Offers a Certificate in Traumatic Stress Studies focused on the treatment of trauma and dissociative disorders in children and adults, and training in the ARC

(Attachment, Regulation and Competency) Framework of treatment planning for children and their caregivers.

www.traumacenter.org/

Trauma-Focused Cognitive Behavioral Therapy® (TF-CBT®)

The official National Therapist Certification Program offers web-based and live training as well as clinical consultation to complete the required certification hours for providing this structured therapy model to children and adolescents.

https://tfcbt.org/

Trauma-Informed Practices and Expressive Arts Therapy Institute

Trauma-Informed Art Therapy® and Trauma-Informed Expressive Arts Therapy® integrate trauma-informed practices, "brain-wise" arts-based interventions, and mind–body research. The Institute is dedicated to professional education and distance learning on creative, trauma-informed practices that focus on the expressive arts.

www.trauma-informedpractice.com/

Veteran/Military-Focused EMDR Training

This specialized EMDRIA-approved training developed by Dr. E.C. Hurley is for Department of Defense and Veterans Affairs therapists and others who work with the military and their families.

http://soldier-center.org

Appendix 2: Trauma-Informed Equine-Assisted Mental Health Trainings

The chapter authors have recommended the following list of trauma-informed trainings. Although this list is not meant to be comprehensive, it does provide a wide range of trauma-informed equine-assisted mental health trainings to choose from. The trainings listed below are ranked alphabetically. Please note that the trainings listed are provided as a courtesy. Trainings from this page do not represent or imply endorsement.

Clinical Skills Intensive Workshop for Mental Health Professionals

By E. Rand Gurley and Nina Ekholm Fry. This four-day clinical and experiential workshop provides the opportunity for mental health professionals who are interested in equine-assisted therapy to discuss clinical theories, case conceptualization, and treatment planning, paired with the opportunity to facilitate equine-assisted sessions with actual clients—all from a trauma-specific perspective. The workshop takes place annually in Priest River, ID, one hour from Spokane, WA.

nina.ekholm-fry@du.edu

EquiLateral™ Certification Course for EMDR Therapists & Equine Professionals

Sarah Jenkins, LPC, CPsychol, EMDRIA-approved training takes attendees step-by-step through the eight phases and three prongs of equine-assisted EMDR, including best practices in treating complex developmental trauma and dissociation.

www.EAEMDR.com

Equine-Assisted Mental Health Practitioner (EAMH) Certificate Program

The EAMH Practitioner Certificate Program at the Institute for Human–Animal Connection, University of Denver is a postgraduate program that prepares mental health professionals to practice ethically and effectively within their scope with education, training, and supervision. Professionals with existing competency in working with trauma learn to specifically enhance trauma treatment principles and techniques in the equine-assisted setting. The certificate program meets the Animal-Assisted Therapy in Counseling Competencies (AAT-C).

http://portfolio.du.edu/equineassistedmentalhealth/

Equus Effect Training

Jane Strong and David Sonatore's curriculum focuses on resilience and relationships skills that warriors, and others making their way from one culture to another, can use to establish healthy relationships at home, work and school. Our relationships with key decision makers in the VA system, veteran service organizations, treatment centers, and other service agencies that support clients' process of moving forward in life, promise a steady stream of veteran participation in this five-week curriculum.

www.theequuseffect.org/training/

EQUUSOMA™: Somatic Experiencing and Equine-Assisted Trauma Recovery

Sarah Schlote training soon to be licensed by the Somatic Experiencing® Trauma Institute, focuses on the integration of trauma-informed principles, psychophysiology, Somatic Experiencing® skills and practices, attachment theory and polyvagal theory into equine-assisted trauma recovery. Additional training in working with structural dissociation and touch in the context of equine-assisted trauma therapy in development.

https://equusoma.com

Generation Farms Equine-Facilitated Wellness Training

Deborah Marshall provides equine-facilitated wellness training incorporating trauma and mindfulness neuroscience and drawing on principles and somatic practices by a number of leading trauma experts, along with a foundation of skills drawn from ecotherapy and the Eponaquest Approach. The training is part of the certification process offered through Equine-Facilitated Wellness Canada.

www.generationfarms.ca

Healing Hooves Equine-Facilitated Wellness Training

Sue McIntosh offers EFW training incorporating the developmental and attachment-based work of Dr. Gordon Neufeld in a multi-species model of work involving horses and other animals. The training is part of the certification process offered through Equine-Facilitated Wellness Canada.

www.healinghooves.ca

IFEAL: Diploma in Equine-Facilitated Psychotraumatology

http://ifealqualifications.com/

LEAP Equine Assisted Programmes Limited

An OFQUAL-regulated Level 5 Diploma in Equine Facilitated Psychotherapy, the only training in the UK designed specifically for mental health professionals. This training includes a module dedicated to working with trauma. LEAP has recently launched TPR™ (Trauma Processing Ride™)—a completely new and innovative, body-based protocol for working with implicit traumatic memory with the help of horses.

info@leapequine.com or www.leapequine.com

Minds-n-Motion: Equine-Assisted Trauma Therapy

Ilka Parent developed a series of skillset training courses that focus on enhancing equine-assisted trauma-therapeutic techniques, particularly when working with combat-related PTSD and complex PTSD, implementing current trauma thera-peutic and psychodynamic concepts.

http://mindsnmotion.net/site/en

The Transitioning Families Therapeutic Reunification Model (TFTRMTM)

Dr. Rebecca Bailey training model is an experiential, educational, solution-focused approach to healing families and individuals. It is an evidence-based, existential model that utilizes the partnership of horses to enhance the treatment and outcome. We are pleased to offer a variety of training experiences for six or more individuals at our Northern California location or for groups of eight or more at locations by request. The TFTRMTM Approach is case specific and is intended to assist a wide variety of individuals and families managing the com-plexities of post traumatic experiences.

admin@transitioningfamilies.com and http://transitioningfamilies.com/

Trauma-Focused Equine-Assisted Psychotherapy (TF-EAP)

Natural Lifemanship (NL) by Bettina Shultz-Jobe and Tim Jobe offers pro-fessional certification, multiple experiential trainings, and online courses in Trauma-Focused Equine-Assisted Psychotherapy and NL for All of Life's Relationships. Grounded in developmental neurobiology and attachment theory, TF-EAP focuses on the cultivation of relationship between client and horse in such a way that attuned connection based on mutual choice and trust is always the goal, leading to therapeutic outcomes including self-regulation and the capacity to experience and form healthy attachment.

www.naturallifemanship.com

Trauma-Focused Equine-Assisted Psychotherapy (TF-EAP)

Bettina Shultz-Jobe and Tim Jobe offer training to understand neurobiology of trauma and relationships, identify relationship patterns, practice new behaviors, and form lasting relationships.

www.naturallifemanship.com

Trauma to Transformation: How Horses Guide Us to Posttraumatic Growth

By Rob Pliskin: A two-day workshop on equine-assisted trauma recovery. The workshop is based on the work of the Posttraumatic Growth Research Group of the Department of Psychology, University of North Carolina-Charlotte, and Mr. Pliskin's experience as an EAGALA professional since 2003. Didactic and experiential work with equines in a group setting.

robpliskin@icloud.com

When Horses Hear the Unspeakable: A Guide to Trauma-Informed Equine Therapy

By Sarah Jenkins: A Web-based course designed for any equine-assisted/facilitated practitioner seeking to expand one's knowledge of the ethics and best practices of working with complex trauma and dissociation, both in and out of the arena.

www.eaemdr.com

Index

Note: Page locators in **bold** refer to tables and page locators in *italics* refer to figures.

accident-related trauma, equine assisted therapy for 125–139; case example 130–136, **132–133, 134**; ethical issues 128–130; multicultural and ethical considerations 137; physical positioning of therapist in relation to client 137; rationale for equine-assisted therapy 128; theoretical approach 126, *126*; tri-phasic trauma treatment model 127–128, *127*

active round pen LEAP© 77–78; case example 78–81, **79–81**

Adverse Childhood Experiences Study 84–86

Ainsworth, M. 10, 56

Altschuler, E.L. 89

American Psychological Association (APA) 19, 21, 125, 126, 154, 186

Anda, R.F. 85, 86

animal-assisted prolonged exposure (AAPE) 89–90

animal rights 129–130

attachment: -based EFPP 109–110, 117; horses providing opportunity to experience safe 109; psychotherapy, neurobiology and 107–109; rupture and repair 10, 13, 15, 24; theory 20, 56, *57 see also* reactive attachment disorder (RAD), trauma-focused EAP for

attachment and Somatic Experiencing® integrated into equine-assisted trauma recovery 3–18; case examples 10–15, 16–18; chronic stress and trauma and impact on attachment 3–5; EQUUSOMA™ biological explanation 5–8; EQUUSOMA™ description 8–9; model of Somatic Experiencing® 8–9; Threshold of Intensity Model 9–10, *9*

autonomic nervous system (ANS) 6, 15, 73, 109

benefits of equine-facilitated psychotherapy 71–73, *72*

body awareness scan LEAP© 75

Boulder Crest Retreat 173–174

Bowen, M. 88

Bowlby, John 10, 20, 56, 88

Broca's area of brain 70

calm in clients with complex trauma and dissociation, increasing tolerance for 44–53; calm as 'dangerous' for clients with unhealed trauma 45–46; case example 47–52, **48–52**; EAP/EFP therapy 45–46; goals and objectives of EAP/EEP intervention 46–47; guidelines in implementing EAP/EFP 46; sample client session note 52; step by step guide to implementing EAP/EEP intervention 47–52, **48–52**; theoretical approach 45; unhealed trauma histories 44–45

Center for Disease Control 3

certification 129

CET *see* chronic early traumatization (CET), experiential equine-assisted focal psychodynamic psychotherapy (EFPP) for

child sexual abuse *see* sexual trauma survivors, equine-assisted group therapy for adolescent

choosing of a horse, client's 59

chronic early traumatization (CET), experiential equine-assisted focal psychodynamic psychotherapy (EFPP) for 107–121; attachment, psychotherapy and neurobiology 107–109; case example 113–115; case example, therapeutic analysis 115–117; equine-assisted psychotherapy 108–109; experiences typical of clients undergoing EFPP 117;

phases of therapy 110, **111–112**; problem
with traditional psychotherapy 108;
theoretical approach 109–110
chronic stress and trauma in childhood:
correlations with increased risk for physical
disease 3; impact on attachment 3–5;
incidence 3
co-regulation 4, 9, 20
cognitive behavioral therapy (CBT):
integration of equine-assisted therapy
with trauma-focused 88; limitations for
relational trauma survivors 69–70;
trauma-focused 86–88, 94
Cohen, J.A. 87, 88
combat-related posttraumatic stress disorder,
using psychodynamic equine-assisted
traumatherapy to treat 186–194; case
example 189–193; integrative treatment
plan 188–189; theoretical approach
186–188
communication, example session 95–97
compartmentalization 20, 21, 55
complex trauma and dissociation, increasing
tolerance for calm in clients with 44–53;
calm as 'dangerous' for clients with
unhealed trauma 45–46; case example
47–52, **48–52**; EAP/EFP therapy
to address 45–46; feeling of calm as
'dangerous' 45–46; goals and objectives
of EAP/EEP intervention 46–47;
guidelines in implementing EAP/EFP
46; sample client session note 52; step
by step guide to implementing EAP/
EEP intervention 47–52, **48–52**;
theoretical approach 45; unhealed trauma
histories 44–45
complex trauma, study of efficacy of
equine-facilitated 89
complex traumatic dissociation: parts work
41; personality states 21; symptoms 19–20
confidentiality 148
Connected Calm Space technique 157–159;
case example 160–167, **161–167**
contraindications and cautions for
equine-assisted therapy 128

*Diagnostic and Statistical Manual of
Mental Disorders* (DSMV) 19, 125
dissociation 69; DSMV definition of disorders
19; personality states 21–22; symptoms
of complex traumatic 19–20; and unmet
needs in infants and children 20–21;
see also complex trauma and dissociation,

increasing tolerance for calm in clients
with; structural dissociation treatment
through equine-assisted trauma therapy
dorsal vagal complex (DVC) 6–8
dual attention stimulus (DAS) 155
dual awareness 25; present time orientation
and fostering 33–37, **34–37**

EC-EMDR *see* equine-connected
eye-movement desensitization and
reprocessing (EC-EMDR)
EFPP *see* experiential/equine-assisted focal
psychodynamic psychotherapy (EFPP) for
chronic early traumatization (CET)
ego-function development 187
ego state work 21–22
EquiLateral™: Equine Assisted EMDR
Protocol 45, 46, 203
equine-connected eye-movement
desensitization and reprocessing
(EC-EMDR) 154–169; blank session
note **170**; case example 160–167,
161–167; Connected Calm Space
technique 157–159; ethical issues in
equine-assisted therapy programs 156;
guidelines in consideration of multicultural
issues and ethics 160; rationale for EAP
155–156; sample client session note
167–168; theoretical approach 154–155
EQUUSOMA™: biological explanation 5–8;
case studies 10–15, 15–18; description 8–9
ethical issues in equine-assisted therapy
programs 58, 128–130, 145, 146–148,
156, 174–175; guidelines in consideration
of 46, 61, 137, 148, 160
experiential/equine-assisted focal
psychodynamic psychotherapy (EFPP)
for chronic early traumatization (CET)
107–121; attachment, psychotherapy and
neurobiology 107–109; case example
113–115; case example, therapeutic
analysis 115–117; experiences typical of
CET clients undergoing 117; phases of
therapy 110, **111–112**; team of therapists
110; therapeutic approach 109–110
eye-movement desensitization and
reprocessing, equine-connected
(EC-EMDR) *see* equine-connected
eye-movement desensitization and
reprocessing (EC-EMDR)

families and trauma 140–153; case example
using Transitioning Families 148–149;

equine-assisted therapies 144–145; ethical considerations in Transitioning Families 146–148; experiential and play therapy 143–144; family therapy 141–142; guidelines in consideration of multicultural issues and ethics 148; loss and attunement exercise 149–151; psychodynamic therapy 142–143; psychoeducation 143; reunification therapy 142; theoretical approaches behind Transitioning Families 141–144; Transitioning Families model and equine-assisted therapy 145–146; Transitioning Families Therapeutic Reunification Model (TFTRM) 141
family therapy 141–142
Felitti, V. J. 84, 85, 86, 104
Figley, Charles 142
Fonagy, Peter 20, 116, 117
Frankl, Viktor 172
freeze state 6–8

Greenberg, L. 146–147
group therapy: with sexually abused children 88–89 *see also* psychodynamic equine-assisted traumatherapy (PEATT) to treat combat-related PTSD; sexual trauma survivors, equine-assisted group therapy for adolescent; Warrior PATHH
gut feelings 71

Hart, O. van der 21, 22, 23, 44, 110
healthy mind, aspects of 126, *126*
herd dynamics and behavior 5, 16–17, 24; inner meeting space technique 27–33, **27–32**
Herman, Judith 5, 23, 26, 44, 126, 127, 188
Horse Inspired Growth and Learning (HIGH) model: case example 178–181, **179–181**; technique 175–178
Horse Sense Skills Cards 94
human–animal interaction studies 23–24

immobility/stillness 6–8
implicit-procedural memory 187
inner meeting space technique 27–33, **27–32**
International Association of Human–Animal Interaction Organizations 145

Janet, Pierre 22

Kaiser Permanente 3
Kline, M. 20

Kolk, B. van der 21, 44, 70, 71, 73, 86, 107, 108, 118, 127, 186, 187

LEAP (Leading Equine Assisted Practitioners) model 70–71, 81; active round pen case example 79–81, **79–81**; active round pen exercise 77–78; body awareness scan 75; limbic restructuring exercises 75–78; meet the herd 75–76, 76–77; reflective grooming exercise 76–77
left and right brains 108, 109, 110
Levine, Peter A. 5, 7, 8, 15, 20
limbic system 73, *74*, 140, 159; case example of client with disorganization in 61–65, **62–66**; RAD and disorganization of 54–56; TF-EAP attempt to re-engage 56
limbic system restructuring 73–74; active round pen case example 79–81, **79–81**; active round pen exercise 77–78; body awareness scan 75; with CET clients 108, 109; Connected Calm Space to promote 159, 160–167, **161–167**; EFP to facilitate 74; exercises to encourage 75–78; meet the herd exercise 75–76, 76–77; reflective grooming exercise 76–77; in subcortical limbic system 108
loss and attunement exercise 149–151

Maher, C. 90, 92
Martin, K.M. 22, 23, 24, 27, 30, 33
meet the herd LEAP© 75–76, 76–77
memory systems 155, 187
mentalization 20, 25, 108, 109, 116
multicultural considerations, guidelines in 46, 61, 137, 148, 160, 178

Naste, T.M. 89
Natural Lifemanship's trauma-focused equine-assisted psychotherapy (TF-EAP) for reactive attachment disorder (RAD) 54–68; blank session note **68**; case example 61–65, **62–66**; choosing a horse to build relationship with 59; description of technique 58–61; ethical issues 58; guidelines in consideration of multicultural issues and ethics 61; reason to treat RAD using 56; sample client session note **66**; secure attachment in 56–58
Natural Lifemanship's trauma-focused equine-connected eye-movement desensitization and reprocessing (EC-EMDR) 154–169; blank session note **170**; case example 160–167, **161–167**;

Connected Calm Space technique
157–159; ethical issues in equine-assisted
therapy programs 156; guidelines in
consideration of multicultural issues and
ethics 160; rationale for EAP 155–156;
sample client session note **167–168**;
theoretical approach 154–155

neocortex 6, 54, 55, 156, 159; case example
of client accessing **161–167**

neurobiology, attachment and psychotherapy
107–109

non-verbal communication 71, 72, 73, 108;
between horse and client 25–26, 109; in
horses 71, 145, 156

oxytocin 24

parasympathetic nervous system 6, 109, 159
parts work for structural dissociation 22–23;
addressing a perpetrator loyal part 38–42,
38–41; description of technique 26; and
equine-assisted trauma therapy 23–26;
fostering dual awareness and present time
orientation 33–37, **34–37**; inner meeting
space technique and case study 27–33,
27–32; techniques and case
examples 27–42

PEATT *see* psychodynamic equine-assisted
traumatherapy (PEATT) to treat
combat-related PTSD

Perry, Bruce 71, 72, 73, 107, 108, 144, 155

play 6; therapy 143–144

polyvagal theory 6

Porges, S.W. 4, 6, 10

post traumatic stress disorder (PTSD)
125–126, 154; in combat veterans 171,
186; studies of effect on horses of clients
with 129 *see also* accident-related trauma,
equine assisted therapy for; psychodynamic
equine-assisted traumatherapy (PEATT) to
treat combat-related PTSD

posttraumatic growth (PTG) in combat
veterans, integrated equine-assisted
psychotherapy for 171–185; blank
session note **185**; case example
178–181, **179–181**; ethical issues
174–175; Horse Inspired Growth and
Learning (HIGH) technique 175–178;
how equine-assisted psychotherapy aids
PTG 173; multicultural guidelines 178;
sample group session note **181–182**;
theoretical approach 172–173; Warrior
PATHH program for 173–174

Prague Declaration 1998 145

present time orientation, and fostering dual
awareness 33–37, **34–37**

prey animals, horses as 71–73, 144, 156

psychodynamic equine-assisted traumatherapy
(PEATT) to treat combat-related PTSD
186–194; case example 189–193;
integrative treatment plan for combat
veterans 188–189; theoretical approach
186–188

psychodynamic therapy and Transitioning
Families Therapeutic Reunification Model
142–143

psychoeducation: for adolescent sexual
trauma survivors 95–96, 97–98; for
families 143; in treating structural
dissociation 27–29

PTG *see* posttraumatic growth (PTG) in
combat veterans, integrated equine-assisted
psychotherapy for

reactive attachment disorder (RAD), trauma-
focused EAP for 54–68; blank session note
68; case example 61–65, **62–66**; choosing
a horse to build a relationship with 59;
description of technique 58–61; ethical
issues 58; goals and objectives of TF-EAP
intervention 58; reason for using TE-EAP
56; sample client session note **66**; secure
attachment in TF-EAP 56–58; theoretical
approach 54–56

reflective grooming LEAP© 76–77

Reichert, E. 88–89

relational trauma, working with 69–83;
active round pen exercise 77–78; benefits
of equine-facilitated psychotherapy
71–73, *72*; body awareness scan 75; case
example 78–79, **79–81**; dissociation for
survival 69; exercises to encourage limbic
restructuring 75–78; LEAP model 70–71;
limbic restructuring 73–74; meet the
herd exercise 75–76, 76–77; rationale
for working with horses 71; reflective
grooming exercise 76–77; talking
cognitive therapy vs. equine facilitated
psychotherapy 69–70

renegotiation 15, 16, 17, 24

reunification therapy 142

riding, horseback: Connected Calm Space case
example 160–167, **161–167**; Connected
Calm Space technique 157–159; focal
psychodynamic therapy and 109–110,
114–115, 116–117; positive effects

of rhythmic 109–110, 155; programs, therapeutic 92–93
right and left brains 108, 109, 110

self-regulation: developing skills of 57–58, 110, 117; scale for scoring **66**
sexual trauma survivors, equine-assisted group therapy for adolescent 84–106; Adverse Childhood Experiences Study and sexual trauma 84–86; case example 99–101, **99–100**; communication, example session 95–97; equine-assisted therapy and trauma 88–90; group therapy literature 88–89; individualized goal sheet 93–95; presentation of symptoms 86–87; prevalence of child sexual abuse 84; program development in subsequent years 102–103, *103*; program outcomes 101–102, *102*; therapeutic riding program 92–93; trauma-focused cognitive behavioral therapy 86–88; trauma-focused equine-assisted therapy, program context 90–93; trust, example session 97–99
Shapiro, Francine 125, 128, 155
Shapiro, Robin 22, 25, 32, 33
Siegel, Daniel 5, 56, 107, 108, 109, 111, *126*, 127
social justice 129–130
Somatic Experiencing® and attachment integrated into equine-assisted trauma recovery 3–18; case examples 10–15, 16–18; chronic stress and trauma and impact on attachment 3–5; EQUUSOMA™ biological explanation 5–8; EQUUSOMA™ description 8–9; model of Somatic Experiencing® 8–9; Threshold of Intensity Model 9–10, *9*
stillness/immobility 6–8
structural dissociation treatment through equine-assisted trauma therapy 19–43; addressing a perpetrator loyal part 38–42, **38–41**; dissociative disorders 19–21; ego state model and structural dissociation 21–22; fostering dual awareness and present time orientation 33–37, **34–37**; inner meeting space technique and case study 27–33, **27–32**; parts work and equine-assisted trauma therapy 23–26; parts work as a treatment approach 22–23; symptoms of disorders 19–20; technique, description 26; techniques and case examples 27–42
sympathetic nervous system 6

TF-CBT *see* trauma-focused cognitive behavioral therapy (TF-CBT)
TF-EAP *see* Natural Lifemanship's trauma-focused equine-assisted psychotherapy (TF-EAP) for reactive attachment disorder (RAD)
TFTRM *see* Transitioning Families Therapeutic Reunification Model (TFTRM)
thresholds of intensity model 9–10, *9*
training, therapist: ethical issues 128–129; general trauma-informed 195–202; trauma-informed equine-assisted mental health 203–206
Transitioning Families Therapeutic Reunification Model (TFTRM) 141; case example 148–149; and equine-assisted therapy 145–146; ethical considerations 146–148; guidelines in consideration of multicultural issues and ethics 148; loss and attunement exercise 149–151; similarities with talk therapy 146; theoretical approaches behind 141–144
trauma-focused cognitive behavioral therapy (TF-CBT) 86–88, 94; integration of equine-assisted therapy with 88
trauma-focused equine-assisted therapy for adolescent sexual trauma survivors 84–106; Adverse Childhood Experiences Study and sexual trauma 84–86; case example 99–101, **99–100**; communication, example session 95–97; equine-assisted therapy and trauma 88–90; group therapy literature 88–89; individualized goal sheet 93–95; presentation of symptoms 86–87; prevalence of child sexual abuse 84; program development in subsequent years 102–103, *103*; program outcomes 101–102, *102*; therapeutic riding program 92–93; trauma-focused cognitive behavioral therapy 86–88; trauma-focused equine-assisted therapy, program context 90–93; trust, example session 97–99
tri-phasic trauma treatment model: case example 130–136, **132–133, 134, 135, 136**; description 127–128, *127*; equine-assisted therapy within 128; multicultural and ethical considerations 137
trust, example session 97–99

vagus nerve 159
ventral vagal complex (VCC) 6, 10
Veterans Administration (VA) 171

veterans, combat *see* posttraumatic growth (PTG) in combat veterans, integrated equine-assisted psychotherapy for; psychodynamic equine-assisted traumatherapy (PEATT) to treat combat-related PTSD

walking around hindquarters of a horse intervention 130–136, **132–133, 134, 135, 136**
Warrior PATHH 171–185; blank session note **185**; at Boulder Crest Retreat 173–174; case example 178–181, **179–181**; ethical issues 174–175; Horse Inspired Growth and Learning (HIGH) technique 175–178; how equine-assisted psychotherapy helps 173; multicultural guidelines 178; sample group session note **181–182**; theoretical approach 172–173
window of tolerance 5; calm to widen client's 45, 47–52, **48–52**; exceeding a client's 41, 46; growing 8–9; structural dissociation and 44–45
Winnicott, Donald 143–144